The Plastic Age

The American Culture

NEIL HARRIS—General Editor

THE PLASTIC AGE (1917–1930)

Edited,
with Introduction and Notes by

Robert Sklar

George Braziller   New York

Acknowledgments

Many persons have contributed to the making of this book. Ellen Frank, my research assistant, brought her energy, imagination, and aesthetic sensibility to the project. Thomas Leonard's fine essay, "The Ethos of Normalcy," provided useful insights on the cultural and moral dimensions of political leadership in the Twenties. Edwin Seaver of George Braziller, Inc., gave me valuable advice and assistance. Howard Harrod provided me with working space in Nashville, Tenn. For assistance in preparing sections of visual documents I am indebted to Mary Yushak of the Film Stills Archive, Museum of Modern Art; Dirk Buys of the University of Michigan Library; and Winthrop Sears, Jr., of the Ford Archives, Henry Ford Museum. My wife, Kathryn Kish Sklar, gave the work at every stage the benefit of her exceptional sense of history and of style.

R. S.

"Our life drives us apart and forces us upon science and invention—away from touch. Or if we do touch, our breed knows no better than the coarse fiber of football. Though Bill Bird says that American men are the greatest business men in the world: the only ones who understand the passion of making money: absorbed, enthralled in it. It's a game. To me, it is because we fear to wake up that we play so well. Imagine stopping money making. Our whole conception of reality would have to be altered."

—WILLIAM CARLOS WILLIAMS, *In the American Grain* (1925)

Preface

"Do not tell me only of the magnitude of your industry and commerce," wrote Matthew Arnold during his visit to the United States in the 1890's; "of the beneficence of your institutions, your freedom, your equality: of the great and growing number of your churches and schools, libraries and newspapers; tell me also if your civilization—which is the grand name you give to all this development—tell me if your civilization is *interesting.*"

The various volumes that comprise THE AMERICAN CULTURE series attempt to answer Matthew Arnold's demand. The term "culture," of course, is a critical modern concept. For many historians, as for many laymen, the word has held a limited meaning: the high arts of painting, sculpture, literature, music, architecture; their expression, patronage, and consumption. But in America, where physical mobility and ethnic diversity have been so crucial, this conception of culture is restricting. The "interesting" in our civilization is omitted if we confine ourselves to the formal arts.

The editors of THE AMERICAN CULTURE, therefore, have cast a wider net. They have searched for fresh materials to reconstruct the color and variety of our cultural heritage, spanning a period of more than three hundred years. Forgotten institutions, buried artifacts, and outgrown experiences are included in these books, along with some of the sights and sounds that reflected the changing character of American life.

The raw data alone, however fascinating, are not sufficient for the task of cultural reconstruction. Each editor has organized his material around definitions and assumptions which he explores in the volume introductions. These introductions are essays in their own right; they can be read along with the documents, or they can stand as independent explorations into social history. No one editor presents the same kind of approach; commitments and emphases vary from volume to volume. Together, however, these volumes represent a unified effort to restore to historical study the texture of life as it was lived, without sacrificing theoretical rigor or informed scholarship.

NEIL HARRIS

Contents

III THE CULTURAL PROSPECT

IV FOUNDATIONS OF THE REPUBLIC

Illustrations

THE AESTHETICS OF INDUSTRY/142.

The Ford River Rouge Plant. Photographs by Charles Sheeler. *Ford Archives, Henry Ford Museum, Dearborn, Michigan.*

FACES OF HARLEM/198.

Drawings from *The Survey* (March, 1925), by Winold Reiss.

TOWN AND COUNTRY/250.

Photographs of the American Environment. *Ford Archives, Henry Ford Museum, Dearborn, Michigan.*

1. New York City during a bus strike, ca. 1920.
2. Detroit from the air, 1927.
3. Detroit street scene, 1923.
4. Commercial Garage, Ridgewood, N.J., ca. 1920.
5. Johnston's Garage, Inc., New Paltz, N.Y., ca. 1920.
6. Interior, F. J. Hedges' Garage, East Hampton, N.Y., ca. 1920.
7. Interior, Drexler Motor Co., Thibodaux, La., late Twenties.
8. South Main Street, Henderson, Tex., ca. 1928.
9. 4-H Club Event, Wayside Inn, Sudbury, Mass., mid-Twenties.
10. Railroad Street, Ironton, Ohio, 1923.
11. A railroad crossing, Carleton, Mich., 1925.

THE GREAT GOD FASHION/298.

Fashion Pages from the *Ladies Home Journal.*

1. June, 1919.
2. June, 1920.
3. June, 1921.
4. November, 1924.
5. November, 1926.
6. November, 1927.
7. November, 1929.
8. February, 1930.

Introduction

ROBERT SKLAR

Most American wars destroyed the creative minds of their era, or swept them into practical tasks: politics, business, law, science. After the Revolution the intellectuals searched breathlessly for native works of art, to prove that independence did not degenerate the mind. All the great post-Civil War writers—Henry and William James, Mark Twain, Henry Adams, William Dean Howells—managed to skip the fighting. The traumas of World War Two produced fifteen postwar years of intellectual timidity and cultural stagnation.

The First World War is the only exception. It destroyed, instead, the official culture which waged and supported the war, smashed it like an old and brittle egg shell, and set free the creative life so long contained within. It was good to the creative minds, providing them with a transforming, often a harrowing experience, but preserving them alive and well to write. The war ended an epoch of sweetness and light, said H. L. Mencken, and he well knew what an epochal moment it was. In the First World War the genteel middle-class cultural structure, which had ruled over American values and ideals for nearly two centuries, raised itself to new heights of rhetoric, energy, repression, and control; and then, untouched and almost unnoticed, it collapsed, never to be the same again.

American culture was newborn in the Twenties. It was a time for naming all things new, a task for language, to which the novelists and poets, the critics and historians, leaped as if predestined. In the span of a decade they created the most brilliant and varied literary culture that America had ever known. Only the times would not stand still. The things named changed their appearance, and needed to be named anew; and the eyes of the beholders saw in a different way, too. The middle-class cultural order, though much weaker, and fragmented, struggled to retain its waning power. Not only was the literary culture newly liberated—the popular culture was being transformed, by new technologies, standardization, mass production, and by the very thrust of cultural uniformity which the middle class had tried in the war to enforce, into a mass culture, uniting American culture as never before through the automobile, movies, and radio.

The literary culture, absorbed in its achievements and its new freedoms, at first paid litttle attention to the new institutions and values of mass culture as they challenged the husks of middle-class order. But by the middle years of the decade, well before the Crash, there was considerable unease among the writers and intellectuals, a sense that through expatriation and indifference they were losing their role as spokesmen and leaders, forfeiting their power to define the values and project the hopes of American society. To whom or to what they were not sure. The Great Crash of October, 1929, seemed to many of them another fortuitous act of Providence, crumbling the money culture as middle-class culture had been thrown off a decade before, providing the writers and intellectuals with the opportunity for commitment and social leadership as they had sought and found artistic freedom a decade before. The literary culture jumped into the social struggle, and the middle class, shattered once more, quietly took a place within the newly dominant structures of mass culture. Within weeks the Twenties atmosphere had disappeared, shaken off, in the grim Depression days, like a bad dream.

II

Who could have guessed the genteel middle-class cultural order would break apart at the end of the First World War, at its greatest hour of triumph? During 1917–1918, the years of American participation in the war, genteel culture exuded nothing but power, confidence, and will. National opinion was united and mobilized as never before to defend civilization against the barbarian attack from the East. There was no generation gap; young men and women fervently volunteered their services, and were in turn exalted by their elders. The important periodicals and organs of opinion stood foursquare behind the war. Dissident intellectuals, Socialists, pro-German elements, were silenced, jailed, or otherwise suppressed with a fervor and thoroughness no era of repression, before or since, has been able to match. For the first time in American history (with the possible exception of John Quincy Adams) a spokesman for genteel culture led the nation from the White House, and as wartime President, the ex-professor Woodrow Wilson seemed to be fulfilling the prophecy he had made long before in a genteel essay: "Some day we shall be of one mind, our ideals fixed, our purposes harmonized, our nationality complete and consentaneous. . . ." Perhaps from moments of supreme glory there is no place to go but down. We need to look at the roots of genteel culture before we can see how easily they came to be pulled out.

For generations genteel culture was so ubiquitous a part of American culture it was like air—hard to see, describe, or criticize. It took an intellectual with as special a background and perception as George Santayana to name it and analyze it, and he did so at a time, 1911, when long-term shifts in the national culture were finally bringing genteel culture to light. Genteel culture in America greatly resembled middle-class cultures in England and Western Europe, but from its formation in the eighteenth century it was shaped by peculiarly American necessities. It had to cope with a highly open and mobile society, and one at least rhetorically and fitfully committed to freedom, equality, and opportunity. Genteel culture, in a word, was the instrument the American middle classes devised to exert some form of social control over those below them and above them on the economic ladder.

The aim was to teach people how to behave, and to do so in the guise of disinterested benevolence—or of noble self-sacrifice. The ultimate weapon of control was the censorious power of social opinion, but the everyday forms of persuasion and manipulation were the schools, literature, the press, the pulpit. The basic trick, the most subtle and challenging, was getting people to adopt the desired manners and morals as if they had been spontaneously generated and freely accepted from within. And it worked, because American society provided real rewards for those who conformed: upward mobility, social acceptance, respectability, comfort, security. There was no conspiracy to run a culture this way: it operated in the usual way of liberal establishments, partly from sincere belief and partly from self-interest; partly from confidence, partly from fear.

Literature played a special role in the operations of genteel culture during the nineteenth century for a number of reasons. Formal education beyond reading and writing was far from universal; the power of the pulpit was in decline; political rhetoric, after the Civil War, was deprecated. But hundreds of thousands of Americans who never heard of Herbert Spencer or Hamilton Fish could recite the whole story of Uncle Tom and Little Eva, if not from Harriet Beecher Stowe's novel, then from the extremely popular dramatization, the condensed version for children, the German and Swedish language editions, the parlor game, or the songs. The printed word was the nineteenth century's pervasive medium,

America the most highly literate of the world's cultures, and fiction the most popular of the arts. For the purveyors and defenders of genteel culture there was both greater ease and greater power in controlling communications rather than institutions: the right men and women in a few important editorships could have an enormous influence in shaping what was said and what was not said in novels, short stories, poetry, history, and popular philosophy.

It works beautifully in theory. But around this calm genteel center American society and culture by the beginning of the twentieth century was changing rapidly and fundamentally. Expanding urban and industrial centers were creating new social and cultural forms, challenging the validity or relevance of the small town old American values that genteel culture put forth. There were new extremes of wealth and poverty, new waves of immigrants who did not share the languages, customs, or religions of Western Europe. By 1900 the new energies of American life seemed to have obliterated the stable and unified forms of the genteel cultural order. Obviously the middle class would not change itself to accommodate alien experience; and the new plutocrats and new immigrants were far less accessible to middle-class social control. In the end, the genteel cultural structure tightened its grip on the narrowing circle of American reality it still controlled. The pressure on writers to conform to genteel norms became more open and intense than ever. The generation of young writers who emerged in the Eighteen-Nineties was decimated by breakdown and early death, and the decade from 1900 to 1910 was one of the bleakest in the history of American literature.,

Of course the middle class had better things to do in the early years of the Progressive Era than worry about the quality of its fiction. The air seemed fouled by dirty politics; it was too much to bear. Those city and state governments which had managed to escape complete corruption were nevertheless outmoded and inept. Middle-class energies poured into political and social movements. According to the historian Robert Wiebe, a whole new middle-class version of social order was forming, based on professional expertise and bureaucratic structures. There was pervasive middle-class disgust with urban immigrant machines and corrupt or ineffective politicians, to be sure, but one may question how deeply or broadly the new bureaucratic and professional ideals had penetrated middle-class thinking. When the former Princeton professor of history and government Woodrow Wilson was nominated by the Democrats in 1912, he built his successful campaign for the presidency on a skillful appeal to genteel sentiment and the promise of reinvigorating the small-town moral and social order.

The real break in middle-class cultural solidarity before the war did not come from the political intellectuals and social theorists of the Progressive movement. Their concern, as Wiebe suggests, was with methods and with functions rather than with values and ends. They remained absorbed, if in a slightly different way from the genteel cultural spokesmen, with the benevolent possibilities of power and control, and they possessed no coherent system of alternative values that could resist the clarion call of Wilsonian rhetoric for "an America united in feeling, in purpose, in its vision of duty, of opportunity, and of service." John Dewey, Thorstein Veblen, Walter Lippmann, and Herbert Croly, among many others, gave up their critical function in response to Wilson's summons to duty and to high resolve.

Those who did not succumb, who had struck out from within at genteel cultural norms and who struggled on against the wartime pressures for conformity, had adopted a wholly different cultural stance. These were men and women born largely in the Eighties—Mencken, Randolph Bourne, Van Wyck Brooks, and Ezra Pound are perhaps the most significant, along with others like Waldo Frank, James Oppenheim, Alfred Kreymborg, Max Eastman, and Floyd Dell. As a group, with a few exceptions, they were remarkably alike: comfortable suburban background, one of the better colleges, European travel or knowledge of European literature and culture. Dewey and Veblen and William James were part of their intellectual background, and they were nurtured on the exhilarating atmosphere of the Progressive years. Their talents and interests led many of them to literary and social criticism rather than to imaginative or theoretical work. With their Western European counterparts—like T. E. Hulme and D. H. Lawrence in England, Guillaume Apollinaire and Marcel Duchamp in France, Herman Hesse in Germany—they were rebelling against the realism and scientism of nineteenth-century literature and thought. They revived a romantic attitude, self-consciously stressing their youth and their disdain for accepted bourgeois values.

Some of the Americans, particularly poets like Pound, became associated with the modern movement in the arts; others identified themselves with international socialism. But on the whole in their brief period of activity before America's entry into the war, these American writers considered themselves cultural nationalists. Their concern was with developing a vigorous new national culture in the United States. They were not so much opposed to middle-class values as to the genteel American version of them. Unlike the genteel arbiters of culture, they were optimistic about the American future and critical of the American past. They took pleasure in the variety and ferment in American culture and social life, and they wanted to create a cultural atmosphere in which social, ethnic, regional, and political differences could express themselves and flourish. They believed they could bring into being a culture unified in diversity. When America entered the war, they resisted but could not prevent a powerful and pervasive genteel middle-class effort to attain cultural unity through uniformity.

The rage for conformity let loose by the declaration of war reflected neither military necessity nor, at least in its fervor and extent, a conscious political choice. It was a cultural phenomenon, because most Americans grasped the purpose of the war in cultural terms. Obviously one can find significant political, economic, and strategic reasons for America's decision to join the Allied side in the war. But Wilson had explained his diplomacy and defined his aims in the language of culture. It was a war to preserve civilization, to make the world safe for democracy, to throw back the barbarian invasion. When the European war had begun in 1914 there may have been a moment of ambiguity in American minds, for every schoolboy knew that American values and institutions were rooted in the ancient forests of German Saxony, from which the Anglo-Saxon people stemmed; and no one could deny the pervasive influence of German culture in such areas as science, medicine, and university life. But in the early months of the war middle-class public opinion gave its loyalty to England.

This required civilization to be redefined and the Germans read out of it. Wartime propaganda depicted the Germans as dark, yellowish-skinned Huns from the Asian steppes, out to destroy the civilization of the blond fair-haired people of the West. In this moment of cultural redefinition the role of genteel culture was greatly enhanced. It was the protector of the English cultural tradition in America, the purveyor of English manners and morals to the American uncouth. As American opinion rallied to the English cause, genteel culture in America—college presidents, clergymen, editors, community leaders in every city and small town—rose purposefully to replant the single standard of Anglo-American culture in every recalcitrant corner of cultural diversity. Germans and Irish, Socialists and Wobblies, atheists and intellectuals, all were to be persuaded or silenced, and the task was carried out all the more thoroughly because disputes over culture and values were more amorphous and vaguely threatening. Never had genteel middle-class culture in America possessed such powers of will and such possibilities for compassion. In one hand cultural warriors carried the fire and arrows of repression and control; in the other they bore the wreaths and garlands of sentimental emotion, the tokens of remembrance for noble self-sacrifice and heroic death in battle.

The genteel drive toward a unanimous national culture was still gathering strength when the war abruptly ended in November, 1918. The Eighteenth Amendment prohibiting the manufacture, sale, or transportation of intoxicating liquors, a genteel effort to extend forms of legal social control from the state to a national level, was completely ratified in 1919, and enforcement procedures set up with the passage of the Volstead Act. The Bolshevik Revolution of October, 1917, in Russia had hardened patriotic sentiment against all forms of radicalism and dissent, and after the war Socialist periodicals continued to be barred from the mails. Five Socialists were expelled from the New York state legislature and a Socialist Congressman from Wisconsin, Victor Berger, was twice prevented from taking his seat. The fear and hatred of left-wing unorthodoxy culminated in the "Red Scare" of January, 1920, with nationwide raids and arrests under the leadership of Attorney General A. Mitchell Palmer. The old methods of cultural control had been enhanced during the war by a new belief in the benevolent powers of force, and the adherents of genteel culture seemed as willing to see their form of social unity enforced by police and federal agents as by editors, ministers, or professors.

But at the moment when genteel culture was consolidating its power over alien and dissenting elements in American society, it was losing its appeal to the social group which had historically provided its foundation —the urban, educated middle class. As they gained the power to coerce, the leaders of genteel culture were giving up their most important moral weapon—the power to convince. Before the war genteel culture had been, if narrow, intelligent and learned within its own bounds. An elite form of sophistication had been one of its prime defenses against cultural intrusions by former newsmen turned literary naturalists or earnest immigrants striving to express themselves. But the rhetoric of war is rarely refined or subtle, and genteel culture far outstripped the usual excesses of war in its frenzy of sentiment and repression.

Ultimately there was a reaction. The young men who had volunteered for battle in the name of sacrifice, glory, and heroism quickly discovered the horrors of trench and gas warfare, the weariness and cynicism among the Allied troops, the corrupt and undemocratic nature of British and French societies, the civilization they had been willing to die to defend. At home wartime inflation struck hardest at the urban middle class with salaries and fixed incomes. As their economic position deteriorated, relative to wage-earning groups in American society, the urban middle class discovered their culture changing form around them. The quality of their culture, and the broad acceptance of its values by all American classes before the war, had been their pride. But when the emotions and social turmoil of war had passed they found their cultural leaders had debased their language and their values by linking them with the most mindless and least sophisticated forms of political opportunism, rural resentment, and ethnic and religious prejudice. Those who had previously given at least silent acquiescence to genteel hegemony now responded to middle-class leadership with open hostility: the rich were disdainful, and immigrant groups rejected an imposed and unnatural cultural identity.

The middle class had lost their control over those who had previously given them cultural allegiance, lost indeed, the firm social and economic status that had served as the foundation of their cultural energy and self-confidence. H. L. Mencken, who had opposed the American entry into the war on the Allied side, had contemplated leaving for Switzerland after the war, believing for a time that his unpopular wartime views had destroyed his literary career in America. But in 1919 his volume of essays, *Prejudices: First Series,* proved to be a popular and widely read book, and by 1920 he was acknowledged as the voice of a new postwar attitude mocking American materialism, enthusiasm, and cultural pretensions. Middle-class readers were applauding his attack on their old middle-class myths.

It was an astonishing moment, a moment when a cultural order that had dominated American life since the eighteenth century lost its hold on the minds of its adherents—lost its persuasive force at the very time it was reaching out to legalize previously informal control over culture. The Twenties was likely the first, and perhaps the only, decade in American culture that lacked an obvious cultural center. This was one of the sources of its enormous cultural diversity and vitality, as many forms—the remnants of genteel culture, a middle-class split into business, rural, scientific, and other cultural fragments, a literary culture, nationality and race cultures, and the new mass culture—danced the game of musical chairs for survival, and possibly for dominance.

III

The flowering of literary culture after the First World War was completely unexpected. The war had raged across the field of culture, bringing the battle right to the writers' own home ground. Some established writers, like Edith Wharton, wrote works of propaganda, though Mrs. Wharton was unique in making French rather than English culture her cause. Writers opposed to American policy in the war, like Theodore Dreiser, equally gave their energies to cultural criticism and radical pamphleteering. Meanwhile, the circle of young critics and cultural nationalists, most of them vigorous opponents of the war, was completely shattered. Bourne, who was thirty-two years old, died in the influenza epidemic in December, 1918. Brooks turned misanthropic; in his first post-war book, *The Ordeal of Mark Twain*, he implied it was impossible to be a writer in America. Mencken made it known that literature no longer interested him as much as it once had; the cultural conflicts of the war had focused his attention on the strange and entertaining phenomenon of democratic culture, and henceforth he would practice social more than literary criticism. The hope of nurturing a vigorous and creative pluralistic American culture had vanished in the rancor and disappointments of war.

The first encouraging sign for postwar literature was the extraordinary reception which greeted *The Education of Henry Adams* when it was published in October, 1918—an irony that that master ironist could have appreciated. Adams had written his autobiography more than a decade earlier, had circulated a few copies privately, and left instructions for its general publication after his death. When he died in the spring of 1918, the Massachusetts Historical Society prepared the manuscript for publication in the fall. Adams' name was barely known to the World War generation, but his voice from the past caught the mood of disillusion when it first began to appear among the educated, urban middle class, and supported it with the weight of tradition and continuity his family represented.

The Education was a long and difficult book, filled with paradox and double meanings, yet its sense of defeat amid every outward sign of victory, its ironic suggestion that those who are best educated are most helpless of all, seemed precisely to forecast the cultural circumstances of the educated middle class after the war. Adams had experienced the disorder they felt all around them, and sought to understand it through a historical theory of multiversity—a theory that might explain why the genteel effort to impose unity on American culture during the war had been so repressive, and ultimately so distasteful to them. For months after the war, to understand themselves, the urban middle class read *The Education of Henry Adams*. They made it the most popular nonfiction book in America, the big best seller and the book most in demand at libraries, from the fall of 1918 to the spring of 1920.

The popularity of *The Education of Henry Adams* was quickly followed by other indications of a significant cultural break with the past. Mencken soared to greater national fame with each new essay satirizing American hypocrisy and pretension. Sherwood Anderson rose suddenly to prominence through his *Winesburg, Ohio,* stories portraying desolate small-town lives. Allegedly torrid sex passages in James Branch Cabell's *Jurgen* generated a clamorous dispute over literary freedom and the power to censor. Large portions of the educated, urban middle class made it unmistakably clear they had ceased to live by the constraints and dictates of genteel culture. They laughed at its prudery and its cultural norms designed to protect the purity of adolescent girls. They threw over its piety toward American institutions and traditions, and welcomed instead any evidence that revealed old heroes as knaves. Their fiercest ridicule was directed against the genteel effort to elevate small-town manners and habits into supreme moral guidelines for life. They rejected any form of middle-class cultural unity that sacrificed the pleasures of city life to country reticence. Their attitude was to have great influence in every area of American social and cultural life in the Twenties, but its effects were felt earliest and most profoundly in literature. The disaffected middle class provided a favorable audience, such as had never before existed in the United States, for a free, serious, and critical American literature.

It was a major reorientation of literary taste, to be sure, not a revolution. Though many of the distinguished old organs of genteel culture—*Harpers, The Atlantic, Scribners, The Century*—slipped temporarily or permanently into irrelevance, *The Saturday Evening Post* grew fat and wealthy by its ability to incorporate new urban middle-class attitudes into the old and reassuring framework of genteel values. Of the many significant works of fiction published in the decade, the books that achieved wide popularity —among them F. Scott Fitzgerald's *This Side of Paradise,* Sinclair Lewis' *Main Street,* John Dos Passos' *Three Soldiers,* Dreiser's *An American Tragedy,* and Ernest Hemingway's *A Farewell to Arms*—all contained some familiar anchor for the middle class, sentiment or sympathy or an acceptable form of morality. Even with its limitations, however, the reading public of the Twenties shared with its best writers an unusual range of common interests and values.

But the path of writers in the Twenties led them away from America, and their appreciative audience of book buyers and readers only helped provide the means. The literary expatriates of the Twenties were seeking a life, more than they were fleeing one. When they cataloged the failures of America it was not the oppressiveness of gentility that bothered them as much as the absence of a literary life—the lack of aesthetic seriousness, of a sustaining criticism, of an artistic community. Even before the war Ezra Pound and T. S. Eliot and Gertrude Stein had gone searching for the literary life America lacked, and when they had not found precisely what they wanted in London and Paris they created it. The young writers of the Twenties were their beneficiaries. They could live a literary life in Paris among an international community of artists. They could produce their own criticism in their little magazines, *This Quarter, Transatlantic Review, Broom, Transition*. And they discovered an aesthetic, modernism, that bound them together less by a doctrine than by a sensibility: style and form are preeminent; language creates its own meanings; literature is its own end.

American literature in the Twenties became the sum of many parts, each writer's quest for a personal style. Modernism imposed no restraints except artistic seriousness. As a literary movement it reached a watershed in 1922, for writers in English, when James Joyce published the great modernist novel, *Ulysses*, and Eliot brought out *The Waste Land*, the great modernist poem. Thereafter every young writer knew the game had changed: Joyce and Eliot made it useless for twentieth-century artists to write nineteenth-century novels and poems. The challenge was most severe to those bright young men who emerged so quickly on the scene in the early Twenties, as much public figures as accomplished writers. Fitzgerald faced it, and slowly achieved the individual style with which he created his 1925 masterpiece, *The Great Gatsby*. Dos Passos met the test, too, emerging as a modernist writer with his 1925 novel, *Manhattan Transfer*. Writers only a year or two younger than Fitzgerald and Dos Passos, like Hemingway or Faulkner or the poet Hart Crane, learned the lessons of Joyce and Eliot outside the public eye, and emerged full grown as heirs of the modernist sensibility.

The achievements of American poetry in the Twenties were even more impressive than those in fiction, but the major poets—Eliot, Wallace Stevens, Robert Frost, Marianne Moore, William Carlos Williams—were older and considerably more experienced than the significant novelists of the Twenties. Moreover, they built on aesthetic and critical traditions, particularly French Symbolism, for which the novelists had no counterpart. And they gained immeasurably, personally or in their craft, from the unique entrepreneurial and critical talents of Ezra Pound. Together the poets and novelists of the Twenties created a body of writing as original and as powerful as any other in American literature. We read them still as contemporaries—Fitzgerald and Hemingway and Faulkner,

Eliot and Stevens and Frost—for pleasure, for beauty, for their sense of man.

Genius, however, exacts a high price. The writers of the Twenties lived deeply within themselves, and the inner tensions and separateness of their literary vocation belied the legends of joyful camaraderie; anyone who retains romantic notions about Twenties literary life should read Hemingway's revengeful memoir, A Moveable Feast. The literary vaudeville was a show of one-man turns, as Edmund Wilson aptly suggested in 1926, but real vaudeville performers always had what writers rarely got, direct communication with their audience. Despite their achievements, writers of the Twenties were beset by more than the usual amount of literary doubts and distress. By 1926 or 1927, many expatriate writers no longer wished to live apart from the mainstream of American life. They wanted to reaffirm their commitment to America, not to accept it as it was, but to change it for the better. Writers went searching for social causes well before the Crash and the Great Depression created social problems they could hardly avoid.

Dos Passos and the poet Edna St. Vincent Millay joined the worldwide effort to save the anarchists Sacco and Vanzetti, who were executed in August, 1927, for a holdup murder committed in South Braintree, Massachusetts, more than seven years earlier; they were sent to their deaths, many intellectuals believed, as innocent men, condemned for their foreign birth and accents, their radical opinions, their lack of patriotism in the war, when they had fled to Mexico to avoid the draft. Dreiser was one of several prominent writers, journalists, and professors to visit the Soviet Union in the late Twenties, and one of many who rekindled his enthusiasm for Socialist alternatives after the Soviet Union altered its bellicose and secretive attitude toward westerners. Eliot and Pound revived the romantic faith in the poet as prophet - or seer for mankind; both men remained abroad, Eliot in England, where he advocated a form of Anglo-Catholic traditionalism, and Pound in Italy, a supporter of Italian Fascism as the true heir to Jeffersonian political doctrines. Fitzgerald and Faulkner, each in his own way, assumed the task that the great nineteenth-century American writers—Cooper and Melville, Hawthorne and James, and Mark Twain—had attempted, imaginatively to portray the fate of American values and ideals in their fiction. Thus the writers of the Twenties erased the line between literature and society they had drawn so rigidly when the decade began.

But it was foolish for writers to think they could return to society on their own terms. By their literary doubts and social commitments they succeeded only in demonstrating their vulnerability, thus reopening old struggles their achievements of the Twenties rightfully should have settled. Genteel culture, flying the banners of humanism, mounted a counterattack on literary modernism as the decade ended, the very moment when a resurgent literary left began its assault on the modernist movement for its arty preciousness and political irrelevance. Ultimately the controversies were settled in the literary and cultural atmosphere of the Thirties, by new schools of criticism which openly or covertly took sides on the political issues of the decade. The literary scene in the Thirties resembled the landscape of feudalism, with universities and left-wing parties serving as fortified castles and towns, waging battle in their specialized literary quarterlies that proclaimed each separate academic or critical or sociopolitical dogma. It was not a hospitable environment for art. Those writers who had tired of their extreme independence found it difficult to maintain any independence at all. Many writers took an active part in the political movements of the Thirties, where they learned that, to be writers, they could rely, after all, only on the separate self.

IV

In 1923 a young writer, Gilbert Seldes, took leave as managing editor of *The Dial,* an influential literary magazine of the Twenties, and wrote a book he published in 1924, *The Seven Lively Arts.* It consisted of essays on popular culture, covering the motion picture comedy, jazz music, comic strips, the circus, vaudeville, and other crowd-pleasing forms of entertainment. Clive Bell called it the book of the epoch, but others thought Bell facetious, one highbrow (as Van Wyck Brooks defined the term back in 1915) gently lampooning another for applying his energy to lowbrow tastes. Other literary persons had flouted their liberation from genteel restraints by taking an interest in common pleasures, though none so elaborately as Seldes. Seldes, however, was quite in earnest. *The Seven Lively Arts* grew out of an intuition—one he was to build on and extend throughout his later career—that popular culture had changed fundamentally after the First World War, and was going through a transformation in the Twenties into a form of culture entirely new. What Seldes was observing and recording in *The Seven Lively Arts* was a process creating the first mass culture in modern society.

Mass culture was launched in the early Twenties as a consequence of the cultural crises generated in America by the First World War. Vast historical forces, to be sure, lay behind the emergence of mass culture in the twentieth century—technological growth, new media, economic development, all those little shifts and great changes in the human and inanimate worlds that social scientists call by such names as industrialization, urbanization, and bureaucratization. But cultures are not produced by forces; they are created by human vision, human needs, human desires, acting upon the technological instruments they have at hand, shaping new technologies to their own ends. Technologies, of course, impose limits, and often when they are developed for one purpose they produce powerful unintended consequences in many other areas of cultural life. The fact is, however, that momentous historical forces have no true life outside the particular environments which give them their social and cultural form. We miss the point if we consider the emergence of mass culture without giving primary weight to the choices made by men.

No cultural crisis engendered by the First World War was more severe —or more fundamental to the nature of American social life—than the ordeal of coercion and rejection suffered by immigrant ethnic and nationality groups. The war, on the domestic front, had seemed to them less a war to save civilization from the Germans than a war to defend Anglo-Saxon America against the foreign-born. They were repeatedly challenged publicly to display their patriotism. Reformers made no secret of the fact that Prohibition was chiefly directed against the notorious drinking habits of immigrant workingmen. Immigrant cultural and social groups were harrassed and disrupted by police and federal agents during the 1919–1920 Red Scare; the Justice Department detained thousands of aliens and illegally deported several hundred alien radicals. In the early Twenties they were subjected to ever increasing hostility from native Anglo-Saxon Americans, a hostility which brought an end to the historic American policy of open entry into the United States, through the enactment of a European quota system—and total exclusion of Asians—in the National Origins Act of 1924. In the cultural disorder of the Twenties, significant portions of Anglo-Saxon old America, of every class and region, fell back on racial and religious prejudice as their answer to the great cultural challenge of modern urban-industrial America—the assimilation of the immigrants, with their enormous variety of languages, religions, customs, and styles, into American cultural life.

Native American culture had faced the challenge before the First World War more in confidence than in fear. Through a process of "Americanization," the immigrants would throw off their peculiar and distinctive traits and learn to live by the cultural norms Anglo-Saxon old Americans taught them. The English Jewish writer Israel Zangwill idealized the process in his melodrama of 1908, *The Melting Pot,* and Zangwill's title entered the American language as the vivid metaphor that explained and justified the great turn-of-the-century migration of Eastern and Southern Europeans to America. But whether the crucible of American life ever would have worked in the expected way can never be known. The war overturned all the old codes and compacts.

In wartime native Americans made new demands on immigrant and nationality groups. They had to accept a new cultural identity at once, to swear allegiance not merely to the United States, but to an idealized version of Anglo-Saxon American values fabricated in the heat of wartime cultural propaganda. Had this been the only concern of ethnic and nationality groups, perhaps the assault on their cultural identity might have been borne. The destruction of European empires in the war, however, quickened old ethnic ties and old national loyalties among the American immigrants. They were like men pulled powerfully forward and backward at the same time; something surely would break if they did not wrench free.

Some groups tried to live with the derogatory label of "hyphenated-American" pasted on them in wartime; they would reside in the United States, supporting the national policies of their home country and preserving the old culture as best they could. Their American-born children, however, rejected that way of life. Moreover, they were drawn into political complications with the new nations of Eastern Europe they had not dreamed of. The only other alternative was to find a new form of cultural identity as Americans, separate from the old concept of assimilation —the melting pot mistake, as an Anglo-Saxon American author of the Twenties called it—and also from the cultural capitulation the nativists demanded. For many among the foreign-born, and especially among their American-born children, the technological changes and new media of the early Twenties presented a completely new and unanticipated opportunity to forge a new relationship to American culture, outside all traditional institutions and forms. They embraced mass culture gladly, and furthered its cause.

The necessary technological conditions for mass culture had been established during the First World War. American industry, far more than British or European, had been geared from its earliest years for mass production and distribution of its products. Yet from the perspective of a federal government suddenly, in 1917, preparing its military forces to fight a modern war, every aspect of the industrial process remained far too chaotic and individualized. The War Industries Board, a federal agency coordinating war production, gave orders to standardize and simplify thousands of products, not only military goods but also consumer items containing materials essential for the war. The impact of the Board's policy helped fundamentally to alter the nature of the American productive system.

The expanding automobile industry had already begun to innovate with new forms of mass production and distribution. By the time of the war everybody in America liked motor cars and wanted to own one. Constructing an automobile, however, was a slow and expensive process, resulting in a price too high for all but the well-to-do. You could either learn to build an inexpensive car, or figure out a way to let people drive their cars while they were still paying for them; the auto industry did both. Henry Ford pioneered with the assembly line and the production of a simple standard model, the Model T; other automobile manufacturers devised a system of installment financing, selling a car in exchange for a small down-payment and a loan agreement covering the remainder, to be paid off in monthly installments, with interest.

Thus nearly everyone who wanted a motor car could buy one—and the enormous success and prestige of the automobile industry in the Twenties was not lost on other manufacturers. They applied the methods of assembly line production and installment financing to every type of consumer goods they could. The greatest innovations came in the manufacturing of electrical products. During the Twenties electric power was extended to four-fifths of American homes, and new electrical appliances in the kitchen or living room—radios, refrigerators, toasters, vacuum cleaners, coffee percolators, and many more—became as ubiquitous as cars on the road. Mass production and mass distribution transformed the daily life of nearly every person in America. Men and women of average or moderate means acquired possessions similar in quality and even in styling to the products owned and used by well-to-do people. Of course no new democracy of material possessions could be complete. A Model T Ford was just a Tin Lizzie next to any handsome roadster or sedan, and a cheap table radio gave more static than satisfaction compared to expensive console models. Yet they performed the same service—your Ford would get you where you were going, and your little radio would pick up programs you wanted to hear.

The effect of such shared experiences and shared opportunities on class distinctions in America was subtle, but profound. Visible class distinctions, enforced by obvious differences in attire, possessions, and life-styles, had always been weaker in America than in Europe, and in the Twenties they became even more attenuated. The wealthy could always maintain their distinctiveness; but in the broad middle ranges of American life old distinctions of income or nationality or religion could be submerged by careful self-schooling in the mass technological norms of dress, habits, manners, and language. The new common standards made it difficult for others to tell at a glance or a sentence what you were or where you came from; their judgment had to become more personal and intangible: Is he neat? Does she have a nice smile? Is he pleasant to be near? In mass culture the old roadblocks to social mobility came down. You could change your name, ignore your religion, leave your background a thousand miles behind. But you could never afford to neglect your appearance. In the Twenties Americans began their grand obsession with cosmetics. The absence of body odor mattered more than the lack of a family tree.

As the advancing technologies of production and distribution made possible common possessions and appearance for the new mass culture of the Twenties, the mass media—radio and movies—forged common bonds of information and values. Commercial radio broadcasting began in November, 1920, and the habit of radio-listening spread as swiftly as electrical lines could be put up—even faster for the enterprising people who bought or built their own wireless sets. Movies dated back to the Eighteen-Nineties, but they had been considered disreputable by respectable people before the war, and they had drawn their audiences largely from the big city working class until D. W. Griffith's two great epics, *The Birth of a Nation* of 1915 and *Intolerance* of 1916, demonstrated the mythic and moral power of movies to genteel arbiters of taste. The movies expanded into a major entertainment industry at the same time as radio, in the greatly altered cultural environment after the war.

Late twentieth-century persons like ourselves may find it difficult to sense the feelings of people experiencing the new electronic media for the first time. They sat in their living rooms or kitchens or bedrooms, while immediate and authentic events of the moment came out of their radio set. Everywhere in the country people heard the newest song by the A & P Gypsies or Will Rogers' latest story or the long tense balloting at the 1924 Democratic Convention. Radio gave them a common fund of experience and information, making Americans more alike than they had ever been before. Or they sat in darkened theaters, watching larger-than-life figures move across a screen, feeling a mood of passivity and empathetic identification that projected them into the places of the actors on the screen, vicariously to share their experiences and emotions. Because of the psychological receptivity they engendered, movies became especially persuasive instructors—moviegoers effortlessly internalized a heroine's smile or an actor's way of walking as naturally as if they had been born with them. The movies gave to America in the Twenties what genteel culture was no longer capable of providing—manners and morals, heroes and heroines. At the movies one could still learn how proper, wellborn, old Americans behaved, and also—what genteel culture never taught— how they misbehaved.

The men who ran radio networks and movie studios never consciously set themselves up in the Twenties as competitors with genteel middle-class culture, but inevitably it worked out that way. The new media were rooted, as Gilbert Seldes recognized, in the popular arts. While they were developing in their early days largely beyond the pale of respectable middle-class notice, movies and radio attracted their entrepreneurial and performing talent from the immigrant and ethnic groups and from exiles from genteel life, the theatre managers, the vaudeville players, the traveling stock company casts. They had already years of experience at finding common denominators pleasing to the varied tastes and feelings of urban populations, and their old abilities worked just as well in the glamorous and profitable new media. When they discovered after the war that they were winning over the middle-class audience to their new media, they happily absorbed the conventions of genteel culture into their popular entertainments.

Hollywood's merger of gentility with the popular arts helped to create the form of several classic silent comedies of the Twenties. Around 1914 Mack Sennett had developed a popular form of slapstick comedy featuring the Keystone Kops, broadly satirizing the working class people who made up the movie audiences of the time. But Sennett's style of burlesque and farce gave way in the Twenties, as Donald W. McCaffrey has pointed out in his *Four Great Comedians*, to situation comedies poking fun at genteel middle-class life. The great silent comedians of the Twenties built several of their most memorable movies on the foundations of genteel comedy—Harold Lloyd in *Grandma's Boy* and *Safety Last*, Buster Keaton in *The Navigator* and many other brilliant comedies, and even Charles Chaplin in his great short film, *The Pilgrim*, of 1923. Like Fitzgerald and Dos Passos and Faulkner, the classic silent comedians learned to build on the hollow shells of genteel convention not to offer false reassurance, but to create art.

Movies and radio forged a new mass culture in the Twenties by absorbing and amalgamating the traditions and cultures of all who created the new media and all who responded to them—ethnic and nationality cultures, the popular arts, and the outward forms at least of genteel culture, if not yet the inner acquiescence. No cultural phenomenon was more remarkable, in a decade marked by nativist sentiment, immigration restriction, and anti-Semitic and anti-Catholic prejudices, than the power of immigrants and children of immigrants—Joseph P. Kennedy and William Fox, Louis B. Mayer and Irving Thalberg, Rudolph Valentino and Greta Garbo and hundreds more, to shape the unified culture that genteel America had spent itself in seeking.

V

During the Twenties the leaders of genteel culture vigorously resisted the encroachments of mass culture upon the American territory they had possessed for generations past. They could still command considerable manpower; but their stock of ammunition was old and barely workable, and they had nothing new or potent to replace it. The small town and rural populations backed them solidly, and that gave them a firm alliance with Congress and the courts. But the urban and the educated flouted their disaffection so openly it would have taken martial law to keep control. Prohibition provides the obvious example. That great triumph of small town virtue was ignored and circumvented in the cities from the moment it became law. Genteel culture had strength enough only to delude itself that its coercive temperance crusade was working beautifully. The principal beneficiaries of the Prohibition Amendment were criminal syndicates from immigrant backgrounds, which prospered and multiplied on the profits and power they reaped from bootleg liquor. Urban Americans learned the passwords to speakeasies; many stocked up on hops, malt, yeast, and sugar, and even distilled corn mash in basement stills.

Urban indifference and urban dominance rankled the small town and rural old Americans throughout the Twenties. Both sides thirsted for confrontation. The most publicized of all the urban-rural conflicts of the decade came at Dayton, Tennessee, in 1925. John T. Scopes, a Dayton schoolteacher, had deliberately broken Tennessee's new state law forbidding the teaching of evolutionary theory in its schools. To Scopes' side rallied modern science, the American Civil Liberties Union, the great defense attorney and agnostic, Clarence Darrow, and the urban press, with Mencken himself in attendance. To assist the state of Tennessee came William Jennings Bryan, three-time Presidential candidate of the Democratic Party, once the voice of silver who would not let mankind be crucified on a cross of gold, now the voice of Biblical fundamentalism, who would not let small town and rural America be dragged down to Hell by the infidel ways of the modern city. You know the script: Darrow humiliates Bryan in a courtroom debate, though the defendent, Scopes, is found guilty. A week later Bryan dies. Both sides leave with a bitter taste in their mouths. The native, Anglo-Saxon middle-class Americans who lived in cities were split from their small-town and rural counterparts by a hostility as deep as any with which the most nativist American greeted the last immigrants to get off the boat at Ellis Island.

The old, comfortable, confident American middle class was split, too, and even more gallingly, by generations. One of the greatest prides of genteel culture had been its power to co-opt and channel its daughters and sons. The young soldiers and their doting sweethearts had gone into war willing to make every sentimental sacrifice and patriotic martyrdom genteel culture asked of them. The truth of war left them bitter and disillusioned, unwilling to suffer genteel leadership a moment longer. It was their younger brothers and sisters, however, who were naturally attuned to the new media and the postwar mood and made the most of them. Not every girl needed to bob her hair, wear short skirts, and call herself a "flapper," nor did every young man need to wear a racoon coat and drive a sporty roadster, to make it clear he wanted to throw off the authority of the past and experiment with new styles and new behavior.

Young people have an uncanny sense of what infuriates their parents: in a decade of strong nativist feeling and race prejudice they gravitated toward the most forbidden emblems of independence, Negro dancing and Negro jazz. It is hard to remember that jazz in the Twenties, which had its roots in "jass" music played in New Orleans bordellos, was as much an affront to their elders as hard rock in the Sixties: and that helps prove an important point about white absorption of Negro culture that LeRoi Jones made in *Blues People*. The young white audience certainly helped support the flowering of Negro music, theater, dance, and letters, the Harlem Renaissance, one of the great cultural achievements of the Twenties. But white interest exacted its price. The disaffected young middle-class whites began by seeking out Negro culture in its own environment. As black culture grew in popularity it was also homogenized for broader tastes, and ultimately it was refashioned by white enter-tainers into an acceptable style for general popular consumption. The first immensely popular radio program in the Twenties was a blackface comedy played by white actors, "Amos 'n' Andy"; and the most famous jazz musician of the Twenties was a white man name Whiteman.

The middle class obviously did not lack ways to control or rationalize the forces of change arrayed against it in the Twenties, yet taken together or separately none of them made up for the firm, coherent culture they had lost. The effusive optimism and unbounded self-confidence of middle class businessmen of the Twenties did help to deflect conflicts within the middle class. Since the Twenties were a period of considerable prosperity, it was natural that businessmen of all regions and conditions would join together in taking credit for it. But business ideology could not in itself put a culture back together again. In earlier periods the ideas and attitudes of businessmen had formed one part of a cohesive middle-class social and cultural order. During the Twenties business ideology dominated middle-class culture nearly by default.

Business optimism, moreover, masked the difficulties the middle classes were going through in making the major economic transformations demanded of them in the Twenties. The war had turned America's world economic role completely around. From a debtor nation before the war, the United States had become the world's principal creditor nation after the war. No one really knew what new policies such a radical change required, so businessmen and congressmen, like anyone else in the same position, continued to pursue the conventional wisdom, believing that their enhanced world economic power was brought about by higher tariffs or superior rectitude. Meanwhile, the gigantic interdependent corporate economy that American capitalists and managers had built was forcing businessmen to discard other and even more dearly held beliefs. Self-reliance, individualism, and independence were as outmoded in the Twenties as the Victorian laced corset. At business conventions and sales meetings all over America sincere and straightforward executives and experts were telling their customers and colleagues to keep smiling and get with the new rules of the game: cooperate, depend on others, play as a member of the team.

Even the Presidents of the United States did their best to preserve the middle class sense of power and confidence; in fact, that's what their middle-class constituents of the Twenties loved them for. We miss entirely why Warren G. Harding and Calvin Coolidge were so extraordinarily popular in their time unless we remember that Americans want character from their presidents more than they want power. Character of the right sort they had in abundance, Harding the handsome small town Ohio newspaper editor, Coolidge the dour son of a Vermont farmer. Moreover, unbelievable as it may seem to modern ears, they both possessed the knack of political rhetoric. Harding's awkward word, "normalcy," conveyed an unimaginable emotional appeal to his audiences in the early Twenties. It seemed to promise them a past they could return to, a cultural order they could reclaim, still powerful, still intact, after the interlude of war. Harding and Coolidge spoke in codes now lost to us, but potent in their time, assuring their listeners that middle-class virtue and moral precepts still ruled America.

The most promising of all middle-class paths out of cultural uncertainty in the Twenties was offered by one of the principal legacies of the prewar Progressive spirit—the faith in experts, in research and scientific method for gaining social knowledge. The middle class was no longer certain what it believed or how it should behave; all right, then, survey research could put together some data on what it did believe and how it actually behaved. Experts could keep them informed on scientific precepts for family life, child raising, relations between the sexes, and any other social need. Social scientists in many fields gladly took up the mantle of cultural leadership that had slipped away from genteel culture. The psychologist John B. Watson was probably the most prominent of all social scientists in the Twenties, both among the public and among his scholarly colleagues. His doctrine of behaviorism, which predicted that all human behavior would someday be understood as specific responses to specific stimuli in the environment, was especially persuasive as an antidote to long years of genteel idealism about the human mind and body. Watson left academic life in the Twenties to become a vice-president of the J. Walter Thompson Advertising Agency.

Social science in the Twenties made perhaps its greatest contribution through scholarly field research into everyday American life. Robert S. Lynd and Helen Merrell Lynd conducted the classic sociological investigation of the era, a study of the social, cultural, and economic life of Muncie, Indiana, published in 1927 as *Middletown: A Study in Modern American Culture*. Students and colleagues of the urban sociologist Robert Park carried out a series of brilliant city investigations in Chicago, among them Harvey Zorbaugh's *Gold Coast and Slum* and Louis Wirth's *The Ghetto*. The government sponsored a major social science research project, the two volume *Recent Social Trends*, covering the Twenties and published in 1932. By the end of the Twenties sociological investigations such as these began to replace literature as the source of norms and lessons for middle-class life. But the Twenties had passed before the middle class had time to put its new knowledge to use.

VI

The great stock market crash of October and November, 1929, ended the Twenties—as a period of time and as a state of mind—with nearly perfect symmetry. Money men panicked; the Left agitated; farmers grew even more restless than they had been during most of the past decade, since the prosperity of the Twenties had largely eluded them. But the spirit of the Twenties did not come crashing down amid tumult and alarms. It collapsed as if with a release of pressure, a rush of escaping air. Most Americans drifted into the early months of the Depression in a state of mild confusion, indecisiveness, and uncomplaining calm.

Radicals were not wrong in calling the Great Crash and the Depression a crisis of capitalism. Millions of workers lost their jobs. Mortgages were foreclosed, and hundreds of thousands of workers and farmers gave up their homes and farms. Bank failures wiped out thousands of savings accounts. Relief and welfare facilities hardly existed. In big cities, breadlines became common sights, and shantytowns for the homeless grew up on the outskirts, derisively named Hoovervilles after President Herbert Hoover, who found no rhetorical codes to hide the reality of economic collapse. Thousands of factory workers left the cities to return to the small towns and farms from which they had set out in the heyday of prosperity. Men and women and especially young people wandered across the country, riding the rails and sleeping in hobo jungles. Millions suffered from undernourishment. Many intellectuals were predicting, publicly or privately, that the United States would go one of two ways, Communist or Fascist. In any case, capitalism was doomed.

Among the people, however, there was astonishingly little sense of catastrophe. It was as if the Crash and the Depression had not generated a crisis, but rather ended one—the cultural crisis that caused such animosities and uncertainties in the Twenties. Adversity rallied people together. As the assembly lines ground to a halt, as construction crews came down from half-finished skyscrapers, the headlong rush into the unknown future seemed momentarily stayed. People had been granted an unexpected chance to catch their breath, time to stop and find out who they were and from where they had come. In the Depression Americans discovered their history and folklore all over again, hunting out the myths and memories that mattered most. Once families had stuck together, neighbors helped each other, strangers met and shared their goods and thoughts with the simplicity and open hearts that seemed to have existed long ago in America, back before the Great War. Americans in the Thirties wished dearly to believe in such social unity and common fellowship, and to regain them in their own lives.

This yearning created a golden opportunity for mass media in the Thirties, and mass culture rapidly emerged as the one true victor in the cultural struggles of the Twenties. Giant entertainment industries, operating with enormous technological complexities, elaborate financial intricacies, and vast arrays of tycoons, yes-men, stars, agents, and hangers-on, projected the simple, everyday American life as the grand cultural theme of the Thirties. The movie director Frank Capra created the image most memorably. In a series of successful films—*It Happened One Night* (1934), *Mr. Deeds Goes to Town* (1936), *Lost Horizon* (1937), *You Can't Take It With You* (1938), and *Mr. Smith Goes to Washington* (1939)—Capra exalted the instincts of the common man and undercut his wisdom in one and the same comic gesture. Any one of Capra's films epitomizes the mass cultural spirit of a decade.

The losers in the cultural competition of the Twenties fell comfortably into place within the new mass culture. The middle class, bankrupted economically and culturally by the Crash, its moral precepts undermined by bank failures and revelations of business chicaneries, its commercial optimism blasted, its experts temporarily stymied, brought along its respectability and the remnants of genteel culture's self-imposed responsibility for standards; the mass media were all too glad to appropriate them. The native-born children of the ethnic and nationality cultures discovered in mass culture their access to the styles and language of cultural assimilation, and in their big city neighborhoods they embraced the brotherhood of motion picture, radio, and comic book legends and lore. Small town and rural America, drawn out of its cultural backwardness by the electronic reach of the new media, gained in prestige during the Depression from all the emphasis on the virtues of little people and everyday lives. In the Thirties many cultures became one culture.

To the Thirties little of the Twenties seemed worth salvaging—not its cultural conflicts, not its intellectual independence and artistic freedom, not its business ideology, not its frenetic sense of frivolous pleasure, of lawless disorder, of uncontrolled change. The spirit of the Twenties sank swiftly into oblivion, and waited for a new generation to resurrect it as legend and as history. The Twenties may always appeal to us as the gay and carefree interlude of legend, but they are more fascinating still in their own true right, for their real weaknesses and strengths, their deep cultural conflicts and their great creative achievements. During the Twenties the dominant structure of twentieth century American culture began to form. The many cultures of that period—their causes, their brilliant life, their consequences—will occupy us for a long time to come.

PART ONE

MASS CULTURE: THE NEW ENVIRONMENT

1. Change Comes to Gopher Prairie

Until the First World War the moral values and social relationships of the small country town were honored by the spokesmen for American middle-class culture as paradigms by which every American, rich or poor, native or immigrant, city dweller or farmer, could guide his conduct. For a generation the growing urbanization and industrialization of American society had challenged the relevance of small-town authority, but in the realm of culture—in fiction and poetry, in the big national magazines, especially in the rhetoric of the Professor-President, Woodrow Wilson—the small town held its own. When the War sapped the energy and shattered the confidence of middle-class cultural control, it ended the reign, once and for all, of small-town moral leadership.

No writer reflected the ambiguous postwar attitude toward the small-town better than Sinclair Lewis (1885–1951). Lewis had been a promising writer of conventional novels and short stories before the publication of *Main Street* in the fall of 1920 transformed him into an internationally famous author, a cultural spokesman, and, a decade later, the first American recipient of the Nobel Prize for literature. He did not anticipate the enormous overnight success of his novel, and he expected the American middle-class reading public to be outraged rather than, as they were, deeply touched, moved almost as by self-discovery. In *Main Street* he captured the vague but complex new sense of the small town's diminished role in American life—revulsion against it and nostalgia for it; a yearning for the new, but a reluctance to part with the familiar. Thousands of American women believed that Lewis's heroine, Carol Kennicott, could only have been modeled directly on themselves.

Four years later, when Lewis was visiting in his hometown, Sauk Centre, Minnesota, he wrote an article for *The Nation,* ostensibly on the attitude of *Main Street's* fictional town, Gopher Prairie, toward the third-party presidential candidacy of Senator Robert M. LaFollette in the election of 1924. "Main Street's Been Paved!" acutely and humorously demonstrates Lewis's ambiguous feelings about small town life. It also offers suggestive insights into the way small-town America was changing during the Nineteen-Twenties under the impact of new technological and cultural forms—the automobile, movies, radio, and mass-produced consumer goods.

Main Street's Been Paved
SINCLAIR LEWIS

When *The Nation* asked me to visit Gopher Prairie, Minnesota, and ask the real he-Americans what they thought of the presidential campaign, I was reluctant. Of all the men whom I met in Gopher Prairie years ago, during that college vacation when I gathered my slight knowledge of the village, Dr. Will Kennicott was the one whom I best knew, and for him I held, and hold, a Little Brother awe. He is merely a country practitioner, not vastly better than the average, yet he is one of these assured, deep-chested, easy men who are always to be found when you want them, and who are rather amused by persons like myself that go sniffing about, wondering what it all means.

I telegraphed the doctor asking whether he would be home, for sometimes in summer he loads his wife and the three boys in his car and goes north for a couple of weeks' fishing. He answered—by letter; he never wastes money by telegraphing. Yes. He was in Gopher Prairie till the middle of August; would be glad to talk with me; knew Carrie (his wife) would enjoy a visit with me also, as she liked to get the latest gossip about books, psychoanalysis, grand opera, glands, etc., and other interests of the intellectual bunch in N. Y.

I arrived in Gopher Prairie on No. 3, the Spokane Flier. Many people will be interested to know that No. 3 is now leaving Minneapolis at 12:04, that the St. Dominick stop has been cut out, and that Mike Lembcke, the veteran trainman so long and favorably known to every drummer traveling out of Mpls., has been transferred to the F line, his daughter having married a man in Tudor.

I was interested to see the changes in Gopher Prairie in the past ten years. Main Street now has three complete blocks paved in cement. The Commercial and Progress Club had erected a neat little building with a

Sinclair Lewis, "Main Street's Been Paved!," *The Nation*, vol. 119, September 10, 1924, pp. 255–260.

room to be used either for pleasure and recreation or for banquets; it has card tables, a pool table, a top-notch radio; and here on important occasions, like the visit of the Congressman or the entertainment of the Twin City Shriners' Brass Band, the ladies of the Baptist Church put up a regular city feed for the men folks. The laws are prettier than they used to be; a number of the old mansions—some of them dating back to 1885—have been rejuvenated and beautified by a coating of stucco over the clapboards; and Dave Dyer has a really remarkable California bungalow, with casement windows, a kind of Swiss chalet effect about the eaves, and one of the tallest radio aerial masts I have seen west of Detroit.

But quite as striking was the change in Dr. Kennicott's office.

The consulting-room has been lined with some patent material which looked almost exactly like white tiling—the only trouble with it, he told me, is that lint and so on sticks to it. The waiting-room is very fetching and comfortable, with tapestry-cushioned reed chairs and a long narrow Art Table on which lie *Vogue*, the *Literary Digest, Photo Play*, and *Broadcasting Tidings*.

When I entered, the doctor was busy in the consulting-room, and waiting for him was a woman of perhaps forty, a smallish woman with horn-rimmed spectacles which made her little face seem childish, though it was a childishness dubious and tired and almost timid. She must once, I noted, have been slender and pretty, but she was growing dumpy and static, and about her was an air of having lost her bloom.

I did not at first, though I had often talked to her, recognize her as Carol, Dr. Kennicott's good wife.

She remembered me, however, by my inescapable ruddiness and angularity; and she said that the doctor and she did hope I'd drop in for a little visit after supper—she was sorry they couldn't invite me to supper, but the new hired girl was not coming along as well as they had hoped, as she was a Pole and couldn't speak a word of English. But I must be sure to come. There would be a really fine concert from WKZ that evening—of course so much of the broadcast stuff was silly, but this would be a real old-time fiddler playing barn-dance music—all the familiar airs, and you could hear his foot stamping time just as plain as though he were right there in the room—the neighbors came in to enjoy it, every Thursday evening. Oh! And could I tell her—— There'd been such an argument at the Thanatopsis Club the other day as to what was the *dernier cri* in literature just now. What did I think? Was it Marcel Proust or James Joyce or *So Big* by Edna Ferber?

She couldn't wait any longer for the doctor. Would I mind telling him to be sure to bring home the thermos bottle, as they would need it for the Kiwanis picnic?

She whispered away. I thought she hesitated at the door. Then the big, trim doctor came out of the consulting-room, patting the shoulder of a frightened old woman, and chuckling, "So! So! Don't you let 'em scare you. We'll take care of it all right!"

From his voice any one would have drawn confidence; have taken a sense of security against the world—though perhaps a sense of feebleness and childishness and absurdity in comparison with the man himself; altogether the feeling of the Younger Brother.

I fumbled at my mission.

"Doctor, a New York magazine—you may not have heard of it, but I remember that Mrs. Kennicott used to read it till she switched over from it to the *Christian Science Monitor*—*The Nation*, it's called; they asked me to go around and find out how the presidential campaign is starting, and I thought you'd be one of the——"

"Look here, Lewis, I've got a kind of a hunch I know exactly what you want me to do. You like me personally—you'd probably take a chance on my doctoring you. But you feel that outside of my business I'm a complete dumbbell. You hope I'm going to pull a lot of bonehead cracks about books and writings and politics, so you can go off and print 'em. All right. I don't mind. But before you lash me to the mast and show me up as a terrible reactionary—that's what you parlor socialists call it, ain't it?—before you kid me into saying the things you've already made up your mind you're going to make me say, just come out and make a few calls with me, will you?"

As I followed him downstairs I had more than usual of the irritated meekness such men always cast over me.

He pointed to a handsome motor with an inclosed body.

"You see, Lewis, I'm doing all the Babbitt things you love to have me do. That's my new Buick coop, and strange to say I'd rather own it— paid for in advance!—than a lot of cubist masterpieces with lop-jawed women. I know I oughtn't to get that way. I know that if I'd just arrange my life to suit you and the rest of the highbrows, why, I'd make all my calls on foot, carrying a case of bootlegged wood alcohol under one arm and a few choice books about Communism under the other. But when it drops much below zero, I've got a curious backwoods preference for driving in a good warm boat."

I became a bit sharp. "Hang it, doctor, I'm not a fool. Personally, I drive a Cadillac!"

This happened to be a lie. The only mechanical contrivance I own is not a Cadillac but a Royal typewriter. Yet I was confused by his snatching away my chance to be superior by being superior to me, and for the second I really did believe I could beat him at motoring-owning as I can beat him at theories of aesthetics.

He grinned. "Yeh, you probably do. That's why you haven't got any excuse at all. I can understand a down-and-outer becoming a crank and wanting to have Bob La Follette or this William X. Foster—or, God! even Debs!—for President. But you limousine socialists, a fellow like you that's written for the real he-magazines and might maybe be right up in the class of Nina Wilcox Putnam or even Harry Leon Wilson, if you did less gassing and drinking and more work and real hard thinking—how you can go on believing that people are properly impressed by your pose of pretending to love all the lousy bums—well, that's beyond me. Well, as I said: Before we go into politics and Coolidge, I want to show you a couple of things to point out what I mean."

He called to Dave Dyer, in the drug-store. Dave is really an amiable fellow; he used to keep me supplied with beer; and we would sit up, talking science or telling dirty stories or playing stud poker, till a couple of hours after everybody else in town had gone to bed—till almost midnight.

Dave came out and shouted: "Glad to see you again, Lewis."

"Mighty nice to see you, Dave."

"I hear you been up in Canada."

"Yuh, I was up there fr little trip."

"Have nice trip?"

"You bet. Fine."

"Bet you had a fine trip. How's fishing up there?"

"Oh, fine, Dave. I caught an eleven-and-a-half pound pickerel—jackfish they call 'em up there—well, I didn't exactly catch it personally, but my brother Claude did—he's the surgeon in St. Cloud."

"Eleven naf pounds, eh? Well, that's a pretty good-sized fish. Heard you been abroad."

"Yes."

"Well. . . . How'd the crops strike you in Canada?"

"Fine. Well, not so good in some parts."

"How long you planning stay around here?"

"Oh, just a couple days."

"Well, glad to seen you. Drop in and see me while you're here."

I was conscious, through this agreeable duologue, that Dr. Kennicott was grinning again. Dave Dyer's amiability had lubricated my former doubtfulness and I was able to say almost as one on a plane of normality with him: "Oh, what are you sniggering at?"

"Oh, nothing, nothing—posolutely Mr. Leopold, absotively Mr. Loeb. (Say, that's a pretty cute one, eh? I got it off the radio last night.) I just mean it always tickles me to see the way you loosen up and forget you're a highbrow when you run into a regular guy like Dave. You're like Carrie. As long as she thinks about it, she's a fierce Forward Looker and Deep Thinker and Viewer with Alarm. But let the hired girl leave the iron on a tablecloth and burn it, and Carrie forgets all about being a Cultured Soul and bawls hell out of her. Sure. You write about Debs, but I'd like to see you acting natural with him like you do with Dave!"

"But really, I'm very fond of Gene."

"Yeh. Sure. 'Gene' you call him—that's the distress signal of your lodge—all you hoboes and authors and highbrows have to say 'Gene.' Well, I notice when you talk to Dave, you talk American, but when you get uplifty on us, you talk like you toted a monocle. Well, climb in."

I considered the sure skill, the easy sliding of the steering-wheel, with which he backed his car from the curb, slipped it forward, swung it about the new automatic electric traffic signal at the corner of Main and Iowa, and accelerated to thirty-five.

"I guess you've noticed the paving on Main Street now," he said. "People that read your junk prob'ly think we're still wading through the mud, but on properly laid cement. the mud ain't so noticeable that it bothers you any! But I want to show you a couple of other things that otherwise you'd never see. If I didn't drag you out, your earnest investigation would consist of sitting around with Carrie and Guy Pollock, and agreeing with them that we hicks are awful slow in finally making Gopher Prairie as old as Boston. . . . Say, do you play golf?"

"No, I haven't——"

"Yeh. Thought so. No Fearless Author or Swell Bird would condescend to lam a pill. Golf is a game played only by folks like poor old Doc Kennicott of G. P., and the Prince of Wales and Ring Lardner and prob'ly this H. G. Wells you're always writing about. Well, cast your eye over that, will you."

We had stopped, here on the edge of Gopher Prairie—this prairie village lost in immensities of wheat and naivetes, this place of Swede farmers and Seventh Day Adventists and sleeve-garters—beside a golf course with an attractive clubhouse, and a half a dozen girls wearing smart skirts and those Patrick sweaters which are so much more charming, more gay, than anything on Bond Street or Rue de la Paix.

And in a pasture beside the golf course rested an aeroplane.

I could say only: "Yes. I see. But why the aeroplane?"

"Oh, it just belongs to a couple more Main Streeters from some place in Texas that are taking a little tourist trip around the golf courses in the country—terrible pair, Lewis; one of 'em is a Methodist preacher that believes hard work is better for a man than whiskey—never would dare to stand up in a bacteriological argument with this give-'em-the-razz scientist friend of yours, DeKruif; and the other is a cowardly lowbrow that got his Phi Beta Kappa at Yale and is now guilty of being vice-president of a railroad. And one other curious little thing: I went into Mac's barber-shop to get my shoes shined this morning, and Mac says to me: 'Afraid you got to let 'em go dusty, Doc—the bootblack is out playing golf.' Now, of course, we're a bad, mean, capitalistic bunch that 're going to vote for that orful Wall Street hireling, Coolidge. In fact, we're reg'lar sadists. So naturally we don't mind playing golf with the bird that blacks our shoes, and we don't mind the hired girl calling us by our first names, while you earnest souls——"

He had forced me to it. "Oh, go to hell!"

He chuckled. "Oh, we'll save you yet. You'll be campaigning for Cal Coolidge."

"Like hell I will!"

"Look, Lewis. May I, as a rube, with nothing but an A. B. from the U of Minn (and pretty doggone good marks in all subjects, too, let me tell you!) inform you that you pulled 'hell' twice in successive sentences, and that the first person singular future indicative of the verb 'to be' is 'shall' and not 'will'? Pardon my hinting this to a stylist like you. . . . Look, I'm not really trying to razz you; I'm really trying the best method of defense, which I believe is attack. Of course you don't think so. If the Japs were invading America, you'd want to have a swell line of soap boxes built along the California coast, and have this bird Villard, and this John Haynes Holmes, and this Upton Sinclair—and prob'ly Lenin and Trotzky and Mother Eddy and some Abrams practitioners and Harry Thaw—all get up on 'em and tell the dear artistic Japs how you love 'em, and then of course they'd just be too *ashamed* to come in and rape our women. But, personally, I'd believe in going out with one grand sweet wallop to meet 'em."

"Doctor, you have two advantages. Like all conservatives, all stout fellows, you can always answer opponents by representing them as having obviously absurd notions which they do not possess, then with tremendous vigor showing that these non-existent traits are obviously absurd, and ignoring any explanation. But we cranks try to find out what is the reality of things—a much less stout and amusing job. And then, while we admit enormous ignorances, you never try to diagnose anything you can't physic or cut out. You like to do an appendectomy, but an inquiry into the nature of 'success'——"

"I've noticed one funny thing in all your writings and stuff, Lewis. Whenever you have to refer to a major operation, you always make it an appendectomy. Have you a particular fondness for 'em, or don't you know the names of any others? I'd be glad to buy you a medical dictionary. All right. I'll quit. Now I want to show you a few other changes in G. P."

He drove back into town; he pointed out the new school-building, with its clear windows, perfect ventilation, and warm-hued tapestry brick.

"That," he said, "is largely Vida Wutherspoon's doing. Remember her and you and Carrie used to argue about education? You were all for having Jacques Loebs and Erasmuses and Mark Hopkinses teaching, and she concentrated on clean drinking-pails. Well, she pounded at us till we built this. . . . Meantime, what've *you* done for education?"

I ignored it, and asked what sort of teachers in this admirably ventilated building were explaining Homer and biochemistry and the glory of God to the youth of Gopher Prairie.

"The teachers? Oh, I guess they're a bunch of dubs like the rest of us; plain ordinary folks. I guess they don't know much about Homer and biochemistry. . . . By the way, in which school are *you* giving your superior notions about Homer and biochemistry, and meanwhile correcting themes, and trying to help the girls that get so inspired by the sort of junk you and Mencken write that they blow home at three G. M., lit to the guards? You hint—of course you haven't met any of 'em but you know it all beforehand—you aren't satisfied with our teaching; we've got a bunch of dumb-bells. . . . Willing to come here and teach Latin, math, and history, so they'll be done right? I'm on the schoolboard. I'll get you the job. Want to?"

At my answer he sniggered and drove on. He showed me the agreeable new station—depot, I think he called it—with its flower-bordered park; the old-fashioned English garden put in by a retired German farmer; and the new State fish-hatchery. He demanded: "Well, how about it? Main Street seem to be existing almost as well as the average back alley of some burg in Italy?"

"Certainly. You have them completely beaten—materially!"

"I see. Well, now we've got one other exhibit that we, anyway, don't think is just 'material'—how birds like you love that word! We've got a baseball team that's licked every town of our size in the State, and we got it by hiring a professional pitcher and coach for five months, and going down into our jeans, without any 'material' return, and paying him three hundred dollars a *week!*"

"How much do you pay your teachers a *month?*" was all I had to say, but it provided voluble, inconclusive debate which lasted the twenty-odd miles to a hamlet called New Prague.

Dr. Kennicott stopped at a peasant-like cottage in the Polish settlement of New Prague, and as he knocked I beheld him change from a Booster to the Doctor. What he did in that house I do not know. I do not understand these big suave men who go in to terrified women and perform mysteries and come out—calm, solid, like stockbrokers. During his fifteen minutes within there was the shriek of a woman, the homicidal voice of a man speaking some Slavic tongue—and as he started off he said to me only: "Well, I think I've got her to listen to reason."

"Good Lord, what reason? What do you mean? What happened in there? Who was the man? Her husband or another?"

I have never seen quite so coldly arrogant a cock of the eyebrow as Kennicott gave me.

"Lewis, I don't mind explaining my financial affairs to you, or my lack of knowledge of endocrinology, or my funny notion that an honest-to-God Vermont school-teacher like Cal Coolidge may understand America better than the average pants-maker who hasn't been over from Lithuania but six months. If you insist on it, of course I shouldn't mind a bit discussing my sexual relations to Carrie. *But* I do not ever betray my patients' confidence!"

It was splendid.

Of course it didn't happen to be true. He had often told me his secrets, with the patients' names. But aside from this flaw it was a noble attitude, and I listened becomingly as he boomed on:

"So! Let that pass. Now, why I brought you out here was: Look at this cross-roads burg. Mud and shacks and one big Ford garage and one big Catholic church. The limit. But look at those two Janes coming."

He lifted his square, competent hand from the steering-wheel and pointed at two girls who were passing a hovel bearing the sign "Gas, Cigarettes, Pop, and EATS"; and those girls wore well-cut skirts, silk stockings, such shoes as can be bought nowhere in Europe, quiet blouses, bobbed hair, charming straw hats, and easily cynical expressions terrifying to an awkward man.

"Well," demanded Kennicott. "How about it? Hicks, I suppose!"

"They would look at home in Newport. Only——"

He exploded. "Sure. 'Only.' You birds always have to pull an 'only' or an 'except' when we poor dubs make you come look at facts! Now, do stop trying to be a wise cracker for about ten seconds and listen to a plain, hard-working, damn successful Regular Guy! Those girls—patients of mine—they're not only dressed as well as any of your Newports or Parises or anywhere else, but they're also darn' straight, decent, hard-working kids—one of 'em slings hash in that God-awful hick eating joint we just passed. And to hear 'em talk—Oh, maybe they giggle too much, but they're up on all the movies and radio and books and everything. And both their dads are Bohemian; old mossbacks; tough old birds with whiskers, that can't sling no more English than a mushrat. And yet in one generation, here's their kids—real queens. That's what we're producing here, while you birds are panning us—talking—talking——"

For the first time I demanded a right to answer. I agreed, I said, that these seemed to be very attractive, probably very clever little girls, and that it was noteworthy that in one generation they should have arisen, in all their radio-wise superiority, from the bewildered peasants one sees huddling at Ellis Island. *Only,* was it Doc Kennicott and Dave Dyer and the rest of Main Street who were producing them? Dr. Kennicott might teach them the preferability of listening to the radio instead of humming Czech folk-songs, but hadn't they themselves had something to do with developing their own pretty ankles, buying their own pretty silk stockings, and learning their own gay manners?

And, I desired to be informed, why was it that to Dr. Kennicott the sleek gaiety of socialistic Slavic girls in New York was vicious, a proof that they were inferior, a proof that no one save Vermont conservatives should be allowed to go through Ellis Island, while the sleek gaiety of movie-meditating Slavic girls on Main Street was a proof of their superiority? Was it because the one part had Dr. Kennicott for physician and the other did not?

There was debate again. I perceived that I had not begun to get my interview; that I was likely to be fired by Mr. Villard. I calmed the doctor by agreeing that his ideas were as consistent as they were practical; and at last I had him explaining Coolidgeism, while he drove back to Gopher Prairie at thirty-five on straight stretches, twenty on curves.

"Well, I hope you're beginning to get things a little straighter now, Lewis. I wanted you to see some of the actual down-to-brass-tacks things we've *accomplished*—the paving on Main Street, the golf course, the silk stockings, the radios—before I explained why everybody around here except maybe a few sorehead farmers who'll vote for La Follette, and the incurable hereditary Democrats who'll stick by Davis, is going to vote for Coolidge. We're people that are doing things—we're working or warring—and in the midst of work or war you don't want a bunch of conversation; you want results.

"Now, first you expect me—prob'bly you've already got it written; darn' shame you'll have to change it—you expect me to pan hell out of Bob La Follette. You expect me to say he's a nut and a crook and a boob and a pro-German. Well, gosh, maybe I would've up till a couple of years after the war. But as a matter of fact, I'm willing—I'm glad to admit he's probably a darn' decent fellow, and knows quite a lot. Maybe it's even been a good thing, some ways, to have a sorehead like him in the Senate, to razz some of the saner element who otherwise might have been so conservative that they wouldn't have accomplished anything. I imagine prob'bly La Follette is a good, honest, intelligent man, a fighter, and a fellow that *does* things. But that's just the trouble. We mustn't be doing too many things, not just now. There's a ticklish situation in the world, with international politics all mixed up and everything, and what we need is men that, even if maybe they haven't got quite so much imagination and knowledge, know how to keep cool and not rock the boat.

"Just suppose a couple of years ago, when Banting was working out insulin for diabetes but his claims weren't confirmed yet, suppose you and all the rest of you Earnest Thinkers, including La Follette, had come to me hollering that I was wrong to go on doing the honest best I could just dieting my diabetes patients. You tell me about Banting—but equally you tell me about some other scientist named, say, Boggs, who had something new for diabetes. What'd I have done? Why, I'd of gone right on being a stingy old conservative and dieting my cases!

"Now, when it proves Banting is right and Boggs is wrong, I follow Banting and kick out Boggs, but I don't do either till I *know*. Boggs might have been a wiz, that took his degree of X. Y. Z. at Jena, but he was premature—he was wrong—he wanted to do too much. Well, La Follette is Boggs, a beaner but plumb wrong, and I and some twenty-thirty million other Americans, we're Coolidge, sitting back and watching, handing it to Banting and such when they prove they've got the goods, but never going off half-cocked.

"The trouble with La Follette isn't that he'd lay down on his job or not understand about railroads and the tariff but that he'd be experimenting all the time. He'd be monkeying around trying to fix things and change things all the time. And prob'bly there's lots of things that do need fixings. But just *now*, in these critical times, we need a driver that won't try to adjust the carburetor while he's making a steep hill.

"So. Not that I mean we're worried—as long as we have a cool head like Cal's at the wheel, with his Cabinet for four-wheel brakes. We ain't been half so worried as you Calamity Howlers. You say that unless La Follette is elected, gosh, the dome of the Capitol will slide off into the Potomac, and Germany will jump on France, and prob'bly my aerial mast will get blown down. Well, far's I can see, most of the folks around here are getting their three squares a day, and the only thing that seems to keep agriculture from progressing is the fact that the farmers can get three bucks a quart for white mule, so they're doing more distilling than manuring.

"Oh, yes, we've had bank failures and there's an increase of tenant-farming. But d' ever occur to you that maybe it's a good thing to close up a lot of these little one-horse banks, so we can combine on bigger and better ones? And about this tenant business; is that any worse than when every farmer owned his own land but had such a big mortgage plastered on it that he didn't really own it at all?

"No, sir, you got to look into these things scientifically. . . . Say, is that left front fender squeaking or do I imagine it? There, don't you hear it now? I do. I'll have Mat fix it. Gosh, how I hate a squeak in a car!

"Now I imagine this sheet *The Nation* tries to let on that the whole country is rising against the terrible rule of Coolidge. And I saw a copy of this *American Mercury*—Guy Pollock lent it to me—where some bird said Coolidge was nothing but a tricky little politician with nothing above the eyebrows. . . . By the way, notice that Ford and Edison and Firestone are going to call on him? Of course those lads, that 're merely the most successful men of affairs and ideas in the country, they're plumb likely to call on a four-flushing accident! Oh, sure!

"Well, now look here. First place, did you ever see a four-flusher that went on holding people's confidence? I never did—Oh, except maybe this chiropractor that blew into town three years ago and darned if he isn't still getting away with it! In the second place, suppose Cal were just a tricky little politician, without a he-idea in his bean. Well, what do you need for the office of President?

"For medicine, and for writing too, I imagine, some ways, you need *brains*. You're working single-handed, no one to pass the buck to, and you got to show results. But a preacher now, all he's got to do is to make a hit with his sermons, and a lawyer simply has to convince the poor cheeses on the jury that his learned opponent is a lying slob. In the same way, for President you need a fellow that can pull the wool over everybody's eyes, whether it's in the primaries back home in Hickville or whether it's dealing with Japan or Russia. If Cal can get by without having any goods whatever, then he's the boy we want, to keep the labor unions in order and kid along the European nations!

"Then, next place. . . . Oh, all this talk is just wasted energy. You know and I know that Coolidge is going to be elected. Be better if they called the election off and saved a lot of money, and damn the Constitution! Why, nobody is interested, not one doggone bit.

"As you ride around the country, do you hear anybody talking politics? You hear 'em talking about Leopold and Loeb, about Kid McCoy, about the round-the-world fliers, about Tommy Gibbons's battle in England, about their flivvers and their radios. But politics—nix! And why? Because they know Coolidge is already elected! Even the unregenerate old Democrats, that would love to have Brother Charlie run the country on the same darned-fool, unscientific, they-say basis on which William Jennings has the nerve to criticize evolution!

"I haven't met one single responsible well-to-do person who's for La Follette. Who've we got boosting him, then? Well, I can tell you—I can tell you mighty darn' quick! A lot of crank farmers that because they don't want to work and keep their silos filled want to make up for it by some one who, they hope, will raise the price of wheat enough so they can get by without tending to business! The fellows that 've always followed any crazy movement—that ran after the Populists and the Nonpartisan League! And a lot of workmen in the cities that think if some crank comes into office they'll all become federal employees and able to quit working!

"But aside from these hoboes—— Well, I guess I've asked a hundred people who they were going to vote for, some around G. P. and some on the smoker down to St. Paul, and ninety out of the hundred say: 'Why, gosh, I haven't thought much about it. Haven't had time to make up my mind. I dunno. Besides, anyway, I guess Cal is going to win.'

"Now, about these so-called 'exposures' of the Attorney General and

so on. Well, I've always suspected there was a lot more to it than you
saw on the surface—lot of fellows trying to make political capital out of
it—and the fact that Wheeler is running with La Follette proves my
contention, and I for one don't propose to let him get away with it, let
me tell you that right now!

"Nope. Unless we have an awful' bad crop failure, and the crops never
looked better than they do this year, we've got you licked. Cal is elected.
It's all over but the shouting."

I called on Kennicott and his wife after six o'clock supper, but I could
not get the talk back to the campaign. Carol hesitated that, yes, she did
admire La Follette, and Davis must be a man of fine manners if he could
be ambassador to the Court of St. James's, but just this year, with so
many bank failures and all, it wasn't safe to experiment, and she thought
she would vote for Coolidge; then some other time we could try changes.
And now—brightening—had I seen *The Miracle* and *St. Joan?* Were
they really as lovely and artistic as people said?

It was time to tune in on the barn-dance music from WKZ, and we
listened to "Turkey in the Straw"; we sat rocking, rocking, the doctor
and I smoking cigars, Carol inexplicably sighing.

At ten I felt that they would rather more than endure my going, and
I ambled up a Main Street whose glare of cement pavement, under a
White Way of resplendent electric lights, was empty save for bored but
ejaculatory young men supporting themselves by the awning-cords in
front of Billy's Lunch Room and the Ford Garage. I climbed to the office
of Guy Pollock, that lone, fastidious attorney whom Carol and I used
once, in the supposition that we were "talking about literature," to
exchange book titles.

He was at home, in his unchanged shabby den, reading Van Loon's
Story of the Bible.

He was glad to see me. With Kennicott I had felt like an intruder; to
Carol I seemed to give a certain uneasiness; but Guy was warm.

After amenities, after questions about the death of this man, the success
of that, I murmured, "Well, there've been a lot of changes in the town—
the pavement and all."

"Yes, a lot. And there's more coming. We're to have a new water
system. And hourly buses to the Twin Cities—fast as the trains, and
cheaper. And a new stone Methodist church. Only—"

" 'Ware that word!"

"I know it. Only—only I don't like the town as well as I used to.

There's more talk, about automobiles and the radio, but there's less conversation, less people who are interested in scandals, politics, abstractions, gallantries, smut, or anything else save their new A batteries. Since Dr. Westlake died, and this fellow Miles Bjornstam went away, and Vida Sherwin's become absorbed in her son's progress in the Boy Scouts, and even Carol Kennicott—Oh, well, the doctor has convinced her that to be denunciatory or even very enthusiastic isn't quite respectable —I don't seem to be awakened by the talk of any one here.

"And in the old days there were the pioneers. They thought anybody who didn't attend an evangelical church every Sunday ought to be lynched, but they were full of juice and jests. They're gone, almost all of them. They've been replaced by people with bath-tubs and coupés and porch-furniture and speed-boats and lake-cottages, who are determined that their possessions of these pretty things shall not be threatened by radicals, and that their comments on them shall not be interrupted by mere speculation on the soul of man.

"Not, understand me, that I should prefer the sort of little people you must find in Greenwich Village, who do nothing but chatter. I like people who pay their debts, who work, and love their wives. I wouldn't want to see here a bunch of superior souls sitting on the floor and dropping cigarette butts in empty hootch glasses. Only—"

He scratched his chin. "Oh, I don't know. But it depresses me so, the perpetual bright talk about gas-mileage and mah jong here. They sing of four-wheel brakes as the Persian poets sang of rose leaves; their religion is road-paving and their patriotism the relation of weather to Sunday motoring; and they discuss balloon tires with a quiet fervor such as the fifteenth century gave to the Immaculate Conception. I feel like creeping off to a cottage in the Massachusetts hills and taking up my Greek again. Oh, let's talk of simpler things!"

"Then tell me your opinion of the presidential campaign. I suppose you'll vote for Coolidge. I remember you always liked books that the public libraries barred out as immoral, but you wanted to hang the I. W. W. and you thought La Follette was a doubtful fellow."

"Did I? Well, this time I'm going to vote for La Follette. I think most of the people who resent, when they go calling, having good talk interrupted by having to listen to morons saying 'Well, good evening, folks!' amid the demoniac static from the loud-speaker—most of them *must* vote for La Follette, and if we don't elect him this year, some time we shall. I have faith that the very passion in the worship of the Great God Motor must bring its own reaction."

"Kennicott feels he has us beaten forever."

"If he has, if the only voice ever to be heard at the altar is Coolidge on the phonograph and the radio, then our grandsons will have to emigrate to Siberia. But I don't believe it. Even the Kennicotts progress— I hope. His ancestors ridiculed Harvey, then Koch, and Pasteur, but he accepts them; and his grandsons will laugh at Coolidge as Kennicott now laughs at the whiskers of Rutherford B. Hayes.

"But meanwhile I feel a little lonely, in the evenings. Now, that the movies have, under the nation-wide purification by fundamentalism and the rigid Vermont ideals of the President, changed almost entirely from the lively absurdities of cowpuncher films to unfaithful wives and ginny flappers in bathing suits, I can't even attend them. I'm going—and, Lord, how I'll be roasted by the respectable lawyers!—I'm going out to campaign for La Follette!

"We must all do it. We've been bullied too long by the Doc Kennicotts and by the beautiful big balloon tires that roll over the new pavement on Main Street—and over our souls!"

2. What the Movies Taught

Before D. W. Griffith's two great epics, *The Birth of a Nation* (1915) and *Intolerance* (1916), respectable middle-class Americans generally regarded the movies as popular entertainment for the working population, to be ignored as beneath notice, or to be censored as potentially harmful to morals. Griffith's achievements demonstrated the artistic possibilities and the myth-making power of motion pictures. Swiftly thereafter, as part of the First World War's cultural transformations, the expanding motion picture industry in Southern California emerged as the first mass cultural medium in America. During the Twenties Americans from every class and region projected toward movies and the movie industry ambitions and values that they had directed elsewhere before the War, or had not felt at all: the dream of instant stardom, of being singled out from a crowd and turned overnight into a star; the more mundane but equally powerful lure of rapid success in the production end of movies through technological wizardry or managerial finesse; the vicarious wish to share in the material luxury and social glamour of Hollywood life among the stars.

At the end of the Twenties the American middle class realized with a rush the powerful influence of a decade's dreams and desires upon their children. Had a whole generation indelibly learned its manners and morals, unattended at Saturday matinees? Educators, sociologists, and psychologists avidly began to study the first generation to grow up under the influence of a mass cultural medium—the young people whom one author called "our movie-made children." A particularly ambitious project, consisting of more than a dozen studies undertaken between 1929 and 1932, was supported by The Payne Fund for the Motion Picture Research Council. One study in the series, *Movies and Conduct* (1933), focused on the impact of movies on youthful behavior. Its author, the sociologist Herbert Blumer (1900–   ), asked more than 1500 college and high school students in Arkansas, North Carolina, New York, and Illinois to write, anonymously, autobiographies of their motion picture experiences. Blumer printed some of the autobiographies as an appendix to his study, identifying their authors by sex, age, school level, and race or nationality. At a time when nearly everything written on the movies

dwelt exclusively on the lives of the stars and the behind-the-scenes operations of the studios, these autobiographies provide one of the rare bits of
evidence we have from the Twenties about *how people actually felt* about, and
responded to, changes in their technology and culture, new ways of spending
their time.

Students' "Motion Picture Autobiographies"

A GIRL OF 22, COLLEGE SENIOR, NATIVE WHITE PARENTS

I have tried to remember the first time that I went to a movie. It must
have been when I was very young because I cannot recall the event.
My real interest in motion pictures showed itself when I was in about
fourth grade at grammar school. There was a theater on the route by
which I went home from school and as the picture changed every other
day I used to spend the majority of my time there. A gang of us little
tots went regularly.

One day I went to see Viola Dana in *The Five Dollar Baby*. The scenes
which showed her as a baby fascinated me so that I stayed to see it over
four times. I forgot home, dinner, and everything. About eight o'clock
mother came after me—frantically searching the theater.

Next to pictures about children, I loved serials and pie-throwing
comedies, not to say cowboy 'n' Indian stories. These kind I liked until
I was twelve or thirteen; then I lost interest in that type, and the spec-
tacular, beautifully decorated scenes took my eye. Stories of dancers and
stage life I loved. Next, mystery plays thrilled me and one never slipped
by me. At fifteen I liked stories of modern youth; the gorgeous clothes
and settings fascinated me.

My first favorite was Norma Talmadge. I liked her because I saw her
in a picture where she wore ruffly hoop-skirts which greatly attracted me.
My favorites have always been among the women; the only men stars
I've ever been interested in are Tom Mix, Doug Fairbanks and Thomas

Excerpts from students' "Motion Picture Autobiographies," in Herbert
Blumer, *Movies and Conduct* (New York, 1933), pp. 220–223, 243–247,
251–257.

Meighan, also Doug McLean and Bill Haines. Colleen Moore I liked for a while, but now her haircut annoys me. My present favorites are rather numerous: Joan Crawford, Billie Dove, Sue Carol, Louise Brooks, and Norma Shearer. I nearly forgot about Barbara LaMar. I really worshiped her. I can remember how I diligently tried to draw every gown she wore on the screen and how broken-hearted I was when she died. You would have thought my best friend had passed away.

Why I like my favorites? I like Joan Crawford because she is so modern, so young, and so vivacious! Billie Dove is so beautifully beautiful that she just gets under your skin. She is the most beautiful woman on the screen! Sue Carol is cute 'n' peppy. Louise Brooks has her assets, those being legs 'n' a clever hair-cut. Norma Shearer wears the kind of clothes I like and is a clever actress.

I nearly always have gone and yet go to the theater with someone. I hate to go alone as it is more enjoyable to have someone to discuss the picture with. Now I go with a bunch of girls or on a date with girls and boys or with one fellow.

The day-dreams instigated by the movies consist of clothes, ideas on furnishings, and manners. I don't day-dream much. I am more concerned with materialistic things and realisms. Nevertheless it is hard for any girl not to imagine herself cuddled up in some voluptuous ermine wrap, etc.

The influence of movies on my play as a child—all that I remember is that we immediately enacted the parts interesting us most. And for weeks I would attempt to do what that character would have done until we saw another movie and some other hero or heroine won us over.

I'm always at the mercy of the actor at a movie. I feel nearly every emotion he portrays and forget that anything else is on earth. I was so horrified during *The Phantom of the Opera* when Lon Chaney removed his mask, revealing that hideous face, that until my last day I shall never forget it.

I am deeply impressed, however, by pathos and pitifulness, if you understand. I remember one time seeing a movie about an awful fire. I was terrified by the reality of it and for several nights I was afraid to go to sleep for fear of a fire and even placed my hat and coat near by in case it was necessary to make a hasty exit. Pictures of robbery and floods have affected my behavior the same way. Have I ever cried at pictures? Cried! I've practically dissolved myself many a time. How people can witness a heart-rending picture and not weep buckets of tears is more than I can understand. *The Singing Fool, The Iron Mask,*

Seventh Heaven, Our Dancing Daughters, and other pictures I saw when very young which centered about the death of someone's baby and showed how the big sister insisted on her jazz 'n' whoopee regardless of the baby or not—these nearly killed me. Something like that, anyway; and I hated that girl so I wanted to walk up to the screen and tear her up! As for liking to cry—why, I never thought of that. It isn't a matter of liking or not. Sometimes it just can't be helped. Movies do change my moods, but they never last long. I'm off on something else before I know it. If I see a dull or morose show, it sort of deadens me and the vim and vigor dies out 'til the movie is forgotten. For example, Mary Pickford's movie—*Sparrows*—gave me the blues for a week or so, as did li'l Sonny Boy in *The Singing Fool.* The poor kid's a joke now.

This modern knee-jiggling, hand-clapping effect used for accompanying popular music has been imitated from the movies, I think. But unless I've unconsciously picked up little mannerisms, I can think of no one that I've tried to imitate.

Goodness knows, you learn plenty about love from the movies. That's their long run; you learn more from actual experience, though! You do see how the gold-digger systematically gets the poor fish in tow. You see how the sleek-haired, long-earringed, languid-eyed siren lands the men. You meet the flapper, the good girl, 'n' all the feminine types and their little tricks of the trade. We pick up their snappy comebacks which are most handy when dispensing with an unwanted suitor, a too ardent one, too backward one, etc. And believe me, they observe and remember, too.

I can remember when we all nudged one another and giggled at the last close-up in a movie. I recall when during the same sort of close-up when the boy friend squeezes your arm and looks soulfully at you. Oh, it's lotsa fun! No, I never fell in love with my movie idol. When I don't know a person really, when I know I'll never have a chance with 'em, I don't bother pining away over them and writing them idiotic letters as some girls I've known do. I have imagined playing with a movie hero many times though; that is while I'm watching the picture. I forget about it when I'm outside the theater. Buddy Rogers and Rudy Valentino have kissed me oodles of times, but they don't know it. God bless 'em!

Yes, love scenes have thrilled me and have made me more receptive to love. I was going with a fellow whom I liked as a playmate, so to speak; he was a little younger than me and he liked me a great deal. We went to the movie—Billie Dove in it. Oh, I can't recall the name but Antonio Moreno was the lead, and there were some lovely scenes which just got me all hot 'n' bothered. After the movie we went for a ride 'n' parked along the lake; it was a gorgeous night. Well, I just melted (as it were) in his arms, making him believe I loved him, which I didn't. I sort of came to, but I promised to go steady with him. I went with him 'til I couldn't bear the sight of him. Such trouble I had trying to get rid of him, and yet not hurt his feelings, as I had led him to believe I cared more than I did. I've wished many times that we'd never seen the movie. Another thing not exactly on the subject but important, I began smoking after watching Dolores Costello, I believe it was, smoke, which hasn't added any joy to my parents' lives.

A GIRL OF 17, HIGH SCHOOL SENIOR, NATIVE WHITE

Rudolph Valentino in *The Shiek* was laughed at by me. I came home and told my parents that I had seen a marvelous actor who sure knew how to ride a horse but he was always mushing over a lady. At a later date, when I had matured by at least two years, I saw the *Son of a Sheik* and came home with a different report. A report very flattering to his ability and method as a lover. I often wondered what it would be like to be in his arms, if he gave wet kisses or dry ones, if he smacked his lips or merely held them tightly, but death took him away and now I've ceased wondering about these wonders.

Three Wise Fools starring Alec B. Francis afforded me much pleasure and took away that misconceived notion of mine that step-parents or guardians were very mean and would make you slave for them as in the story of Cinderella. *Black Oxen* with Corinne Griffith made me believe more in the extraordinary powers of chemistry as did *Tol'able David* starring Richard Barthelmess. *Bluebeard's Eighth Wife*, featuring Gloria Swanson, greatly appealed to me and in one respect was very beneficial. Up until then, movie picture titles were ignored by me. But that title about Bluebeard, and I had read the fairy tale, developed my sense of why is a movie title and what is its relation to a movie. From that time on I have never yet seen a picture whose title I have not fitted to it to my own satisfaction. I will only skim over the historical pictures I saw, namely, *Paul Revere's Ride, Abraham Lincoln, Man Without a Country, Covered Wagon,* and *The Vanishing American,* as I did not care for them in the least. The Duncan Twins in *Topsy and Eva* I will also ignore for the reason that my anticipation of the show was so great that I was doomed to disappointment in the realization of it.

William Haines in *Brown of Harvard* was the first really impressive college picture I saw, and I then resolved to refrain from molesting freshmen when I am an upper classman in college. However, I do not want the reader to get the idea that I am still of the same opinion.

William Boyd in *The Volga Boatman* was the realized movie ideal of my thoughts. That was the most perfect picture I have ever seen. Photography, direction, acting, subtitling, accuracy of details, truth of plot, truth of historical event, truth in scenic backgrounds, correct costuming—everything combined to make a truly perfect picture! I still don't know if I received anything of real value from that picture, but if anyone would quiz me on any detail, whether of action or description or detail, I could answer correctly. I only saw it once but I was so entranced by it that I overlooked nothing. I forgot nothing, I remembered everything.

The War Pictures, and I believe I am right in capitalizing what I did, have convinced me of the real evils of war, of the ideas that though war is a menace, disarmament can never be fully and thoroughly put into effect.

Barbed Wire with Pola Negri, *The Legion of the Condemned,* and *The Big Parade* served as the founders of those ideas. One incident from *The Big Parade* I would like to requote here. John Gilbert is in a shell-hole, anxiously awaiting the return of his buddy from No Man's Land. His nerves are on edge; the cannons roaring about him and the shells bursting in air arouse his hatred of the general's orders; he hates himself for staying there like the general told him to do instead of going out to find and aid his buddy. Then on top of all this tension a soldier from the trench crawls into the shell-hole to tell him to quit standing there and pacing but to lie down so that the enemy will not spy their dugout. "Orders from the general" the soldier said. And then John Gilbert rose, jumping out of the dugout, he pauses long enough to draw himself up to the stature of a real man and to fire back, "Orders! Orders! Who's fighting this war—Men or Orders?" And with that he leaves to seek out his buddy from God knows where. I shall never forget that bit of philosophy nor shall I ever forget the incident causing supposedly that bit of wisdom.

Underworld pictures such as *The Dragnet, London After Midnight, Twelve Miles Out,* (this was not exactly an underworld picture, but inasmuch as it dealt with hi-jackers, rumrunners, etc., I have classed it as such), and *Streets of Sin* are in my opinion utterly worthless and in some cases ruinous for the unsettled youths. It gives too many ideas to become one of those gunmen because they believe they have found some new and ingenious method of outwitting the police, and then, wouldn't it be fun to realize their William S. Hart child ideals by going out and shooting and capturing and escaping and then not have to pay any penalty? Many people maintain that pictures of that type are instructive rather than destructive. They believe that youth upon viewing pictures of that type will profit by seeing that the gunman pays the penalty, but it has been proved time and again that youth loves to be inventive, adventurous—wants to always outwit somebody. And then people say that those underworld pictures are so instructive (and again I am sarcastic!).

John Gilbert in *Masks of the Devil* I would like to say several things about. By chance, the day after I had viewed that show my English teacher used it as an example of something I cannot just now recall, but then she started to tell what she thought of the show. She said it was immoral—immoral in the sense of truth, because, she said it was not true; it was a lot of "bunk." I then raised my hand, and upon being called on, said that if that show was not truth, then all fiction books are also immoral and every one knows that if fiction was so immoral, it would not be handed down from one generation to another. Her answer was that they were different sorts of truths. That was a teacher's point of view of that show. I, as a pupil, claim that it was immoral in the sense of pollution. If the reader has seen this show, I am leaving it to him to decide whether the younger generation or the older generation has a better interpretation of movies and their morals. *The Noose* and *The Wheel of Chance*, melodramas in a sense, were exceedingly similar. *The Wheel of Chance* was adapted from the book, *Roulette*, and its philosophy was that life is like the roulette wheel—one either wins or loses—there is no semi-loss and semi-gain; that we're just the little ball that spins around on this wheel of life, uncertain where we are to fall, yet always molding our landing places.

The last show that I am going to mention is the show that so accurately pictured the viewpoints of the younger generation—*Our Dancing Daughters* starring Joan Crawford. In Joan Crawford the true spirit of the younger generation was shown. No matter what happened she played fair. She even lost her man and in the eyes of the older generation they think that when a modern young miss wants her man back she'd even be a cutthroat, but Joan Crawford showed that even in a crisis like that she was sport enough to play fair! And "play fair" is really the motto of the better class of young Americans, and even in the best products there is always a blemish so why must the younger generation be so shamefully thought of. I hope many of these women who are scandalized at the actions of the modern miss saw that show and, if they did not change their beliefs after seeing it, then, it does not mean that the movie was a failure but that they are the failures not to recognize so obvious a truth.

And now, I hope I have convinced the reader of this: that movies are godsends, and to express my sentiments, long may they live and long may they stay in the land of the free and the home of the brave!

COLLEGE GIRL, 18, NATIVE BORN OF WEALTHY SWEDISH PARENTS

Upon going to my first dance I asked the hairdresser to fix my hair like Greta Garbo's. Of course I did not tell the hairdresser that I was copying this intriguing and fascinating actress or she would think I had gone insane. I, the "nicest" girl, whom mothers to this day set as an example to their daughters and young sons. Oh, the unconscious cruelty of father when he forbade me pleasures other children had and have, and I partly made up this injustice to myself by seeing a picture once or twice a year and living them over and over again. I lived the life of the heroine and used my little sister for the rival or unpleasant character, very seldom the good character. The rival afforded me more opportunity to be dramatic. In speaking on graduation day I did my best to finish with the swaying-like curtsy which Pola Negri taught me from the stage.

Somehow or other Dolores Costello has not taught me mannerisms, but what beauty is. When I see her I cannot help but truly believe that there is a God, creator of the beautiful. She brings to me that deep feeling of beauty and all that goes with beauty—love, truth, sympathy, etc.

Only at one time did the movies decide my yielding to a temptation which my better self condemned. I regret it very much. I had been fond of a dark boy, somewhat like John Gilbert, who had proposed many times while I was a sophomore in high school. He seemed perfect to me at the time. His family are among the best known aristocrats and he was supposedly intelligent. How I dislike him for this lack of the "supposed intelligence." He did not realize what he was asking me to do but they are not all of that type. One evening after he had built more alluring castles than usual, I decided it would be romantic to run away with him. No longer would I be under my dear but misunderstanding father's strict rules.

At that time we lived some distance from here in an enormous home with a beautiful garden surrounding it. My "hero" was to wait near the thick bushes, and to help me to get out through the windows as soon as it was dark. I had scarcely flashed the light as the signal, when father came into my room. He had been told by the gardener or someone else that somebody was lurking among the trees. He came to warn me about closing my windows, and found me with my clothes packed. No one outside of father, the boy, and I will ever know this, but it hurt all of us.

Because my father had been very strict in his beliefs, regarding marriage, rights of women, and these beliefs gave me many chances to rebel unsuccessfully, I was in a mood to listen and see other beliefs. Sometimes before this again unsuccessful rebellion I had seen a runaway marriage which had impressed me tremendously. I did think that having a hero like this dark boy to protect me from father's anger and strictness would be heaven. Curiously enough I was more interested in the details of escaping—how the girl got her clothes down, how she got down, what he did to help her down—all these details I watched more carefully than the rest of the play in the runaway marriage.

My reactions toward the movies, so different from those of my sister, may be due to my desire to be above my friends. I have always been ahead, at least two years, in school. Before sixteen I was graduated from high school, and I did none of the things I would have liked to do. I have always been known as reserved and quiet among others outside of the family, or as a speaker among the various foreign clubs, or as a serious student, but at times I wanted to play with those of my age. I would have given all my toys or anything to be with others on the street. And all this pent-up grief, desire for play, anticipated joy in company with others of my age has been unfulfilled. Only after I had been to a movie did I release these emotions when no one saw me or heard me except my little sister. I felt so much better after having been naughty Pola Negri for a few moments, or Vilma Banky without being reprimanded by that old governess or father's sister. After being "naughty," undignified and unladylike, as father would say, I would see Dolores Costello or through her see Sister Cecelia and settle down again for a few days. I would not relive some old picture again until I had been thwarted in or refused my desires. Dolores Costello has an influence over me which is similar to that of father when he is sad and dreams of past days.

Do I day-dream? I think that my "confession" thus far shows much day-dreaming. I have (most of the time) imagined myself as someone above many, where others may come to me for help. I imagine myself advising parents in some big institution not to be too strict with their children, to allow them time to play even with the dirtiest little boy or girl. How would I have enjoyed to run down the street with even a colored girl or boy of my size. I have always dreamed of marrying a poor man, contrary to father's life plans, and through this poor man of meeting hard-working, honest people whom I shall be able to help with whatever I have. And because there is every possibility that these dreams may come true, I cling to my dream world woven about the movies I have seen. Just what I would like to do would be something like this: I should like to build a big factory of some kind, and enable students, children of laborers, to become well educated through their earnings, in part-time work.

Although I feel very intensely the pain, joy, sorrow of the heroine, or the struggling character, I do not, and cannot cry. I don't think that I have cried but twice, just dry, painful sobs, and that was days after the funeral when I realized what death at home meant. How many times tears would have been a blessing instead of those painful choking feelings in my chest somewhere. Scenes of sorrow, as in *Resurrection* where the lovers are in the power of love and by force are separated, and the girl is starving because she cannot find work anywhere; in the poor family scene, the struggles, joy, grief; in a picture *Divorce*, or something like that, where the child dies of neglect because the parents are too busy fighting for a divorce to care for the child,—all these come back to me. These scenes become a part of me and teach me unselfishness, kindness, and sympathy. Many times these scenes or the recollections of them mean nothing until trouble or pain comes to me and I recall the pains or troubles which I saw in some picture.

When I discovered I should like to have this coquettish and coy look which all girls may have, I tried to do it in my room. And surprises! I could imitate Pola Negri's cool or fierce look, Vilma Banky's sweet but coquettish attitude. I have learned the very way of taking my gentlemen friends to and from the door with that wistful smile, until it has become a part of me. I have been disgusted with the flirting and vamping in the movies. And yet, haven't I done it to one? Yes, but I console myself, that it wasn't with anyone, or everyone, but the one.

Has anyone not admired a passionate lover? I certainly did when I was in high school; and John Gilbert gave me reason to admire a passionate lover. He made me wonder what it feels like to be loved in that manner. And this unconscious yearning became conscious when I met one who was almost my ideal. But this yearning, as many of father's "not nice" yearnings, had to be satisfied by living and experiencing them in the movies, until recently since I have been engaged. But if I see any more of these passionate fiery movies I will not be able to resist the pleas to become a wife before next quarter. These passionate pictures stir such longings, desires, and urges as I never expected any person to possess. Just the way the passionate lover held his sweetheart suggests so many beautiful and intimate relations, which even my reacting a scene does not satisfy any more. I cannot believe myself that I am "I" any more; because when I first entered high school these scenes gave me unpleasant and guilty feelings. I would determine that I would never see them again. And now they come back clearly to me, but in such a different light. I actually want to experience these scenes, and see beauty in them.

A BOY OF 17, HIGH SCHOOL SENIOR, NATIVE BLACK PARENTS

The earliest movie stars that I can remember were Wm. S. Hart and Tom Mix who played entirely in Western stories. I liked to see them shoot the villain and save the girl and "live happily ever after." It caused me to shout as loudly, or louder, than the rest. Following them came Douglas Fairbanks, who seemed so carefree and light that he won nearly everyone with his personality. He would jump, use a lasso, thrust a sword, and fight in a way to satisfy any child's desire for action. Now I have no special star but I think Emil Jannings is a great actor because he seems to put his heart and soul into his work.

As a boy, I went with nearly every one to the theater; my mother, father, sister or brother, relatives, and friends. Usually I went in the afternoon or evening, anywhere from one to five times a week. Now I still go with my relatives occasionally but mostly with friends or alone.

I cannot recall anything that I have done that I had seen in the movies except try to make love. It happened that when I was small there were no boys in my neighborhood and I had to go several blocks before I could play with some my size or age. But there were a few girls in my neighborhood my size. Seeing Douglas Fairbanks woo his maiden I decided to try some of "Doug's stuff" on one of the girl friends. I know I was awkward and it proved more or less a flop.

Several times on seeing big, beautiful cars which looked to be bubbling over with power and speed, I dreamed of having a car more powerful and speedier than all the rest. I saw this car driven by myself up to the girl friend's door and taking her for a ride. (I was then eight years old and in my dreams I was no older.) Then too, I saw Adolphe Menjou, the best dressed man in the world, try in various ways to kill me because I had won his title. Perhaps the picture that left the most depressing picture on my mind was one in which a murdered man was thrown over a high cliff from a mountain top. I could see that dead body falling, falling to the rocky depths far below and squash into almost nothing. Some nights I dreamed of falling and other nights I had nightmares from dreaming of the same thing, awoke in a cold sweat, and was not able to go to sleep again till dawn. Whenever I saw anyone looking down from some rather high place or some workman in the precarious position, I had a sickly feeling in the pit of my stomach and averted my eyes.

The most heartbreaking picture that I ever saw and which caused me to shed uncontrollable tears was *Over the Hill,* starring Mary Carr. She was ill treated by all her children except one and had to go to the poorhouse and scrub daily. This picture caused me to see my mother in a new light and make a vow that I would always protect and provide for her as long as I or she lives. This mood lasted until the comedy, when I soon forgot it, but I have always kept my vow.

I have not adopted any mannerisms from the movies but I have tried to act like the actors of a picture for a short time after seeing the picture. Such actions were trying to act like a screen drunkard, a hero cowboy who shot and killed the villain and rode triumphantly away with the fair one. I used to go to "wild western" pictures and observe the Indians grab their hearts, or put their hands over their hearts, turn all away around and fall dead after they had been shot while resisting the unlawful Americans. When my chums played cowboy or cops and robbers, I tried to imitate these Indians in falling. Of course, many besides myself, I suppose, have tried to imitate Charles Chaplin or Douglas Fairbanks but I became so proficient in imitating Charles Chaplin that I became to be known as Charles in the neighborhood in which I formerly lived which made me dream of the time when I, Charles Chaplin, would be the star of the silver screen. Douglas Fairbanks gave me an inspiration to jump, fight, use long whips, ride, use rapiers and to be as happy and as full of life as he seemed to be.

While imitating these stars I became interested in love pictures and went to see them as often as I could. This liking developed after seeing such stars as Wallace Reid, Norma Talmadge, Rudolph Valentino, Mary Pickford, and Pola Negri. These actors stirred within me a desire to do an ardent love scene with a girl. The first girl that I tried this on said that I was crazy. The second girl wasn't interested. But the third girl actually thought that I really meant what I was saying about her eyes and lips and she permitted me to try out everything that I had planned and this occasion proved successful in more ways than one.

Occasionally I used to think constantly of such actors as Wallace Reid,

Rudolph Valentino, or Pola Negri; especially the latter whose bewitching eyes instilled within me many ungodly thoughts that never were voiced.

I cannot say that I received any temptations from the movies but I did get one real ambition. That being, to fly and be an aviator. This desire originated from such pictures as *Wings*, *The Flying Fleet*, and *Lilac Time*, all of which featured airplanes. Now I visit all the aviation exhibits and "talks" possible. The most interesting show I have yet seen is the one that was at the Chicago Coliseum. I visit the municipal airport often and just the sound of an airplane's motor is enough to start one thinking of that time when I am going to have a powerful plane of my own and see all the world by means of it.

Another ambition that I had was to be a "Jackie Coogan" at the age of eight. I thought I would be more of a star than Jackie himself. I dreamed of the time when I would be a great star and have a great deal of money because of it. Then I could buy a tiny automobile, just my size, that would run as fast as any big car. I would also have some ponies, a beautiful home for my mother and myself and be a veritable "lady's man." (All this time I was eight years old.)

Sometimes from seeing such pictures as *The Birth of a Nation* I would not but feel the injustice done the Negro race by other races. Most of the bad traits of unintelligent Negroes are used in many pictures and a lovable or educated character is rarely pictured.

At other times, *West Point*, a picture of college life and a military training school, stirs within me a desire to go to college or some military or naval school away from home and serve my country as best I can.

In crime pictures, as in real life, the criminal not only becomes the hero on the screen but outside the theater as well. At other times the criminal's life is such that the audience simply abhors being such a character. If there were more of the latter type of picture I am of the opinion that there would be far less crime.

3. Ideals and Idols

What possible image can we have of movies in the Twenties? There is as yet no critical or historical canon for American movies, and if there were, it could not avail us much without ready access to the films themselves, as we have for other art forms of the Twenties—novels, poems, plays, music, paintings. We are left with legends—of Valentino or Stroheim or Fairbanks; with stills, suggesting, at their best, a world we cannot enter; and occasionally with the experience of a film. The nostalgic mystique of silent movies has long since disappeared. It did not last beyond the early years of talking pictures, when the advent of sound seemed permanently to have destroyed visual subtlety in Hollywood films. At times it takes a willing eye to grasp the aesthetics of silent movies, and not every silent film deserves the effort. But for a few silent film directors, the need to tell their stories in pictures without spoken words brought out extraordinary powers of artistry—in the composition of shots, in the expressive photography of faces and crowds, in the flow and structure of visual action. The silent movies of D. W. Griffith and Josef von Sternberg, of the comedy actor-directors Charles Chaplin and Buster Keaton, among others, will maintain a permanent place among the great achievements of the American movies.

The audiences of the Twenties, of course, cared most about the stars. And there was no little irony in their adulation for the movies' alluring heroines and dashing heroes. Because native middle-class Americans before the First World War had considered movies disreputable, the positions of power in the movie industry—financier, producer, director, star—were left open to outsiders and minorities in American society, immigrants, Catholics, and Jews. At a time in the Twenties when nativist sentiments and hostile feelings against Catholics and Jews were running high, middle-class American movie-goers were enjoying movies financed by men like Joseph P. Kennedy and Louis B. Mayer, directed by Sternberg and Stroheim or Murnau, and starring Valentino or Garbo or Dietrich. Such was the power of the silver screen.

The following stills from movies of 1919 to 1931 present some of the significant actors and actresses, movies, and directors of the Twenties.

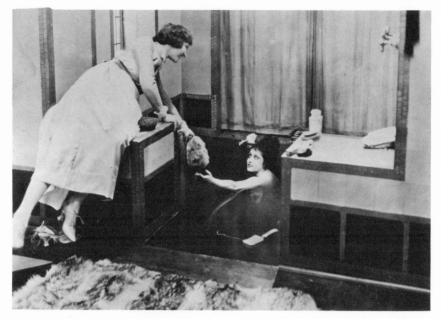

1. *Gloria Swanson in Cecil B. DeMille's* Male and Female, *1919.*

2. *Richard Barthelmess and Lillian Gish in D. W. Griffith's* Broken Blossoms, *1919.*

3. *Richard Barthelmess in Henry King's* Tol'able David, *1921.*

4. *Douglas Fairbanks in* The Mark of Zorro, *1921.*

5. *Erich von Stroheim in* Foolish Wives, *1922*

6. *King Vidor directing John Gilbert in* The Big Parade, *1925*

7. *D. W. Griffith directs Mae Marsh in* The White Rose, *1923.*

8. *Buster Keaton in* The Navigator, *1924.*

9. *George O'Brien and Janet Gaynor in F. W. Murnau's* Sunrise, 1927.

10. *Vilma Banky and Rudolph Valentino in* Son of the Sheik, 1926.

11. *John Gilbert and Greta Garbo in* Flesh and the Devil, *1926.*

12. *George Bancroft, Evelyn Brent, and Larry Semon in Josef von Sternberg's* Underworld, *1927.*

13. *Charles Chaplin in* The Circus, *1928.*

14. *Emil Jannings in Josef von Sternberg's* The Last Command, *1928.*

15. *Jean Harlow, James Cagney, and Edward Woods on the set of* The Public Enemy, *1931.*

16. *Marlene Dietrich and Gary Cooper in Josef von Sternberg's* Morocco, *1930.*

4. America on the Road

Twentieth century man may so readily accept the vast alterations in consciousness brought about by technological change, chiefly because he remains unaware of them. Only in retrospect can we look back and see how differently we used to think and act. The automobile is a valid case in point. When the automobile became a pervasive artifact of American life in the Twenties, it provided millions of Americans with a mobile extension of the self, a machine that could go when and where an individual driver wished to direct it. With an automobile life expanded. You could travel faster to more distant places, go and come at your whim, alone or with others. Surely there were psychic responses to such new powers and new dimensions of time and space. One searches in vain, however, for proof of it in books and magazines of the Twenties. As with the movies, they comment abundantly on the technical and commercial aspects of auto driving—tire-changing and gas mileage, the joys and problems of tourism, auto camps and the new motels, road conditions, model changes, sales resistance and how to overcome it, the effect of the automobile on country stores (their business went down as farmers drove to town for Saturday shopping). But how did it feel to be on the highway in a closed car, driving to an unfamiliar town, a distant campground, a roadhouse; high speeds, new mores, strange faces, what were they like? Those who wrote on automobiles in the Twenties leave it to our imagination.

   Most later accounts of the automobile's impact on American culture rely heavily on the interviews and observations gathered by Robert S. Lynd (1892–   ) and Helen Merrell Lynd (1896–   ) in their intensive sociological survey of Muncie, Indiana—*Middletown: A Study in Modern American Culture*. The Lynds wished to study the changes in social and cultural life in a small American city from 1890 to 1924. As their research progressed it focused more directly on the effects of industrialism on community life. Their field work and writing took them more than five years, and was financed by the Institute for Social and Religious Research. *Middletown* is the most widely known of several important social research projects at the end of the Twenties that indicate a shift in the way Americans learned about and evaluated their culture. In the late Twenties they began increasingly to look toward sociological research and field studies for information on the nature of American life, and normative judgments on its quality and direction.

Middletown
ROBERT S. and HELEN MERRELL LYND

Although lectures, reading, music, and art are strongly intrenched in Middletown's traditions, it is none of these that would first attract the attention of a newcomer watching Middletown at play.

"Why on earth do you need to study what's changing this country?" said a lifelong resident and shrewd observer of the Middle West. "I can tell you what's happening in just four letters: A-U-T-O!"

In 1890 the possession of a pony was the wildest flight of a Middletown boy's dreams. In 1924 a Bible class teacher in a Middletown school concluded her teaching of the Creation: "And now, children, is there any of these animals that God created that man could have got along without?" One after another of the animals from goat to mosquito was mentioned and for some reason rejected; finally, "The horse!" said one boy triumphantly, and the rest of the class agreed. Ten or twelve years ago a new horse fountain was installed at the corner of the Courthouse square; now it remains dry during most of the blazing heat of a Mid-Western summer and no one cares. The "horse culture" of Middletown has almost disappeared.[1]

Nor was the horse culture in all the years of its undisputed sway ever as pervasive a part of the life of Middletown as is the cluster of habits that have grown up overnight around the automobile. A local carriage manufacturer of the early days estimates that about 125 families owned a horse and buggy in 1890, practically all of them business class folk. "A regular sight summer mornings was Mrs. Jim B—— [the wife of one of the city's leading men] with a friend out in her rig, shelling peas for dinner while her horse ambled along the road." As spring came on each year entries like these began to appear in the diaries:

[1] Two million horse-drawn carriages were manufactured in the United States in 1909 and 10,000 in 1923; 80,000 automobiles were manufactured in 1909 and 4,000,000 in 1923.

Robert S. Lynd and Helen Merrell Lynd, *Middletown: A Study in Modern American Culture* (New York, 1929), pp. 251–263.

"April 1, '88. Easter. A beautiful day, cloudy at times but very warm, and much walking and riding about town."

"May 19, '89. Considerable carriage riding today."

"July 16, '89. Considerable riding this evening. People out 'cooling off.'"

"Sept. 18, '87. Wife and myself went to the Cemetery this afternoon in the buggy. Quite a number of others were placing flowers upon the graves of their dear ones. . . ."

But if the few rode in carriages in 1890, the great mass walked. The Sunday afternoon stroll was the rule.

Meanwhile, in a Middletown machine shop a man was tinkering at a "steam wagon" which in September, 1890, was placed on the street for the first trial. . . .

"The vehicle has the appearance of an ordinary road wagon, when put in motion," said the newspaper, "though there is no tongue attached. It is run on the principle of a railroad locomotive, a lever in front which guides the vehicle being operated by the person driving. The power is a small engine placed under the running gears and the steam is made by a small gasoline flame beneath a fuel tank. Twenty-five miles an hour can be attained with this wonderful device. The wagon will carry any load that can be placed on it, climbing hills and passing over bad roads with the same ease as over a level road. The wagon complete cost nearly $1,000."

In other cities other men were also working at these "horseless wagons." As late as 1895 Elwood Haynes of Kokomo, Indiana, one of the early tinkerers, was stopped by a policeman as he drove his horseless car into Chicago and ordered to take the thing off the streets. In 1896 the resplendent posters of the alert P. T. Barnum featured in the foreground a "horseless carriage to be seen every day in the new street parade"—with elephants, camels and all the rest of the circus lost in the background while the crowd cheers "the famous Duryea Motorwagon or Motorcycle."

The first real automobile appeared in Middletown in 1900. About 1906 it was estimated that "there are probably 200 in the city and county." At the close of 1923 there were 6,221 passenger cars in the city, one for every 6.1 persons, or roughly two for every three families.[2] Of these 6,221 cars,

[2] These numbers have undoubtedly increased greatly since the count was made.

As a matter of fact, by far the greater part of the wide diffusion of the automobile culture one observes today in Middletown has taken place within the last ten or fifteen years. There were less than 500,000 passenger automobiles registered in the entire United States in 1910 and only 5,500,000 in 1918, as over against 15,500,000 in 1924. (Cf. *Facts and Figures of the Automobile Industry, 1925 Edition,* published by the National Automobile Chamber of Commerce.)

41 per cent. were Fords; 54 per cent. of the total were cars of models of 1920 or later, and 17 per cent. models earlier than 1917. These cars average a bit over 5,000 miles a year. For some of the workers and some of the business class, use of the automobile is a seasonal matter, but the increase in surfaced roads and in closed cars is rapidly making the car a year-round tool for leisure-time as well as getting-a-living activities. As, at the turn of the century, business class people began to feel apologetic if they did not have a telephone, so ownership of an automobile has now reached the point of being an accepted essential of normal living.

Into the equilibrium of habits which constitutes for each individual some integration in living has come this new habit, upsetting old adjustments, and blasting its way through such accustomed and unquestioned dicta as "Rain or shine, I never miss a Sunday morning at church"; "A high school boy does not need much spending money"; "I don't need exercise, walking to the office keeps me fit"; "I wouldn't think of moving out of town and being so far from my friends"; "Parents ought always to know where their children are." The newcomer is most quickly and amicably incorporated into those regions of behavior in which men are engaged in doing impersonal, matter-of-fact things; much more contested is its advent where emotionally charged sanctions and taboos are concerned. No one questions the use of the auto for transporting groceries, getting to one's place of work or to the golf course, or in place of the porch for "cooling off after supper" on a hot summer evening; however much the activities concerned with getting a living may be altered by the fact that a factory can draw from workmen within a radius of forty-five miles, or however much old labor union men resent the intrusion of this new alternate way of spending an evening,[3] these things are hardly major issues. But when auto riding tends to replace the traditional call in the family parlor as a way of approach between the unmarried, "the home is endangered," and all-day Sunday motor trips are a "threat against the church"; it is in the activities concerned with the home and religion that the automobile occasions the greatest emotional conflicts.

Group-sanctioned values are disturbed by the inroads of the automobile upon the family budget.[4] A case in point is the not uncommon practice of

[3] "The Ford car has done an awful lot of harm to the unions here and everywhere else," growled one man prominent in Middletown labor circles. "As long as men have enough money to buy a second-hand Ford and tires and gasoline, they'll be out on the road and paying no attention to union meetings."

[4] What a motor car means as an investment by Middletown families can be gathered from the following accepted rates of depreciation: 30 per cent. the first year, 20 per cent. more the second, 10 per cent. more each of the next three years. The operating cost of the lightest car of the Ford, Chev-

mortgaging a home to buy an automobile. Data on automobile ownership were secured from 123 working class families. Of these, sixty have cars. Forty-one of the sixty own their homes. Twenty-six of these forty-one families have mortgages on their homes. Forty of the sixty-three families who do not own a car own their homes. Twenty-nine of these have mortgages on their homes. Obviously other factors are involved in many of Middletown's mortgages. That the automobile does represent a real choice in the minds of some at least is suggested by the acid retort of one citizen to the question about car ownership: "No, sir, we've *not* got a car. That's why we've got a home." According to an officer of a Middletown automobile financing company, 75 to 90 per cent of the cars purchased locally are bought on time payment, and a working man earning $35.00 a week frequently plans to use one week's pay each month as payment for his car.

The automobile has apparently unsettled the habit of careful saving for some families. "Part of the money we spend on the car would go to the bank, I suppose," said more than one working class wife. A business man explained his recent inviting of social oblivion by selling his car by saying: "My car, counting depreciation and everything, was costing mighty nearly $100.00 a month, and my wife and I sat down together the other night and just figured that we're getting along, and if we're to have anything later on, we've just got to begin to save." The "moral" aspect of the competition between the automobile and certain accepted expenditures appears in the remark of another business man, "An automobile is a luxury, and no one has a right to one if he can't afford it. I haven't the slightest sympathy for any one who is out of work if he owns a car."

Men in the clothing industry are convinced that automobiles are bought at the expense of clothing,[5] and the statements of a number of the working class wives bear this out:

"We'd rather do without clothes than give up the car," said one mother of nine children. "We used to go to his sister's to visit, but

---

rolet, Overland type, including garage rent and depreciation, has been conservatively figured by a national automotive corporation for the country as a whole at $5.00 a week or $0.05 a mile for family use for 5,000 miles a year and replacement at the end of seven years. The cost of tires, gas, oil, and repairs of the forty-seven of the workers' families interviewed who gave expenditures on cars for the past year ranged from $8.90 to $192.00.

[5] "The *National Retail Clothier* has been devoting space to trying to find out what is the matter with the clothing industry and has been inclined to blame it on the automobile. In one city, to quote an example cited in the articles, a store 'put on a campaign that usually resulted in a business of 150 suits and overcoats on a Saturday afternoon. This season the campaign netted seventeen sales, while an automobile agency across the street sold twenty-five cars on the weekly payment plan.' In another, 'retail clothiers are unanimous in blaming the automobile for the admitted slump in the retail clothing trade.' " (*Chicago Evening Post*, December 28, 1923.)

by the time we'd get the children shoed and dressed there wasn't any money left for carfare. Now no matter how they look, we just poke 'em in the car and take 'em along."

"We don't have no fancy clothes when we have the car to pay for," said another. "The car is the only pleasure we have."

Even food may suffer:

"I'll go without food before I'll see us give up the car," said one woman emphatically, and several who were out of work were apparently making precisely this adjustment.

Twenty-one of the twenty-six families owning a car for whom data on bathroom facilities happened to be secured live in homes without bathtubs. Here we obviously have a new habit cutting in ahead of an older one and slowing down the diffusion of the latter.[6]

Meanwhile, advertisements pound away at Middletown people with the tempting advice to spend money for automobiles for the sake of their homes and families:

"Hit the trail to better times!" says one advertisement.

Another depicts a gray-haired banker lending a young couple the money to buy a car and proffering the friendly advice: "Before you can save money, you first must make money. And to make it you must have health, contentment, and full command of all your resources. . . . I have often advised customers of mine to buy cars, as I felt that the increased stimulation and opportunity of observation would enable them to earn amounts equal to the cost of their cars."

Many families feel that an automobile is justified as an agency holding the family group together. "I never feel as close to my family as when we are all together in the car," said one business class mother, and one or two spoke of giving up Country Club membership or other recreations to get

[6] This low percentage of bathtubs would not hold for the entire car-owning group. The interviewers asked about bathtubs in these twenty-six cases out of curiosity, prompted by the run-down appearance of the homes.

While inroads upon savings and the re-allocation of items of home expenditure were the readjustments most often mentioned in connection with the financing of the family automobile, others also occur: "It's prohibition that's done it," according to an officer in the Middletown Trades Council; "drink money is going into cars." The same officer, in answering the question as to what he thought most of the men he comes in contact with are working for, guessed: "Twenty-five per cent. are fighting to keep their heads above water; 10 per cent. want to own their own homes; 65 per cent. are working to pay for cars." "All business is suffering," says a Middletown candy manufacturer and dealer. "The candy business is poor now to what it was before the war. There is no money in it any more. People just aren't buying candy so much now. How can they? Even laboring-men put all their money into cars, and every other branch of business feels it."

a car for this reason. "We don't spend anything on recreation except for the car. We save every place we can and put the money into the car. It keeps the family together," was an opinion voiced more than once. Sixty-one per cent. of 337 boys and 60 per cent. of 423 girls in the three upper years of the high school say that they motor more often with their parents than without them.[7]

But this centralizing tendency of the automobile may be only a passing phase; sets in the other direction are almost equally prominent. "Our daughters [eighteen and fifteen] don't use our car much because they are always with somebody else in their car when we go out motoring," lamented one business class mother. And another said, "The two older children [eighteen and sixteen] never go out when the family motors. They always have something else on." "In the nineties we were all much more together," said another wife. "People brought chairs and cushions out of the house and sat on the lawn evenings. We rolled out a strip of carpet and put cushions on the porch step to take care of the unlimited overflow of neighbors that dropped by. We'd sit out so all evening. The younger couples perhaps would wander off for half an hour to get a soda but come back to join in the informal singing or listen while somebody strummed a mandolin or guitar." "What on earth *do* you want me to do? Just sit around home all evening!" retorted a popular high school girl of today when her father discouraged her going out motoring for the evening with a young blade in a rakish car waiting at the curb. The fact that 348 boys and 382 girls in the three upper years of the high school placed "use of the automobile" fifth and fourth respectively in a list of twelve possible sources of disagreement between them and their parents suggests that this may be an increasing decentralizing agent.

An earnest teacher in a Sunday School class of working class boys and girls in their late teens was winding up the lesson on the temptations of of Jesus: "These three temptations summarize all the temptations we encounter today: physical comfort, fame, and wealth. Can you think of any temptation we have today that Jesus didn't have?" "Speed!" rejoined one boy. The unwanted interruption was quickly passed over. But the boy had mentioned a tendency underlying one of the four chief infringe-

[7] As over against these answers regarding the automobile, 21 per cent. of the boys and 33 per cent. of the girls said that they go to the movies more often with their parents than without them, 25 per cent. and 22 per cent. respectively answered similarly as regards "listening to the radio," and 31 per cent. and 48 per cent. as regards "singing or playing a musical instrument." On the basis of these answers it would appear that the automobile is at present operating as a more active agency drawing Middletown families together than any of these other agencies.

ments of group laws in Middletown today, and the manifestations of Speed are not confined to "speeding." "Auto Polo next Sunday!!" shouts the display advertisement of an amusement park near the city. "It's motor insanity—too fast for the movies!" The boys who have cars "step on the gas," and those who haven't cars sometimes steal them: "The desire of youth to step on the gas when it has no machine of its own," said the local press, "is considered responsible for the theft of the greater part of the [154] automobiles stolen from [Middletown] during the past year." [8]

The threat which the automobile presents to some anxious parents is suggested by the fact that of thirty girls brought before the juvenile court in the twelve months preceding September 1, 1924, charged with "sex crimes," for whom the place where the offense occurred was given in the records, nineteen were listed as having committed the offense in an automobile. Here again the automobile appears to some as an "enemy" of the home and society.

Sharp, also, is the resentment aroused by this elbowing new device when it interferes with old-established religious habits. The minister trying to change people's behavior in desired directions through the spoken word must compete against the strong pull of the open road strengthened by endless printed "copy" inciting to travel. Preaching to 200 people on a hot, sunny Sunday in midsummer on "The Supreme Need of Today," a leading Middletown minister denounced "automobilitis—the thing those people have who go off motoring on Sunday instead of going to church. If you want to use your car on Sunday, take it out Sunday morning and bring some shut-ins to church and Sunday School; then in the afternoon, if you choose, go out and worship God in the beauty of nature—but don't neglect to worship Him indoors too." This same month there appeared in the *Saturday Evening Post,* reaching approximately one family in six in Middletown, a two-page spread on the automobile as an "enricher of life," quoting "a bank president in a Mid-Western city" as saying, "A man who works six days a week and spends the seventh on

[8] In any consideration of the devotion to "speed" that accompanies the coming of the automobile, it should be borne in mind that the increased monotony for the bulk of the workers involved in the shift from the large-muscled hand-trades, including farming, to the small-muscled high-speed machine-tending jobs and the disappearance of the saloon as an easy means of "tellin' the world to go to hell" have combined with the habit-cracking, eye-opening effect of service in the late war to set the stage for the automobile as a release. The fact that serviceable second-hand cars can be bought for $75.00 and up, the simplicity of installment payment, "the fact that everybody has one"—all unite to make ownership of a car relatively easy, even for boys. Cf. the incident cited above of the boy who wanted to "swap in his Ford for a Studebaker that will go seventy-five miles an hour."

his own doorstep certainly will not pick up the extra dimes in the great thoroughfares of life." "Some sunny Sunday very soon," said another two-page spread in the *Post*, "just drive an Overland up to your door—tell the family to hurry the packing and get aboard—and be off with smiles down the nearest road—free, loose, and happy—bound for green wonderlands." Another such advertisement urged Middletown to "Increase Your Week-End Touring Radius." [9] If we except the concentrated group pressure of war time, never perhaps since the days of the camp-meeting have the citizens of this community been subjected to such a powerfully focused stream of habit diffusion. To get the full force of this appeal, one must remember that the nearest lakes or hills are one hundred miles from Middletown in either direction and that an afternoon's motoring brings only mile upon mile of level stretches like Middletown itself.

> "We had a fine day yesterday," exclaimed an elderly pillar of a prominent church, by way of Monday morning greeting. "We left home at five in the morning. By seven we swept into ———. At eight we had breakfast at ———, eighty miles from home. From there we went on to Lake ———, the longest in the state. I had never seen it before, and I've lived here all my life, but I sure do want to go again. Then we went to ——— [the Y.M.C.A. camp] and had our chicken dinner. It's a fine thing for people to get out that way on Sundays. No question about it. They see different things and get a larger outlook."
>
> "Did you miss church?" he was asked.
>
> "Yes, I did, but you can't do both. I never missed church or Sunday School for thirteen years and I kind of feel as if I'd done my share. The ministers ought not to rail against people's driving on Sunday. They ought just to realize that they won't be there every Sunday during the summer, and make church interesting enough so they'll want to come."

But if the automobile touches the rest of Middletown's living at many points, it has revolutionized its leisure; more, perhaps, than the movies or any other intrusion new to Middletown since the nineties, it is making leisure-time enjoyment a regularly expected part of every day and week rather than an occasional event. The readily available leisure-time options of even the working class have been multiplied many-fold. As one working class housewife remarked, "We just go to lots of things we couldn't go

---

[9] Over against these appeals the Sunday of 1890 with its fewer alternatives should be borne in mind: as a Middletown plumber described it, "There wasn't anything to do but go to church or a saloon or walk uptown and look in the shop windows. You'd go about hunting saloons that were open, or maybe, if you were a *hot* sport, rent a rig for $1.50 for the afternoon and take your girl out riding."

to if we didn't have a car." Beefsteak and watermelon picnics in a park or a near-by wood can be a matter of a moment's decision on a hot afternoon.

Not only has walking for pleasure become practically extinct,[10] but the occasional event such as a parade on a holiday attracts far less attention now.

> "Lots of noise on the street preparing for the 4th," reports the diary of a Middletown merchant on July 3, 1891. And on the 4th: "The town full of people—grand parade with representatives of different trades, an ox roasted whole, four bands, fireworks, races, greased pig, dancing all day, etc." An account in '93 reports: "Quite a stir in town. Firecrackers going off all night and all this day—big horse racing at the Fair Ground. Stores all closed this afternoon. Fireworks at the Fair Grounds this evening."

Today the week before the Fourth brings a pale edition of the earlier din, continuing until the night before. But the Fourth dawns quietly on an empty city; Middletown has taken to the road. Memorial Day and Labor Day are likewise shorn of their earlier glory.

Use of the automobile has apparently been influential in spreading the "vacation" habit. The custom of having each summer a respite, usually of two weeks, from getting-a-living activities, with pay unabated, is increasingly common among the business class, but it is as yet very uncommon among the workers.[11] "Vacations in 1890?" echoed one substantial citizen. "Why, the word wasn't in the dictionary!" "Executives of the 1890 period *never* took a vacation," said another man of a type common in Middletown thirty-five years ago, who used to announce proudly that they had "not missed a day's work in twenty years." Vacations there were in the nineties,

---

[10] Sunday afternoon motorists today report only an occasional anachronism of a person seen walking about town. A newcomer to Middletown remarked, "I was never in a city where people walk so little. They ride to work, to a picture show or to dances, even if they are going only a few blocks." One business class woman says that her friends laugh at her for walking to club meetings or downtown.

In the early nineties street car rides were somewhat of an event and "trolley parties" were popular. "Saturday afternoon out with ma and Trese car riding and walking," writes the young baker in his diary, and a news note in June, 1890, states that "tickets for free street car ride were given out Sunday morning at the First Christian Church for Sunday School children."

[11] Not all of the business class are paid while on vacation, e.g., many retail clerks are not paid, but the custom is usual.

The growth of the vacation habit is reflected in the fact that the Woman's Club met with unabated vigor all through the summer in 1890. In 1900 it took the first vacation in its history for July and August. Commencing with 1914 it has closed earlier and earlier, and since 1919–20 has closed for the three months from June 1.

nevertheless, particularly for the wives and children of those business folk who had most financial leeway. Put-In Bay, Chautauqua, country boarding-houses where the rates were $5.00 a week for adults and $3.00 for children, the annual conference of the State Baptist Association, the Annual National Christian Endeavor Convention, the annual G.A.R. encampment, all drew people from Middletown. But these affected almost entirely business class people. A check of the habits of the parents of the 124 working class wives shows that summer vacations were almost unknown among this large section of the population in the nineties. In lieu of vacations both for workers and many of the business class there were excursions: those crowded, grimy, exuberant, banana-smelling affairs on which one sat up nights in a day coach, or, if a "dude," took a sleeper, from Saturday till Monday morning, and went back to work a bit seedy from loss of sleep but full of the glamour of Petoskey, or the ball game at Chicago. Two hundred and twelve people from Middletown went to Chicago in one week-end on one such excursion. One hundred and fifty journeyed to the state capital to see the unveiling of a monument to an ex-governor—"a statesman," as they called them in those days. Even train excursions to towns fifteen, twenty, and forty miles away were great events, and people reported having "seen the sights" of these other Middletowns with much enthusiasm.

Today a few plants close for one or two weeks each summer, allowing their workers an annual "vacation" without pay. Others do not close down, but workers "can usually take not over two weeks off without pay and have their jobs back when they return." Foremen in many plants get one or two weeks with pay. Of the 122 working class families giving information on this point, five families took one week off in 1923 and again in 1924, seven others took something over a week in each year, twelve took a week or more in only one of the two years. No others had as extensive vacations as these twenty-four, although other entire families took less than a week in one or both years, and in other cases some members of the families took vacations of varying lengths. Of the 100 families for whom income distribution was secured, thirty-four reported money spent on vacations; the amounts ranged from $1.49 to $175.00, averaging $24.12.

But even short trips are still beyond the horizon of many workers' families, as such comments as the following show:

> "We haven't had a vacation in five years. He got a day off to paint the house, and another year they gave him two hours off to get the deed to the house signed."
> "Never had a vacation in my life, honey!"

"Can't afford one this year because we're repairing the house."

"I don't know what a vacation is—I haven't had one for so long."

"We like to get out in the car each week for half a day but can't afford a longer vacation."

But the automobile is extending the radius of those who are allowed vacations with pay and is putting short trips with the reach of some for whom such vacations are still "not in the dictionary."

"The only vacation we've had in twenty years was three days we took off last year to go to Benton Harbor with my brother-in-law," said one woman, proudly recounting her trip. "We had two Fords. The women slept in the cars, the men on boards between the two running boards. Here's a picture of the two cars, taken just as the sun was coming up. See the shadows? And there a *hill* back of them."

5. Radio Fans Talk Back

Radio, which began commercial broadcasting in November, 1920, was an even more powerful medium of mass cultural diffusion than movies or the automobile. It was accessible to a much larger audience—to the ill and the infirm, the very young and the very old, those who could not easily go out to enjoy the pleasures of a movie or an auto ride. It could be listened to in the privacy of one's home, in casual indoor attire, or played as background to housework or study. Though weather conditions sometimes made driving or movie-going inconvenient, radio was always available.

Moreover, radio possessed unmatchable immediacy and reality: it was "live," you listened to events the very moment they were taking place. That was William Jennings Bryan's voice and not an actor's, the real crack of Babe Ruth's bat, and the real roar of the Yankee Stadium crowd. As you sat by your receiving set, hearing the World Series or a national political convention, you could know that millions of others were listening in just as you in every part of America. After he broadcast the 1924 Democratic convention, Graham McNamee observed that alert politicians were already beginning to shape their platform speaking styles to please their unseen audience.

McNamee (1888–1942) was the most popular radio announcer of the Twenties, whose broadcasting voice carried baseball, boxing, football, political conventions, and national election results from coast to coast. He began his career as a baritone, singing light and grand opera, and made his debut as a soloist at Aeolian Hall in New York in 1920. In 1923 he entered radio broadcasting. Quickly he sensed that an announcer should be more than a disembodied voice introducing events, should rather be a personality in his own right, providing a distinctive point of view toward the action he describes, filling in the dead moments with colorful comments and chatter. It may have been McNamee's engaging personality, as well as the important events he broadcast, which prompted the flood of letters from radio listeners McNamee discusses in You're on the Air, written in collaboration with the author and publicist Robert Gordon Anderson (1881–1950).

You're on the Air
GRAHAM McNAMEE

After a while cutting off the studio or putting it on the air becomes automatic, but at first, like all the others, I sometimes forgot to press the little button on the end of the control wire and people tuning in would hear things that were never meant to be heard. One night I made a rather impatient remark, and someone rushed in from the monitor's booth exclaiming, "That went out on the air!" Other doors from the offices opened, and others, too, politely informed me, "That went out on the air!" I had finally composed myself and was about to begin broadcasting again when the tenth man rushed in with this warning, "Say Mac, that went out on the air," and losing my temper, I shot back, rather rudely, it must be confessed—"Get out of here, Luf, or I'll break your head."

Next morning our mail was flooded with letters asking why the announcer was going to break Llufrio's head; what had Luf done, and so on.

It was in the fall of the year 1923, that the letter-writing habit really took hold of the fans; and now we not only have case after case filled with these letters, but thousands of specially selected ones bound in russia leather and also a very amusing collection in what we call the "Coffee File."

The name was chosen because of an incident in the Harvard-Princeton game in the fall of 1925 when, rather excited over some play, my associate, Carlin, dropped our thermos bottle filled with coffee through a crack in the stand just as he was handing it to me. I must have expressed my disgust and disappointment rather forcibly, as I was cold from the frosty weather—and all this time the "mike" was on.

Many letters came in from fans amused over the accident, and a still greater number after another mishap in a World Series game when the rain suddenly came down and spoiled my new suit. Just to entertain people I jokingly mentioned this fact, never dreaming what would be the result—not only a host of sympathetic letters but many offers from cloth-

Graham McNamee, *You're on the Air* (New York, 1926), pp. 30–32, 172–189.

ing houses and individuals for new suits. Had I accepted one tenth of these I might have been the Beau Brummel my family say I'm not.

❂   ❂   ❂

"I could write you in ink, but you ain't worth it."

So wrote a fan in pencil on bright pink paper with a pinker border.

Ordinarily, one would think, little attention would be paid to such a missive, but the fact that it, and others of the same type, are in our files and carefully classified indicates the close inspection we give, and the importance we attach, to the daily mail from the "fans."

The average letter of 1923 was usually some informal note scribbled on any old paper, and too, frequently revealed the sender as ignorant not only of grammar and rhetoric but even of the simplest spelling. The few that came in from persons of education were just hasty notes written on the spur of the moment at the close of a program.

Gradually, however, the mail increased in quality and constructive criticism, showing a real, and, in many instances, an intelligent desire to help in program building. Many of the daily letters now are carefully type written, are dictated to stenographers, and not infrequently display at the top a very well-known letter head.

We cannot, of course, adopt all the suggestions; practical considerations of which the senders cannot be aware often prevent. But frequently we do follow them, and the result has had a noticeable effect on both the type and the handling of our entertainment. And as has already been indicated, it isn't only the letters from people of note that we examine; for often the letter sent in by some laborer or ignorant foreigner, painfully spelled out, is more significant than those more perfectly expressed. Even the children's scrawls were read with care.

And while this mail improved in tone, so, also, it increased in bulk; until now we have a whole room devoted to the files, all carefully sorted and arranged. Many of the more important we have bound up in leather; and even the abusive ones are carefully kept, like the one quoted at the head of this chapter and the card which came last Christmas morning:

"Holiday greetings to the smallest, meanest-principled man in New York, is the wish of one who holds for you nothing but contempt!"

After reading that one over several times I came to the conclusion that the sender didn't think so very much of me. Still, out of it I really got a big kick. Radio, I thought, must be pretty powerful to arouse such feeling.

Not only is the intensity of feeling on the part of the radio fans astonishing, but frequently also their accuracy of information. They follow artists and programs as closely as sport fans follow their heroes, form sheets, and score cards; and the announcer has to be on the alert to keep from slipping.

One evening I announced that John Powell, the famous pianist, was making his debut before the microphone. Before the finish of the program we received not only one but several telephone calls, and the next day many letters, telling us that I had been wrong, that this had *not* been Mr. Powell's debut. And an even more astonishing thing about it was that they not only corrected us on this point, but one and all gave time, date, and place of the previous appearance (at Carnegie Hall), and some even added that he had played the MacDowell "Concerto" for piano and orchestra, with von Hoogstraten conducting.

Not only are the abusive letters startling, but also the requests we receive by mail and often by telephone to broadcast the deaths of loved ones, or to advertise on the air for relatives that have disappeared. Frequently the voices pleading with us for such services are actually incoherent from grief.

Some have a more humorous note, even though they are sincere enough, when they ask our help in locating missing dogs and cats, pet ponies and goats; or garnet pins, engagement rings, sets of false teeth, and stolen tin lizzies. Such requests, needless to say, we cannot heed.

One distracted person asked us to find someone who could tell of an effective remedy for hiccoughs from which her husband was suffering. One could easily imagine the result, for everyone has a pet remedy for this affliction—and our mail would have been swamped, our phone system absolutely stalled, with recommendations for standing on one's head, kicking one's heels in the air, and so on.

But it must not be supposed that these letters are as a rule frivolous; the great majority are written in deadly earnest, as witness those referred to above and the hosts that come in trying to use our services as a matrimonial bureau. Here's one chap that asks for "a single maiden never wed." It, that is the letter (we couldn't supply the other), follows:

"Dear Mr. McNamee:

"Knowing that your great station and its very pleasing official voice reaches into many homes and distant places, it occurred to me that, in view of the fact that I have given the early years of my life to educational advancement by studying nights and working by day, I am now in the thirties, in the best of health, with several degrees and now completing a course in Radio Engineering.

"I own a farm on the highway to—, built my own home and garage, but am waiting for a suitable bird to put in the nest. I have partitioned off nothing so far, but want a Protestant girl of settled habits, strong moral fiber, of German, Scotch, or American parentage of the old school, who can cook the old-fashion way, loves children, nature, flowers, who will be a real mother and home-maker.

"Probably among your many listeners there is a *single maiden, never wed,* who is looking for such an opportunity, for I am a bachelor self-made in every sense.

Yours,

"P. S. You may read my letter to your listeners."

Not so many pages back, we were speaking of the part radio plays in all our lives—sometimes it seems to play hob with domestic arrangements, as complained the correspondent who wrote us that our program of the night before had been all too delightful. Her husband had called all the family to the set, leaving the evening meal smoking on the table. When they returned, their two pet cats were licking up the last scrap; and these radio fans had to go practically dinnerless. Our customer, however, was reasonable and didn't claim damages.

Two dogs caused the catastrophe described in another letter. Ernest Thompson Seton, the famous naturalist, in the course of his radio lecture, had occasion to imitate the bellow of a wild bull calling to its mate. Evidently it was a real call of the wild, for our correspondent's two great police dogs, which had been blinking by the fireplace, suddenly dove for the horn and before he could pry them off, they had completely demolished it.

This fan, too, was fair enough, and didn't ask us for damages or to supply a new set. "I am not a poor man," he wrote, "and am able to buy one. But just the same I don't think it's quite fair for you to have wild animals in your studio without announcing it to your customers. And I'd greatly appreciate it, if next time you'd let me know when you're going to have a menagerie at WEAF, and so save me some money."

It was our rule to announce at the beginning of the evening's program that our wave length was 492 meters; later we changed it to 610 kilocycles, but this change was only in terms, for the two measurements are synonymous. It served, however, to prove the power of the imagination, for one fan wrote in requesting us to please go back to meters, for ever since we had been using kilocycles his reception had been poor.

But the World Series letters are, perhaps, the most human of all. Here are some cue lines from a few we have selected at random, showing as motley and picturesque an assemblage as one could hope to picture:

1. A farmer in Vermont: "Listening through a regular blizzard."
2. A veteran of the civil war: "I ran the bases in fourteen and a half seconds. Tim Murmane held the watch."

3. An Ohio Judge: "We adjourned court for fear we would get your report and mine mixed in a damage case."

4. A sailor at anchor off Pennock Light: "On an ocean-going barge in a howling Nor-Easter."

5.. "Fifty pairs of head phones at Fort Monmouth."

6. "A veterans' hospital." (263 signatures).

7. A boy: "From the sound of your voice I was satisfied that you were coo-coo, too."

8. From George: "I bet you had a good soar throat when you were done talking."

9. "A bunch of T.B.'s who depend entirely on radio for contact with outside world"—signers all girls. A postscript, alluding to an incident in the World's Series is added: "How many quarts of water went down your neck?"

10. A Virginia Farmer: "Your allusion to rain was so real that my wife hurried out and brought in the cushions from the porch."

11. An old guide in a remote hunting lodge of the Adirondacks.

12. A man in bed with a broken neck.

13. "A hundred stranded hulks, all dry docked."

14. A good Samaritan who saw "three hundred men, all laborers, with dinner buckets in their hands, assembled in a street where a merchant had set up a loud-speaker."

15. A Massachusetts boy with infantile paralysis, for whom someone sent a wire.

16. From Corsopolis: "I don't know just what it means, but it's all about the 'World's Serious Games.'"

17. A cigar store in Rutland, Vermont: A word of thanks with many signatures written on wrapping paper.

18. A Past Commander of the G. A. R.: "I am eighty-two, but I never miss a ball game and I never miss a circus. Nigger-like I'll follow a brass band half around town and don't associate with Old Men. I keep young!"

19. A high school Junior Master: "I wonder if you know you used the expression 'who will he send out' instead of 'whom'?"

20. My grandfather-in-law in Missouri whom I had never met.

21. A Widow of Providence: "I felt like flying with red flannel for your poor sore throat. We love you.

"This is not a flapper, but a very comely widow who stands without hitching."

22. "I am sick, and a shut-in, and I like you."

23. A deaf man "whose life has been an eternal silence for twenty-five years, and who now, over the radio, hears every word."

In giving a rounded report one must not overlook the dissenting letters, many threatening physical violence.

A Pittsburgh fan wrote me: "We would appreciate it if you would not constantly remind us that the score was Washington 4; Pittsburgh 0."

Another appealed to the office: "For the love of mike" (an unconscious witticism), "take McNamee out. My batteries are valuable and I can get jokes from the newspapers."

The Washington fans took the series quite as much to heart. Wrote one:

"You utterly and miserably failed in your rôle. You announced, yes, but spent more time telling about your personal discomforts (as if we cared a damn) than you did about who was at bat and what he was doing.

"You failed in 1924, but, My God! you get worse as you get older! Stick to music and weather reports, but let the Chicago man handle the large athletic events for the good of us all."

An associate judge in the capital seemed to feel the same way, though he expressed his feelings in a little different fashion.

"It would have been excellent," he wrote, "had you been mindful of your audience and its divergent sympathies, and divested yourself of your very evident prejudice in favor of Pittsburgh.

"No doubt any complimentary letter will be exhibited to your employers. Will you be man enough to show them this too?"

Well, Judge, there it is.

Now these letters came in on all sorts and hues of paper, even on birch bark. They contained prose, poetry, and *vers libre,* and were done in script, pen, plain pencil, blue pencil, type; and not a few were printed by hand with marginal decorations.

But the one, after all, that I value most, is quite simple in character. It is from a hospital and significant enough of the pleasure radio gives so many afflicted millions to print in full:

"Mr. Graham McNamee,
    Station WEAF,
        195 Broadway, N. Y.
"Please accept our sincere thanks for your wonderful broadcasting of the first game of the 1924 season between the Giants and the Brooklyn Dodgers. Your knowledge of the game and your colorful description made a hit here; and it was no ordinary bunt but a powerful wallop that has had us talking ever since.

"The Hospital is really a home for some eight hundred patients, a majority of whom are playing their last game and waiting for the exit gates to open. Their little Main Street is quite narrow, and the radio is bringing the world to their feet, as it were.

"I wish you could see all these helpless men listening to your voice; some are blind and many bed-ridden, but the smile on their faces as the game progressed certainly would repay you, had you any doubts as to the success of your reception.

"One old fellow remembers McGraw when he played on the Olean,

N. Y., team, and another was the chum of Willie Keeler. Everyone, in fact, has a baseball remembrance, and whenever we want to start a fight we get Johnny and Jimmy, who are here twenty years, to talk about Merkle and the time he failed to touch second. Both claim the Cubs stole that game and none dare to dispute them.

"As Roxy would say, 'God Bless You.' "

We often hear of the reunions of friends brought about by radio after long separations. This letter which comes close home, unfortunately arrived too late:

"My dear Mr. McNamee:

"Many years ago, I knew a baby of your name, whose mother's name was Annie and whose father's name was John. They were, at the time, very pleasant neighbors of mine. But in the natural migration of families from one place to another, we drifted to different neighborhoods and to different cities.

"A few years ago, however, Mrs. McNamee came to Washington and proved that she had not forgotten the one-time friendship by the fact that she looked me up, and came to see me.

"During this visit, I asked after the baby boy. She happily told me that he had developed a splendid voice, which, at the time, was being trained. Since then, our lives have again fallen into different channels, but my interest in her was revived by the pleasure I experienced listening to your voice over the radio during the National Democratic Convention. We were very ardent and constant 'listeners in,' and will remember for some time your cheery 'Good morning, Ladies and Gentlemen of the Radio Audience.'

"I would like very much to know if you are that boy whom I knew so long ago, and, if so, to know something of your mother.

"Thanking you for the great pleasure you gave us during the Convention, I am,

"Most sincerely,"

Within the past two years there were, however, several reunions that were happily consummated by radio. One I particularly recall was that of a man of sixty with a girl he had known in his youth. They had been engaged, but through some misunderstanding had separated, and for years did not see each other.

Meantime, both had married, their respective helpmates had died, and his one-time fiancée became an elocutionist, often speaking over the radio. After his wife's death he bought a set and, happening to tune in one night, was amazed to hear his boyhood sweetheart. From time to time he listened to the familiar voice, as it spoke from various cities, then he summoned up courage enough to write to her in care of one of the stations from which she broadcast. She answered—several times; they met—

several times; and now—well, if she ever broadcasts again, it will be under a name quite different from the old one.

But I must not linger over these old records and files which bring back such pleasant memories, though I'd like to quote from the poems sent in—there are many very clever ones—and particularly the letters from people all over the country commenting on the political broadcastings. One came from a dear old lady—I have never seen her but I'm sure she was that—who wrote in that she could neither walk nor see to read or write, but she was going to try and write me just the same "about those conventions." As radio widened her horizon, so she and the women in turn will widen the political horizon of this country, if hers and the countless other intelligent queries are any indication.

There is one other, in fact, a whole series of letters between Mrs. Ballington Booth and a burglar, that must not be overlooked, since they are stranger and more compelling than the most fascinating fiction.

The burglar had been planning another little assignment—so he wrote in his first letter of confession—when, on passing down the street, he stopped to listen to a loud-speaker, while Mrs. Booth was broadcasting. She was telling of her work in the prisons for the convicted men; and somehow her talk seemed aimed directly at him. It sank in a little; yet still he went on maturing his plans.

The night for the job came; he jimmied his way through the window of the house and, flashing his pocket battery this way and that, made his way to the safe. Suddenly he heard a voice—and paused, startled. The place was deserted, the family having gone, as he knew, to the country. Then he smiled—of course—it was the loud-speaker! They had forgotten to turn it off. So he got down on his knees and to work once more. But there was something about that voice—yes it was Mrs. Booth's again! He listened—his fingers seemed to have lost their cunning—and as the voice went sweetly and persuasively on, somehow he could not continue. This time the message sank in; and quietly collecting his tools and packing them in his kit, he climbed over the window sill and "turned to the right."

6. Simplicity Sells

The vastly enlarged part played by advertising in American business during the Twenties was in many ways a symptom of the developing mass culture of those years. Advertising, of course, was also an important force in its own right for shaping mass perceptions and unifying public attitudes and values. The need for new methods and increased use of advertising came about because of the changes in American social and industrial structures during the First World War. Manufacturing in the United States had always been shaped by the relatively egalitarian and prosperous aspects of American life, leading industry to concentrate on quantity production and wide distribution of goods. The war enormously accentuated these features of American industry. During the war the federal War Industries Board enforced standardization and simplification in many areas of product design and manufacture. Wartime inflation narrowed the gap in living standards between salaried workers and wage earners, while war production demands brought thousands of women, Negroes, and other marginal economic groups into the industrial process. A new mass consumer base was thereby created to support the intensified trend toward uniformity and mass production in manufacturing. The new practice of installment buying on credit brought more and more products within the range of average incomes.

Through advertising, manufacturers got the news of their products' virtues to the mass consumer audience of potential buyers. But what was the nature of this broad, amorphous consumer class? How could its wants be known, its tastes influenced? To answer these questions, specialists in advertising emerged in the Twenties. One such advertising authority was Kenneth M. Goode (1880–1958), who published eight books on advertising during his career, and teamed with the writer and publicist Harford Powel, Jr. (1887–1956) in one of his earliest efforts, *What About Advertising?*. In a chapter entitled "The Sea of Humanity," they provided the facts about the American buying public that manufacturers and advertisers were looking for.

What About Advertising?
KENNETH M. GOODE and HARFORD POWEL, JR.

In the United States are about 118,000,000 people. Dropping the 5,500,000 who can't read or are in jails or hospitals, we have 112,500,000 left. Subtracting 23,000,000 boys and girls under fourteen, we find, roundly, 90,000,000 people still within range of ordinary advertising artillery.

These 90,000,000 people comprise every able person over fourteen. Necessarily, therefore, they include the proprietors and clerks of all retail stores. Also all middlemen, salesmen, and advertisers. In fact, 11,000,000 of the 90,000,000 are supposed to live, one way or another, by helping distribute goods. So, concentrated in this 90,000,000 we find not only all customers, but America's whole army of wholesalers, jobbers, retailers, and store clerks. This 90,000,000 contains, therefore, all the "sales resistance."

As customers of the 1,300,000 retail stores in the United States are 1,304,300 Smiths, 1,024,000 Johnsons, 730,500 Browns, 684,700 Williamses and 658,300 Jones. And Millers, Davises, Andersons, Wilsons, and Moores by the quarter million. Customers, on one hand, owners and clerks, jobbers and salesmen on the other, they twine and intertwine. No large advertiser need, therefore, consider any particular difference between his consumers and distributors. Where they are not actually identical, the law of averages makes them practically identical in all mental and social characteristics.

Admirable market surveys have sorted out the bank accounts of these Browns, Andersons, and Joneses. They have classified the 1,304,300 Smiths down to their last dime. Yet few advertisers seem to have any vivid picture of the John Smiths who own that dime. If every advertiser had to go to a town meeting at the little red schoolhouse and personally repeat his copy word for word, face to face, to a hundred Johnsons, Millers, and Williamses, there would be a lot of different advertisements in next month's magazines.

Kenneth M. Goode and Harford Powel, Jr., *What About Advertising?* (New York, 1927), pp. 102–118.

First, as to education. Out of every 100 American children of school age, we are told:

36 are not attending school at all
54 are attending public elementary school
7 are attending public high school
3 attend public night school, vocational school, etc.
2 only enter college or university
1 only remains in college to graduate

This means, first, that only 64 per cent of the youth of America, coming customers, are at school at all. Even this 64 per cent does not receive a complete public-school education. Their schooling averages only seven and one-half years. College and university education reaches but two Americans in every hundred; and of those two, only one completely.

Or, taking the method of Dr. Brigham, and following the education of one thousand typical American boys, all of whom together enter the first grade:

1,000 boys enter 1st grade
  970 of them enter 2nd grade
  940 "   "   " 3rd grade
  905 "   "   " 4th grade
  830 "   "   " 5th grade
  735 "   "   " 6th grade
  630 "   "   " 7th grade
  490 "   "   " 8th grade

Of our original one thousand boys:

230 boys enter 1st-year high school
170 of them finish 2nd-year high school
120 of them finish 3rd-year high school
95 of them graduate from high school

Of the original one thousand boys: '

50 boys enter 1st-year college
40 of them finish 2nd-year college
20 of them finish 3rd-year college
10 of them remain in college to be graduated

Although the various "Alpha" intelligence tests rate the college freshman above the average man on the street, we don't find even the college graduate—the select one-out-of-every-hundred schoolboys—any great highbrow. A recent graduating class at Princeton voted "If" their favorite poem; *Tom Jones* their favorite novel; Maxfield Parrish their favorite artist; Douglas Fairbanks their favorite movie actor; *Saturday Evening Post* their favorite magazine, and tied Sabatini with Booth Tarkington as their favorite author. Up at Yale the seniors were even more conservative. Tennyson is the favorite poet; Tarkington gives way to Dickens, Stevenson, and Dumas. *The Tale of Two Cities* is the favorite novel, and D'Artagnan the favorite character in fiction.

In a canvass of our American schools to discover the most popular "recitations," the National Educational Association found that Longfellow led five out of eight grades; Stevenson, one; Scott, one; Wordsworth, one. Thirty-six thousand children in seventeen states voted *Tom Sawyer, Little Women,* and *Black Beauty* their favorite books. Long afterward through the same law of averages, young readers of *The Youth's Companion* voted with complete unanimity for *Tom Sawyer, Little Women,* and *Treasure Island.* Each branch of the New York Public Library has always out fifteen to twenty-five copies of *David Copperfield, Vanity Fair,* and *The Scarlet Letter.* Year in and year out one great New York department store reports *David Copperfield* its one best-selling book!

The president of a great university says that not one voter in twenty has any intelligent idea of why or what he voted for in any national election. A few years ago 700,000 of the Epworth League voted the greatest ten men in history as follows:

1—Thomas Edison
2—Theodore Roosevelt
3—William Shakespeare
4—Henry W. Longfellow
5—Alfred Tennyson
6—Herbert Hoover
7—Charles Dickens
8—General Pershing
9—Lloyd George
10—Andrew J. Volstead

Because the "intelligence" [1] of the average American—which is exactly our 90,000,000 sales resisters—is generally reckoned in terms of boys and girls slightly under high-school age and education, a list like that may be worth the attention of any advertiser. For the same reason he will be interested in an examination in current events at the Knoxville High School.

Not 500 in 1,047 of these Knoxville students were able to locate the District of Columbia. Asked "What is an Electoral College?" one said, "It's a college where you take what you want." Ninety-five per cent of the senior class failed to answer this question at all. Asked "What member of

---

[1] Meaning of course, *literate* intelligence, that is, ability to cope with *words.*

royalty died recently?" four said "Queen Elizabeth," and nine said "Bryan." Mrs. Miriam Ferguson, then Governor of Texas, caused considerable disagreement. She was called "A singer recently admitted to grand opera"; "Football player"; "Baseball player"; "Writer"; "Movie star"; and finally, "Husband of the Governor of Texas." Nine said Mary Roberts Rinehart was a famous actress, while one declared Sir Walter Scott wrote the "Star-spangled Banner." Speaking of "Ma" Ferguson reminds us of another test conducted by a certain well-known pictorial periodical among another 1,650 high-school students, this time scattered all over the country. Mrs. Ferguson was mistaken by some for Babe Ruth and by others for the President of Mexico. One hundred and eighty— more than 10 per cent—failed to recognize a portrait of President Coolidge. Incidentally, only about 15 out of 1,047 of the Tennessee students knew the name of the Mayor of Knoxville—their own home city.

If Knoxville seems too extreme, turn to a similar examination in a Wisconsin Normal School where one of the prospective teachers called Steinmetz "a kind of piano"; Frances E. Willard "an American pugilist"; Mussolini "a region in southern Eurasia" and Fiume "a mountain in Japan." "Teapot Dome," to one of these young women was "an old tomb discovered in Egypt," while another affronted all Massachusetts by describing Henry Cabot Lodge as "a place where societies meet."

Or, drop down into North Carolina, where the state university instructors find that "many students who get into college cannot understand ordinary written English." One freshman there preferred "David Copperfield's novels to those written by Dickens." An upper-classman reported that "Diabetes was Milton's Italian friend." Another upper-classman, that "Lincoln's mind growed as his country kneaded it."

Or, skip eastward to the metropolis, where, speaking of 800 applicants for admission to the New York Bar, Mr. Allan Fox reported George Washington as the only figure in American history that most of them could identify. The majority of the candidates knew nothing of English literature or history. Asked whether they had ever read any biography, some of them last fall were answering, "Yes, the Private Life of Helen of Troy."

Not so long ago, reading was the nation's only means of culture. Advertising then had practically a monopoly on the news of new goods. Powerful as the printed word still is, the news supremacy of our publications is seriously threatened by at least two new ways of scattering ideas over the nation. Six million radio sets, no doubt, average an hour or two apiece every day. And for every publication in America, there is already a motion-picture theater. Probably 10,000,000 people a day see a picture. In the course of a fortnight, therefore, every person in the United States either in person or by proxy, sees at least one film. So, quite aside from additional competition for attention and in distributing fresh news, the effect of radio and movies on popular habits of thought and expression must be considered by any advertiser. Their short, staccato, picture-and-title, flippant, flash technique, infinitely reinforced by its debasement in the daily millions of tabloids, threatens within ten years to disturb even our serious literature. The mental standard for the moving-picture producer is the intelligence of the fourteen-year-old child. Professor Francis B. Tyson, of the University of Pittsburgh, holds the actual appeal more nearly adapted to a child about twelve years.

The public taste in melody is as simple as its taste in motion pictures. Advertisers who lean toward the Wagnerian·form of expression might profit by a glance at what may be the most representative "request" program ever put on the radio. The New York Edison Company selected it from many hundreds of suggestions. But the vote on popular solos is illuminating. Strangely enough it was led by Balfe's supposedly forgotten "Then You'll Remember Me." Then Tosti's "Good-bye"; Bartlett's "A Dream"; Herbert's "Falling in Love."

Skipping from music to perfumes, out of several thousand people tested by Macy's, under direction of Professor Poffenberger, choices ran in this order:

Women	Men
Lilac	Lilac
Oriental bouquet	French bouquet
Jasmine	Jasmine
French bouquet	Oriental bouquet
Violet	Rose
Rose	Violet

And from perfumes to colors. Preferences, in general, are supposed to run:

Women	Men
Violet	Blue
Blue	Violet
Green	Red
Red	Green
Orange	Orange
Yellow	Yellow

Pure colors are preferred to tints and shades. Yellow stands always near the bottom, red at or near the top. Women generally prefer red, and men blue. Taking greater refinements, E. J. G. Bradford found, by testing a large number of people, that they liked in order: dark blue, gray-green, chocolate brown, light gray-blue, slate gray, with bluish tinge. They cared least for yellowish green, pink, bluish green. In combinations, men seem to prefer green-and-blue, red-and-blue, blue-and-purple, and even yellow-and-blue; women are more conventional with red-and-blue, red-and-green, yellow-and-blue.

After forcing himself to recognize the extreme mental simplicity of the vast majority of his audience, and their pathetic lack of adult mental nourishment, the advertiser must next realize that any workable relation between wealth and education went with the war. Our present install-ment selling, whereby anybody can buy anything, wipes out the last of the old buying "power" distinctions. This, of course, applies only to actual *ability* to purchase. Taste, culture, knowledge, and appreciation of fine achievements still foregather in favorable environment. Certain adver-tisers will find these smaller "class" groups, based today on true con-geniality of interest far more valuable than those formerly based on a supposition of superior wealth.

But, you may say, through natural selective machinery, any worth-while publication will have readers notably above average. Anybody who pays several dollars a year for magazines must be of more than ordinary wealth and intelligence. True of all publications twenty years ago, it is still true of many. Don't however, overlook the law of large numbers. As soon as any business starts dealing with human beings in hundreds-of-thousand lots, it surrenders then and there to the law of averages. Just as there is no difference between the water of the Atlantic and Pacific, so there is no difference between circulation as it gets into millions. All the same sea of humanity; its atoms are the average man. Some humorist asks, "Who is this 'average man' we hear so much about?" The question is justified. But the answer is easy: *he* is! Except for a very few eccentricities, each of us is average. Therefore, on any given point other than the single common resemblance that first classified them—and even that may prove negligible —any given 100,000 American citizens are far more likely to act exactly like any other 100,000 American citizens than to be in the slightest degree different.

Suppose we admit, for example, that magazine readers generally are about the same sort of people who would buy the 7 per cent preferred stock of a first-class public utility corporation. Here are the occupations of those who bought a recent issue of these securities *in lots of 50 shares or more:*

Accountants	166	Messengers	91
Bakers	153	Metal workers	157
Barbers	155	Nurses	274
Butchers	115	Painters	182
Carpenters	483	Plasterers	60
Chauffeurs	601	Plumbers	257
Clerks	2,987	Policemen	347
Domestics	623	Printers	335
Draftsmen	149	Railroad men	312
Dressmakers	372	Seamen	51
Electricians	582	Secretaries	314
Factory workers	1,058	Bankers and brokers	65
Foremen	518	Dentists	63
Housekeepers	4,029	Doctors	146
Laborers	499	Lawyers	77
Machinists	499	Managers	496
Mail carriers	115	Manufacturers	153
Mechanics	530	Merchants	926
Engineers	558		

Just about the average crowd you might meet in your favorite store. Or reading your pet newspaper. Again, you might say that people who buy magazines are the sort who will buy high-grade automobiles. The Paige Detroit Company found that 13.2 per cent of their cars were sold to workmen. And, unless you are content to disconsider one family in every four, you too will have to do business with workmen. Wage earners in the United States today own $70,000,000 worth of stocks in the industries employing them. Americans are a working people; even among the very wealthiest class, personal business activity brings in nearly half the income. On the other hand, Americans are thrifty. Of the people who paid taxes in 1924 on less than $5,000 income 6,300,000 had, over and above their earnings, an average "outside" income of $500.

In New York City, roughly speaking, one family in seventeen has an income of $150 a week. Seven families out of every eleven have less than $150 a week, but more than $60. One family in three lives on less than $60 a week. The average current income for the whole United States in 1926, divided evenly among, men, women, and babes in arms, would have given each $770. No advertiser can go far wrong calculating his per-family average at $75 a week—with two people working to produce it. To reach much above that eleven dollars-a-day-per-family income, he will have to set his selective advertising machinery wastefully enough to throw out twelve out of every thirteen families!

Hardly less interesting than the shift of purchasing power from the few very wealthy to the many wealthy enough is the relation of women to buying. One authority has drawn up a domestic life table of one thousand average American girls.

Age
15–18	110 in 1,000 marry
18–24	300 " " work; 500 marry
24–35	190 " " work; 790 marry
35–45	150 " " work; 830 keep house
45–55	140 " " work; 860 keep house or are independent
55–65	130 " " work; 210 are widows
65	420 " " dead; 500 widows, 140 work (60 widows)

But a woman doesn't necessarily have to marry to be a buyer. Even by the 1920 census there were more than 4,000,000 women earning their own living in other than household duties. The first dozen classifications of that date may still be of interest—they include nine out of every ten working women:

Teachers	639,241
Stenographers	564,744
Saleswomen, clerks, floorwalkers, and overseers	535,609
Clerical workers	472,163
Bookkeepers and cashiers	345,746
Dressmakers (not in factory) and tailoresses	267,347
Women farmers and stock-raisers	253,836
Telephone operators	178,379
Trained nurses	143,664
Retail dealers	78,980
Music teachers	72,678
Milliners and millinery dealers	69,598

Whether married or getting pay for their work, women are the nation's purchasing agents. Woman is generally admitted to be directly responsible for four out of every five sales—and probably has something to say even in the fifth. For beautifying themselves, they spend nearly $2,000,000,000 a year. All in all they are supposed to pour each year at least $32,000,000,000 into retail stores.

A recent survey conducted in various types of retail stores in New York City, shows how completely the woman buys for the whole family.

	Per cent of purchases by	
	Men	Women
Department store	18	82
Drug store	22	78
Grocery store	19	81
Silks	2	98
Pianos	22	78
Leather goods	33	67
Automobiles	59	41
Hardware	51	49
Electrical supplies	20	80
Men's socks	25	75
Jewelry	10	90
Men's neckwear	37	63

In the matter of their own clothes, an investigation made for R. H. Macy & Co., Inc., by a number of savings banks, shows, in the face of the funny papers, the average American woman spends only about 6 per cent of her husband's pay on her own clothes. The whole matter of clothes expense in families of five, with incomes varying from $2,000, is shown by this table:

Size of family income	Dollars spent on clothes for family	Dollars spent on clothes for wife
$ 2,000	$ 384.00	$ 109.36
3,000	591.00	195.00
5,000	700.00	238.00
7,000	889.00	311.15
10,000	1,190.00	452.20
15,000	1,180.00	720.00
20,000	2,400.00	1,080.00
25,000	3,000.00	1,500.00

Turning to the other side of the family, the *American Legion Weekly* asked 1,000 supposedly representative men about their clothes.

> 294 out of 1,000 men buy 1 suit a year
> 509 " " " " " 2 suits " "
> 171 " " " " " 3 " " "
> 44 " " " " " 4 " " "
> 7 " " " " " 5 " " "
> 4 " " " " " 6 " " "

As to prices paid for suits:

12 out of 1,000 pay less than $25	
91 " " " " from $25–$35	
296 " " " " " $35–$45	
471 " " " " " $45–$60	
95 " " " " " $60–$75	
49 " " " " over $75	

Having started with schoolboys and spared a moment to grown men and women, we return to youth again. Surveys show that in buying, as well as in all other things, youth must be served. Buyers between the ages of twenty and forty are found to be responsible for sales approximating:

56 per cent in ready-to-wear goods
58 per cent in dress goods
62 per cent in underwear
64 per cent in hosiery
64 per cent in furniture
64 per cent in musical instruments
67 per cent in rugs

These figures, it must be admitted, sound reasonable. In the first place, the ages between twenty and forty mark practically two-thirds of all our activities in every direction; in the second place, most of those over forty who are ever going to have luxuries are already comfortably fixed, compared with the younger generation.

All these 1,304,300 Smiths, 1,024,200 Johnsons, 730,000 Browns, young or old, married or single, live in 29,000,000,000 homes.

220 out of 1,000 of these homes have radio receivers
450 " " " " " " " phonographs
550 " " " " " " " automobiles
600 " " " " " " " telephones

The average normal American, broadly speaking, celebrates his twenty-fifth birthday by shutting shop mentally and refusing to accept any new ideas. He has then the literate capacity of a twelve- or fourteen-year old child. Many an advertiser may be discouraged to realize that copy aimed anywhere above the comprehension of an eighth-grade schoolboy cuts his audience in half, while any argument over the head of a college freshman misses nine out of ten of his possible prospects. A crowd that can rank Edison above Shakespeare, and Herbert Hoover over Charles Dickens, isn't likely to be much swayed by subtle nuances. Once again the advertiser must seek his simple, sure-fire appeal. To find that appeal he must keep his eye on his audience, the way it buys, reads, talks, as it swings back and forth in tidal waves of action. Consider the words of "Chick" Sale, master student of American vaudeville audiences.

> My object is to touch the something that is in all of us—the laugh we have at others for their simple-minded folly because we know that we are simple-minded ourselves in many things. We are hicks at heart. That explains my success. I give people pictures of what they would be but for the grace of God and the rapid transit companies.

Your average audience—which means *any* American audience as soon as you reach into the hundred thousands—is like that: $8-, $10-, $12-a-day workers; thirteen- or fourteen-year-old minds scarcely equal to second-year high school. Each gets a book every four months where public libraries reach them; four out of five haven't even this service. And one out of three families have no books in their home. They like Tosti's "Goodbye," *David Copperfield*, "The Big Parade," "Abie's Irish Rose." They all go to the movies every other week; and about one in four listens to the radio perhaps an hour a day. They like dark blue as a color and lilac as a scent. Writing themselves, they use a vocabulary generally fewer than a thousand words although each can understand, in reading, maybe six times that many. In their aggregate action the element of intellect is practically negligible. How, and why, then, do they act? What effect does advertising have on them? What do the 1,304,303 Smiths and the 730,500 Browns really know about advertising?

7. What to Buy, and Why

By the end of the Twenties more than two-thirds of American homes were equipped with electricity, as compared to less than one-fifth before the First World War. Domestic life was transformed by the introduction into millions of households of the electrical appliances that have since become staples of modern living—refrigerators, vacuum cleaners, fans and heaters, coffee percolators, waffle irons, heating pads, washing machines, sewing machines, irons, toasters, radios. These new products were accompanied by scores of other re-designed machines and environments, from the automobile to the orange juicer, from the typewriter to the bathroom.

It was the job of advertisers to inform the public about what was newly available and why they ought to buy it, and no medium in the Twenties better served this end than *The Saturday Evening Post*. In 1926 a black-and-white full page ad in the *Post* cost $6,000, but it was well worth it. The *Post*'s average weekly circulation during the Twenties approached two and one-half million, and each issue was read, far more than most magazines of the time, by both men and women, by adults and by the young. Late in the Twenties most issues of the *Post* ran over two hundred pages, with three-fifths of the magazine taken up by ads—and the *Post* refused all ads for cigarettes or liquor. To its writers the *Post* paid as much as $6,000 for a short story and $60,000 for a serial. Under the editorship of George Horace Lorimer, from 1899 to 1936, the *Post* presented to its middle-class audience a congenial and definitive image of themselves and their society, an image of genteel culture and values attuned to industrial and commercial change: they were progressive yet traditional, innovative yet steady, daring yet conventional, comfortable yet hard-working, light-hearted but serious, practical-minded but not without a generous, redeeming streak of sentiment. Amid its stories and articles the *Post* provided an agreeable setting for the pleasures and values offered in the ads which are reprinted here, and in thousands of others like them.

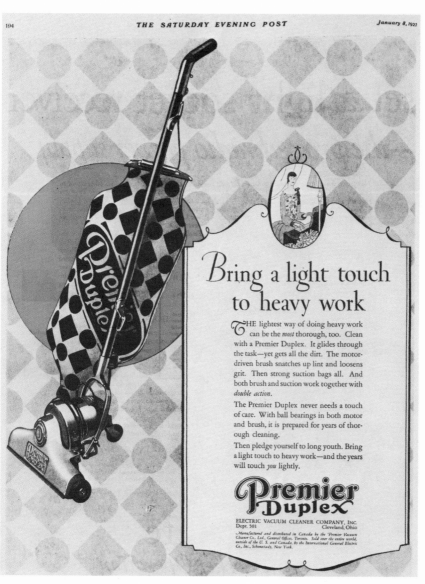

Bring a light touch to heavy work

THE lightest way of doing heavy work can be the *most* thorough, too. Clean with a Premier Duplex. It glides through the task—yet gets all the dirt. The motor-driven brush snatches up lint and loosens grit. Then strong suction bags all. And both brush and suction work together with *double action.*

The Premier Duplex never needs a touch of care. With ball bearings in both motor and brush, it is prepared for years of thorough cleaning.

Then pledge yourself to long youth. Bring a light touch to heavy work—and the years will touch *you* lightly.

Premier Duplex

ELECTRIC VACUUM CLEANER COMPANY, INC.
Dept. 501   Cleveland, Ohio

Manufactured and distributed in Canada by the 'Premier Vacuum Cleaner Co., Ltd., General Offices, Toronto. Sold over the entire world, outside of the U. S. and Canada, by the International General Electric Co., Inc., Schenectady, New York.

1. The Saturday Evening Post, *January 8, 1927.*

100

WHEN that boy of yours "takes all day" in the bathroom you merely realize more acutely the importance of having *enough bathrooms to go round.* And why not have them? Let your plumbing dealer show you what a joyous bathroom you can have in almost no space at all. See if his careful estimate is not lower than your "guess." And mention Kohler Plumbing Fixtures, those with the name "Kohler" fused in superbly white enamel, if you want the best—at no higher cost. . . . Write for the booklet of Kohler Ware.

KOHLER CO., Founded 1873, KOHLER, Wis.   •   *Shipping Point, Sheboygan, Wis.*   •   *Branches in Principal Cities*

KOHLER OF KOHLER
Plumbing Fixtures

The American Club in Kohler Village, the most beautiful industrial community in America

2. The Saturday Evening Post, *January 15, 1927.*

3. The Saturday Evening Post, *February 5, 1927.*

102

Where can you find so much *for* $750

※ *50 miles and more an hour.*
5 to 25 miles in 8 seconds.
25 miles to the gallon.
Full-sized, with ample seating capacity for all passengers.
Mohair plush upholstery.
Chrysler smartness and beauty of line and color.
Low-swung bodies.
Special spring front engine mounting.

CHRYSLER "50"

IN these features* and in scores of others, the Chrysler "50" reveals quality and value which single it out as far and away the greatest offering ever made in a car at this price.

Contrast these features with what you find in any other four-cylinder car—or any six approximating the Chrysler "50" in price. Either by mental comparison or by actual demonstration.

It then becomes perfectly plain that—at or near $750—only the Chrysler "50" gives these values.

CHRYSLER MODEL NUMBERS MEAN MILES PER HOUR

4. The Saturday Evening Post, *May 7, 1927.*

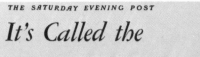

5. The Saturday Evening Post, *February 9, 1929.*

RADIO
by VICTOR

scores the most sensational success in the history of the industry...

Again a glorious Victor triumph — an achievement that set a new high mark in radio reproduction... Victor micro-synchronous Radio!

Here is the radio, and the only radio, backed by thirty years of matchless experience and undisputed leadership in the field of sound reproduction. Victor-Radio is the product of the most painstaking and specialized craftsmanship. It is the first and only micro-synchronous radio.

Now the words "sensitivity" and "selectivity" take on new meaning. Here is radio music such as you have never heard before...startling new realism, warmth and color..."acoustic symmetry" — throughout the entire musical scale!

Victor micro-synchronous balance makes the ideal of the radio engineers a reality. A child can operate Victor-Radio. Every station is in plain sight. For the first time radio tuning is *instant* – and *accurate*.

Victor-Radio can be had separately or combined with the marvelous new improved Victor-Electrola ...in exquisite, compact Victor-built cabinets... giving you music from the air that will change your radio viewpoint...music from records that is utterly beyond words...music that *duplicates* the original performance of the artist.

Only unparalleled Victor resources could bring you Victor quality at list prices so sensationally low. Only $155* for the Victor-Radio Console; only $275* for the Victor-Radio Electrola. Victor Talking Machine Division – Radio-victor Corporation of America, Camden, N. J., U. S. A.

Victor-Radio

Victor-Radio Console with Victor Full-Vision Super-Automatic Station Selector: All stations plainly and permanently visible...just slide the knob to right or left—you have exactly the station you want. List price $155, Less Radiotrons.

6. The Saturday Evening Post, *July 20, 1929.*

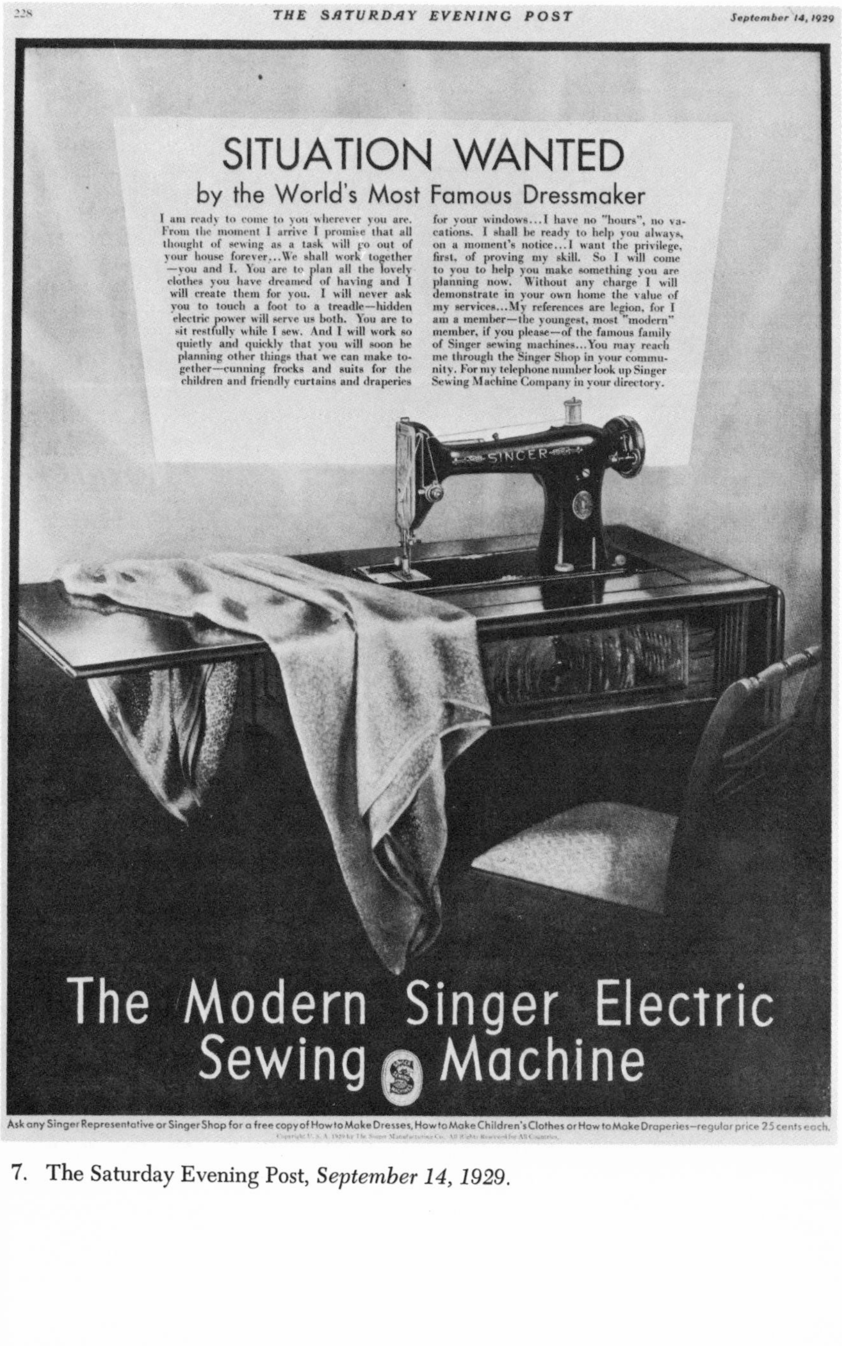

7. The Saturday Evening Post, *September 14, 1929.*

PART TWO

LETTERS AND
LEADERSHIP

8. The Dream of a National Culture

In the half-decade before America's entry into the First World War, American writers and intellectuals were gradually breaking free from genteel culture's tight control over literary expression. The most innovative work was being created in London and Paris by prewar expatriates like Ezra Pound, T. S. Eliot, and Gertrude Stein, though their significance was not widely recognized until after the war. At home, the important new literary figures were middle-aged writers and poets like Theodore Dreiser, Edgar Lee Masters, and Sherwood Anderson. All three had been held back by small-town constraints or genteel repressions, but in the prewar years they produced novels, stories, and poems in a powerful style of vernacular realism.

The younger writers of the prewar literary movement tended to be critics, rather than creators of fiction or poetry. Van Wyck Brooks (1886–1963) was a leader of this group, and also representative in his background—childhood in a suburban town, education at a prominent Eastern university, travel in Europe, extensive knowledge of European literature and the arts. Brooks' European experience gave him the perspective for a double-pronged attack on American genteel middle-class culture: it had failed to create an American aesthetic, it had prevented the formation of a democratic culture. But Brooks and his fellow critics foresaw the emergence around them of a renaissance in American arts, a movement led by the young and founded on the diversity and vitality of commonplace American life. As literary and cultural critics they hoped to assist in the creation of a true national culture, a culture built on the bedrock of everyday experience, rather than enforced from above. In September, 1916, with support from a wealthy patron, Brooks, James Oppenheim, Waldo Frank, and other young critics started a monthly magazine, *The Seven Arts,* which quickly became the leading spokesman for the doctrines of aesthetic liberation and cultural nationalism. Brooks began contributing essays to *The Seven Arts* on national culture. "The Culture of Industrialism," the fifth in a series of seven, appeared in April, 1917, the month the United States entered the war.

The Culture of Industrialism
VAN WYCK BROOKS

If we are dreaming of a "national culture" today it is because our inherited culture has so utterly failed to meet the exigencies of our life, to seize and fertilize its roots. It is amazing how that fabric of ideas and assumptions, of sentiments and memories and attitudes which made up the civilization of our fathers has melted away like snow uncovering the sordid facts of a society that seems to us now so near the lowest rung of the ladder of spiritual evolution. The older generation does not recognize its offspring in the crude chaotic manifestations of the present day, but I wonder if it ever considers this universal lapse from grace in the light of cause and effect? I wonder if it ever suspects that there must have been some inherent weakness in a culture that has so lost control of a really well-disposed younger generation, a culture which, after being dominant for so long, has left in its wake a society so little civilized? What is the secret of its decay? And how does it happen that we, whose minds are gradually opening to so many living influences of the past, can feel nothing but the chill of the grave as we look back over the spiritual history of our own race?

It was the culture of an age of pioneering, the reflex of the spirit of material enterprise—that is the obvious fact; and with the gradual decay of the impulse of enterprise it has itself disintegrated like a mummy at the touch of sunlight. Why? Because it was never a living, active culture, releasing the creative energies of men. Its function was rather to divert these energies, to prevent the anarchical, sceptical, extravagant, dynamic forces of the spirit from taking the wind out of the myth of "progress," that myth imposed by destiny upon the imagination of our forebears in order that a great uncharted continent might be subdued to the service of the race.

For the creative impulses of men are always at war with their possessive impulses, and poetry, as we know, springs from brooding on just those aspects of experience that most retard the swift advance of the practical mind. The spirit of a living culture, which ever has within it some of the

Van Wyck Brooks, "The Culture of Industrialism," *The Seven Arts*, vol. 1, April, 1917, pp. 655-666.

virus of Pascal's phrase: "Caesar was too old to go about conquering the world; he ought to have been more mature"—how could this ever have been permitted to grow up, even supposing that it might have been able to grow up, in a people confronted with forests and prairies and impelled by the necessities of the race to keep their hearts whole and their minds on their task? No, it was essential that everything in men should be repressed and denied that would have slackened their manual energy and made their ingenuity a thing of naught, that would have put questions into their minds, that would have made them static materially and dynamic spirtually, that would have led them to feel too much the disparity between the inherited civilization they had left behind and the environment in which they had placed themselves, that would have neutralized the allure of the exterior ambition which led them on.

Puritanism was a complete philosophy for the pioneer and by making human nature contemptible and putting to shame the charms of life it unleashed the possessive instincts of men, disembarrassing those instincts by creating the belief that man's true life is altogether within him and that the imagination ought never to conflict with the law of the tribe. It was this that determined the character of our culture, which cleared the decks for practical action by draining away all the irreconcilable elements of the American nature into a transcendental upper sphere.

European critics have never been able to understand why a "young nation," living a vigorous, primitive life, should not have expressed itself artistically in a cognate form; and because Whitman did so they accepted him as the representative poet of America. So he was; but it is only now, long after the pioneer epoch has passed and the "free note" has begun to make itself heard, that he has come to seem a typical figure to his own countrypeople. In his own time Whitman was regarded with distrust and even hatred because, by releasing, or tending to release, the creative faculties of the American mind, by exacting a poetical coöperation from his readers, he broke the pioneer law of self-preservation. By awakening people to their environment, by turning democracy from a fact into a principle, his influence ran directly counter to the necessities of the age, and his fellow-writers justly shunned him for hitting in this way below the belt. In fact had Whitman continued to develop along the path he originally marked out for himself he might have seriously interfered with the logical process of the country's material evolution. But there was in Whitman himself a large share of the native pioneer nature, which made it impossible for him to take experience very seriously or to develop beyond a certain point. As he grew older, the sensuality of his nature led him astray in a vast satisfaction with material facts, before which he purred like a cat by the warm fire. This accounts for the reconciliation which occurred in later years between Whitman and his literary contemporaries. They saw that he had become harmless; they accepted him as a man of talent; and making the most of his more conventional verse, they at last crowned him provisionally as the "good gray poet."

For the orthodox writers of the old school had a serious duty to perform in speeding the pioneers on their way; and they performed it with an efficiency that won them the gratitude of all their contemporaries. Longfellow with his lullabies, crooning to sleep the insatiable creative appetites of the soul, Lowell, with his "weak-wing'd song" exalting "the deed"—how invaluable their literature was to the "tired pioneer," forerunner of the "tired business man" of the present day and only a loftier type because, like the tired soldier of the trenches, it was in response to the necessities of the race that he had dammed at their source the rejuvenating springs of the spirit! Yes, it was a great service those old writers rendered to the progress of this country's primitive development, for by unconsciously taking in charge, as it were, all the difficult elements of human nature and putting them under chloroform, they provided a free channel for the *élan* of their age.

But in so doing they shelved our spiritual life, conventionalizing it in a sphere above the sphere of action. In consequence of this our orthodox literature has remained an exercise rather than an expression and has been totally unable either to release the creative impulses of the individual or to stimulate a reaction in the individual against his environment. Itself denied the principle of life or the power of giving life, it has made up for its failure to motivate the American scene and impregnate it with meaning by concentrating all its forces in the exterior field of aesthetic form. Gilding and idealizing everything it has touched and frequently attaining a high level of imaginative style, it has thrown veils over the barrenness and emptiness of our life, putting us in extremely good conceit with ourselves while actually doing nothing either to liberate our minds or to enlighten us as to the real nature of our civilization. Hence we have the meticulous technique of our contemporary "high-class" magazines, a technique which, as we know, can be acquired as a trick, and which, artistic as it appears, is the concomitant of a complete spiritual conventionality and deceives no sensible person into supposing that our general cleverness is the index of a really civilized society.

II

This total absence of any organic native culture has determined our response to the culture of the outer world. There are no vital relationships that are not reciprocal and only in the measure that we undergo a cognate experience ourselves can we share in the experience of others. To the Catholic, Dante, to the aristocrat, Nietzsche, to the democrat, Whitman, inevitably means more than any of them can mean to the scholar who merely receives them all through his intellect without the palpitant response of conviction and a sympathetic experience. Not that this "experience" has to be identical in the literal sense; no, the very essence of being cultivated is to have developed a capacity for sharing points of view other than our own. But there is all the difference between being actively and passively cultivated that there is between living actively or passively emotional lives. Only the creative mind can really apprehend the expressions of the creative mind. And it is because our field of action has been preëmpted by our possessive instincts, because in short we have no national fabric of spiritual experience, that we are so unable today to think and feel in international terms. Having ever considered it our prerogative to pluck the fruits of the spirit without undergoing the travail of generating them, having ever given to the tragi-comedy of the creative life a notional rather than a real assent, to quote Newman's famous phrase, we have been able to feed ourselves with the sugar-coating of all the bitter pills of the rest of mankind, accepting the achievements of their creative life as effects which presuppose in us no causal relationships. That is why we are so terribly at ease in the Zion of world culture.

All this explains the ascendancy among our fathers of the Arnoldian doctrine about "knowing the best that has been thought and said in the world." For, wrapped up as they were in their material tasks, it enabled them to share vicariously in the heritage of civilization, endowing them, as it were, with all the pearls of the oyster while neatly evading in their behalf the sad responsibility of the oyster itself. It upholstered their lives with everything that is best in history, with all mankind's most sumptuous effects quite sanitarily purged of their ugly and awkward organic relationships. It set side by side in the Elysian calm of their bookshelves all the warring works of the mighty ones of the past. It made the creative life synonymous in their minds with finished things, things that repeat their message over and over and "stay put." In short, it conventionalized for them the spiritual experience of humanity, pigeon-holing it, as it were, and leaving them fancy-free to live "for practical purposes."

I remember that when as children we first read Carlyle and Ruskin we were extremely puzzled by their notes of exasperated indignation. "What are they so angry about?" we wondered, and we decided that England must be a very wicked country. Presently, however, even this idea passed out of our heads, and we came to the conclusion that anger and indignation must be simply normal properties of the literary mind (as they are, in a measure) and that we ought to be grateful for this because they produce so many engaging grotesqueries of style. Our own life was so obviously·ship-shape and water-tight—was it possible that people in other countries could have allowed their life to become less so? Unable as we were to decide this point, we were quite willing to give the prophets the benefit of the doubt, as regards their own people. But it was inconceivable that for us they meant any more by their contorting rages than the prophets of the Bible meant, whose admirably intoned objurgations we drank in with perfect composure on Sundays.

Consequently, those very European writers who might, under normal circumstances, have done the most to shake us out of our complacency have only served the more to confirm us in it. Our immediate sphere of action being sealed against them, their influence has been deflected into "mere literature," where it has not been actually inverted. For in so far as our spiritual appetites have been awake, it has only gone to convince us, not that we are unenlightened ourselves, but that other people are wicked. This incidentally explains the charge of hypocrisy that has been brought against the Anglo-Saxon mind in general ever since the industrial epoch began, a charge that has followed Puritanism as inevitably as trade has followed the flag; and it explains also the double paradox that while our reformers never consider it necesary to take themselves in hand before they set out to improve the world, our orthodox literary men, no matter what models they place before themselves, cannot rise above the tribal view of literature as either an amusement or a soporific.

How natural, then, that the greatest, the most "difficult" European writers should have had, as Carlyle and Browning and Meredith had, their first vogue in America! How natural that we should have flocked about Ibsen, patronized Nietzsche, found something entertaining in every kind of revolutionist, and welcomed the strangest philosophies (the true quite as readily as the false)! For having ourselves undergone no kindred creative experience for them to corroborate and extend, we have ever been able to escape their slings and arrows with a whole skin. They have said nothing real to us because there has been nothing in our own field of reality to make their messages real.

III

As a result of this immemorial inhibition of our humane impulses, this deliberate obliviousness to the facts of life, personal and social alike, the younger generation find themselves in a very peculiar position. For having, unlike Europeans of any class, no fund of general experience in their blood, as it were, to balance the various parts of their natures, they are incapable of coördinating themselves in a free world. So long as their creative and their possessive, their spiritual and their material, instincts frankly face in opposite directions they are able to make some sort of "go" of life, as their fathers did before them. But the whole spirit of our age tends to make this dualism more and more difficult. When, therefore, their instincts face about and confront one another and attempt to make some sort of compact, the material instinct inevitably comes out on top, because the material instinct alone is acquainted with the life of action. Their inherited and acquired culture drops away from them like a dream in the dawn and their consciousness immediately contracts into a field of reality that is restricted almost solely to the primary biological facts. This accounts for the brutality of so much of our contemporary realism; it accounts for the general poverty and chaos of our spiritual life.

Not that we only have suffered in this way, but that we have suffered more completely in certain respects than other countries. The world over the industrial process has devitalized men and produced a poor quality of human nature. By virtue of this process the orthodox culture of the world fell, during the nineteenth century, into the hands of the prig and the aesthete, those two sick blossoms of the same sapless stalk, whose roots have been for so long unwatered by the convictions of the race. But in Europe the great traditional culture, the culture that has ever held up the flame of the human spirit, has never been gutted out. The industrialism that bowled us over, because for generations our powers of resistance had been undermined by Puritanism, was no sooner well under way in Europe than human nature began to get its back up; and a long line of great rebels reacted violently against its dessicating influences. Philologists like Nietzsche and Renan, digging among the roots of Greek and Semitic thought, artists like Morris and Rodin, rediscovering the beautiful and happy art of the Middle Ages, economists like Marx and Mill, revolting against the facts of their environment, kept alive the tradition of a great society and great ways of living and thus were able to assimilate for human uses the positive by-products of industrialism itself, science and democracy. They made it impossible for men to forget the degradation of society and the poverty of their lives and built a bridge between the greatness of the few in the past and the greatness of the many, perhaps, in the future. Thus the democracies of Europe are richer than ours in self-knowledge, possessing ideals grounded in their own field of reality and so providing them with a constant stimulus to rise above their dead selves, never doubting that experience itself is worth having lived for even if it leads to nothing else. And thus, however slowly they advance, they advance on firm ground.

For us, individually and socially, nothing of this kind has been possible. It has been the very law of our life that our ways should be kept dark, that we should not be awakened to the hideousness of our civilization, that the principles in the light of which we are supposed to stand should remain abstract and impersonal. It seems to me wonderfully symbolic of our society that the only son of Lincoln should have become the president of the Pullman Company, that the son of the man who liberated the slaves politically should have done more than any other, as *The Nation* pointed out long ago, to exploit them industrially. Our disbelief in experience, our habitual repression of the creative instinct with its consequent overstimulation of the possessive instinct, has made it impossible for us to take advantage of the treasures our own life has yielded. Democracy and science have *happened to* us abundantly, more abundantly than to others because they have had less inertia to encounter; but like children presented with shining gold pieces we have not known how to use them. Either we have been unable to distinguish them from copper pennies, or else we have spent them in foolish ways that have made us ill. Our personal life has in no way contributed to the enriching of our environment; our environment, in turn, has given us personally no sense of the significance of life.

IV

Thus we see today, emerging from his illusions, the American as he really is: obscure to himself and to others, a peasant, and yet not a peasant, an animal, but full of gentleness and humor, physically sane but neurotic from the denial of his impulses, a ragbag of inherited memories and unassimilated facts, a strange, awkward, unprecedented creature, snared by his environment, helplessly incapable of self-determination in a free world—in a word, "low-brow," and aware of it. As I visualize him, rather dimly, he has "made his pile" or has otherwise "fixed things" more or less so that he has time to come out into the open and look around a little. He is rather jocose about this because he is not used to it. Things in general puzzle him so much that he cannot work up very much interest in them. The wheels of his natural self are too rusty to generate any friction. Presently, therefore, reminded that he is wasting time, he turns back again to his old habits—only to find that they in turn no longer appeal to him as they formerly did. *Things*, in short, repel him now instead of engaging him; they have worked up a momentum of their own; they scarcely require his coöperation even. And so he has to turn about once more and face that blank within himself where a world of meanings ought to be.

Now is it possible that all the poets and artists of history, whose function it has been to create and manifest these meanings, are unable to fill up this blank in his mind? Our industrial conception of culture assumes that they can do so, out of hand, and that by a process of injection from the outside, by means of indiscriminate lecturing and the like, the fact that life is a miraculous and beautiful thing can be somehow pumped into the middle of his soul. But how does he himself feel about the matter? He knows that by this process only the upper levels of his brain are touched, and that they are touched only by minds in which the true fires of life have never been lighted.

That is why we feel today that it is the real work of criticism in this country to begin *low*. For the American mind will never be able to recapture the wisdom of the world except by earning it, and it can only earn this wisdom through its own ascent upward on the basis of these primitive facts to which it has been gradually awakened. Between the apparently civilized vision of life of our best conventional story-writers and the really civilized vision of writers like Anatole France there yearns a gulf that is wide and deep, and we shall have to descend to the bottom of that gulf before we can begin the exhilarating climb to our own true heights. There are plenty of writers, of course, who imagine that they can get across from peak to peak by aeroplane, as it were, by dazzling flights of sophistication; but they do not achieve their aim and something within them tells them that they do not. They divine, as we all divine, that the only strictly organic literature of which at the moment this country is capable is a literature that is being produced by certain minds which seem, artistically speaking, scarcely to have emerged from the protozoa. That our life contains a thousand elements to which these writers just now fail to do justice is quite beside the point.

Not that we are Hottentots, or even peasants, although our arrested development somewhat resembles that of peasants. No, we are simply at the beginning of our true national existence and we shall remain there, stock still, as we have already remained for a century and a half, until we have candidly accepted our own lowest common denominator. But once we have done that, we shall begin to grow, and having begun to grow we shall grow quickly. For we already possess elements that belong to every level of development, even the highest—some even that are higher than the highest and put heaven to shame. They are all there, but they are not grouped in the right order; and so they have no cumulative effect. As soon as the foundations of our life have been reconstructed and made solid on the basis of our own experience, all these extraneous, ill-regulated forces will rally about their newly found center; they will fit in, each where it belongs, contributing to the essential architecture of our life. Then, and only then, shall we cease to be a blind, selfish, disorderly people; we shall become a luminous people, dwelling in the light and sharing our light.

9. Idealists in Battle

America's entry into the First World War in April, 1917, shattered the hopes of the young critics and writers who were dreaming of a national culture. They might have expected the rhetorical extravagance and the virulent repression of dissent from leaders of the genteel culture, who had emotionally sided with England since the European war began, and had defined America's role in the war as nothing less than the savior of civilization. But when the older generation of intellectuals came out avidly and uncritically for the war, it was a stunning blow.

Among the supporters of the war were college professors who had taught them art and values, magazine editors who had encouraged their essays, respectable Anglo-Saxon Socialists who had provided models of courage and trenchant political thought. As the young critics saw it, it was not simply these few men who had failed, or even a generation. What had failed them were the American traditions they had counted on for ideas, for continuity, for support, for public understanding. Thus the war destroyed the very foundations of their cultural optimism.

For some, like John Reed, a new hope could be found in the Bolshevik Revolution. Reed made his way to Moscow, wrote *Ten Days that Shook the World,* and died there in 1920 of typhus. For others, like Randolph Bourne, it was a time to take nothing for granted, to go back to the beginning and rethink every issue anew.

Born in 1886, the same year as Van Wyck Brooks, Bourne had worked for six years before he could afford to enter Columbia in 1909. His experience as a factory worker gave him a deeper knowledge of everyday American life than many of his literary colleagues possessed, and he wrote extensively on the schools, on urban culture, and on the lives of workers, as well as on literature and ideas. It was the breadth and firmness of Bourne's sense of American society that gave his wartime essays like "The War and the Intellectuals" their special authority and power for his associates. When *The Seven Arts* folded after its subsidy was withdrawn, they looked for his intellectual leadership and analysis of the postwar scene in his other outlet,

The Dial. But Bourne was stricken during the influenza epidemic of late 1918, and in December he died of pneumonia.

The War and the Intellectuals
RANDOLPH BOURNE

To those of us who still retain an irreconcilable animus against. war, it has been a bitter experience to see the unanimity with which the American intellectuals have thrown their support to the use of war-technique in the crisis in which America found herself. Socialists, college professors, publicists, new-republicans, practitioners of literature, have vied with each other in confirming with their intellectual faith the collapse of neutrality and the riveting of the war-mind on a hundred million more of the world's people. And the intellectuals are not content with confirming our belligerent gesture. They are now complacently asserting that it was they who effectively willed it, against the hesitation and dim perceptions of the American democratic masses. A war made deliberately by the intellectuals! A calm moral verdict, arrived at after a penetrating study of inexorable facts! Sluggish masses, too remote from the world-conflict to be stirred, too lacking in intellect to perceive their danger! An alert intellectual class, saving the people in spite of themselves, biding their time with Fabian strategy until the nation could be moved into war without serious resistance! An intellectual class, gently guiding a nation through sheer force of ideas into what the other nations entered only through predatory craft or popular hysteria or militarist madness! A war free from any taint of self-seeking, a war that will secure the triumph of democracy and internationalize the world! This is the picture which the more self-conscious intellectuals have formed of themselves, and which they are slowly impressing upon a population which is being led no man knows whither by an indubitably intellectualized President. And they are right, in that the war certainly did not spring from either the ideals or the prejudices, from the national ambitions or hysterias, of

Randolph Bourne, "The War and the Intellectuals," *The Seven Arts,* vol. 2, June, 1917, pp. 133–146.

the American people, however acquiescent the masses prove to be, and however clearly the intellectuals prove their putative intuition.

Those intellectuals who have felt themselves totally out of sympathy with this drag toward war will seek some explanation for this joyful leadership. They will want to understand this willingness of the American intellect to open the sluices and flood us with the sewage of the war spirit. We cannot forget the virtuous horror and stupefaction which filled our college professors when they read the famous manifesto of their ninety-three German colleagues in defence of their war. To the American academic mind of 1914 defence of war was inconceivable. From Bernhardi it recoiled as from a blasphemy, little dreaming that two years later would find it creating its own cleanly reasons for imposing military service on the country and for talking of the rough rude currents of health and regeneration that war would send through the American body politic. They would have thought anyone mad who talked of shipping American men by the hundreds of thousands—conscripts—to die on the fields of France. Such a spiritual change seems catastrophic when we shoot our minds back to those days when neutrality was a proud thing. But the intellectual progress has been so gradual that the country retains little sense of the irony. The war sentiment, begun so gradually but so perseveringly by the preparedness advocates who came from the ranks of big business, caught hold of one after another of the intellectual groups. With the aid of Roosevelt, the murmurs became a monotonous chant, and finally a chorus so mighty that to be out of it was at first to be disreputable and finally almost obscene. And slowly a strident rant was worked up against Germany which compared very creditably with the German fulminations against the greedy power of England. The nerve of the war-feeling centered, of course, in the richer and older classes of the Atlantic seaboard, and was keenest where there were French or English business and particularly social connections. The sentiment then spread over the country as a class-phenomenon, touching everywhere those upper-class elements in each section who identified themselves with this Eastern ruling group. It must never be forgotten that in every community it was the least liberal and least democratic elements among whom the preparedness and later the war sentiment was found. The farmers were apathetic, the small business men and working-men are still apathetic towards the war. The election was a vote of confidence of these latter classes in a President who would keep the faith of neutrality. The intellectuals, in other words, have identified themselves with the least democratic forces in American life. They have assumed the leadership for war of those very classes whom the American democracy has been immemorially fighting. Only in a world where irony was dead could an intellectual class enter war at the head of such illiberal cohorts in the avowed cause of world-liberalism and world-democracy. No one is left to point out the undemocratic nature of this war-liberalism. In a time of faith, skepticism is the most intolerable of all insults.

Our intellectual class might have been occupied, during the last two years of war, in studying and clarifying the ideals and aspirations of the American democracy, in discovering a true Americanism which would not have been merely nebulous but might have federated the different ethnic groups and traditions. They might have spent the time in endeavoring to clear the public mind of the cant of war, to get rid of old mystical notions that clog our thinking. We might have used the time for a great wave of education, for setting our house in spiritual order. We could at least have set the problem before ourselves. If our intellectuals were going to lead the administration, they might conceivably have tried to find some way of securing peace by making neutrality effective. They might have turned their intellectual energy not to the problem of jockeying the nation into war, but to the problem of using our vast neutral power to attain democratic ends for the rest of the world and ourselves without the use of the malevolent technique of war. They might have failed. The point is that they scarcely tried. The time was spent not in clarification and education, but in a mulling over of nebulous ideals of democracy and liberalism and civilization which had never meant anything fruitful to those ruling classes who now so glibly used them, and in giving free rein to the elementary instinct of self-defence. The whole era has been spiritually wasted. The outstanding feature has been not its Americanism but its intense colonialism. The offence of our intellectuals was not so much that they were colonial—for what could we expect of a nation composed of so many national elements?—but that it was so one-sidedly and partisanly colonial. The official, reputable expression of the intellectual class has been that of the English colonial. Certain portions of it have been even more loyalist than the King, more British even than Australia. Other colonial attitudes have been vulgar. The colonialism of the other American stocks was denied a hearing from the start. America might have been made a meeting-ground for the different national attitudes. An intellectual class, cultural colonists of the different European nations, might have threshed out the issues here as they could not be threshed out in Europe. Instead of this, the English colonials in university and press took command at the start, and we became an intellectual Hungary where thought was subject to an effective process of Magyarization. The reputable opinion of the American intellectuals became more and more either what could be read pleasantly in London, or what was written in an earnest effort to put Englishmen straight on their war-aims and war-technique. This Magyarization of thought produced as a counter-reaction a peculiarly offensive and inept German apologetic, and the two partisans divided the field between them. The great masses, the other ethnic groups, were inarticulate. American public opinion was almost as little prepared for war in 1917 as it was in 1914.

The sterile results of such an intellectual policy are inevitable. During the war the American intellectual class has produced almost nothing in the way of original and illuminating interpretation. Veblen's *Imperial Germany;* Patten's *Culture and War,* and addresses; Dewey's *German Philosophy and Politics;* a chapter or two in Weyl's *American Foreign Policies;*—is there much else of creative value in the intellectual repercussion of the war? Is it true that the shock of war put the American intellectual to an unusual strain. He had to sit idle and think as spectator not as actor. There was no government to which he could docilely and loyally tender his mind as did the Oxford professors to justify England in her own eyes. The American's training was such as to make the fact of war almost incredible. Both in his reading of history and in his lack of economic perspective he was badly prepared for it. He had to explain to himself something which was too colossal for the modern mind, which outran any language or terms which we had to interpret it in. He had to expand his sympathies to the breaking-point, while pulling the past and present into some sort of interpretative order. The intellectuals in the fighting countries had only to rationalize and justify what their country was already doing. Their task was easy. A neutral, however, had really to search out the truth. Perhaps perspective was too much to ask of any mind. Certainly the older colonials among our college professors let their prejudices at once dictate their thought. They have been comfortable ever since. The war has taught them nothing and will teach them nothing. And they have had the satisfaction, under the rigor of events, of seeing prejudice submerge the intellects of their younger colleagues. And they have lived to see almost their entire class, pacifists and democrats too, join them as apologists for the "gigantic irrelevance" of war.

We have had to watch, therefore, in this country the same process which so shocked us abroad,—the coalescence of the intellectual classes

in support of the military programme. In this country, indeed, the socialist intellectuals did not even have the grace of their German brothers
and wait for the declaration of war before they broke for cover. And
when they declared for war they showed how thin was the intellectual
veneer of their socialism. For they called us in terms that might have
emanated from any bourgeois journal to defend democracy and civilization, just as if it was not exactly against those very bourgeois democracies
and capitalist civilizations that socialists had been fighting for decades.
But so subtle is the spiritual chemistry of the "inside" that all this intellectual cohesion—herd-instinct become herd-intellect—which seemed
abroad so hysterical and so servile, comes to us here in highly rational
terms. We go to war to save the world from subjugation! But the German intellectuals went to war to save their culture from barbarization!
And the French went to war to save their beautiful France! And the
English to save international honor! And Russia, most altruistic and self-
sacrificing of all, to save a small State from destruction! Whence is our
miraculous intuition of our moral spotlessness? Whence our confidence
that history will not unravel huge economic and imperialist forces upon
which our rationalizations float like bubbles? The Jew often marvels that
his race alone should have been chosen as the true people of the cosmic
God. Are not our intellectuals equally fatuous when they tell us that our
war of all wars is stainless and thrillingly achieving for good?

An intellectual class that was wholly rational would have called insis-
tently for peace and not for war. For months the crying need has been
for a negotiated peace, in order to avoid the ruin of a deadlock. Would
not the same amount of resolute statesmanship thrown into intervention
have secured a peace that would have been a subjugation for neither
side? Was the terrific bargaining power of a great neutral ever really
used? Our war followed, as all wars follow, a monstrous failure of diplomacy. Shamefacedness should now be our intellectuals' attitude, because
the American play for peace was made so little more than a polite play.
The intellectuals have still to explain why, willing as they now are to use
force to continue the war to absolute exhaustion, they were not willing to
use force to coerce the world to a speedy peace.

Their forward vision is no more convincing than their past rationality.
We go to war now to internationalize the world! But surely their League
to Enforce Peace is only a palpable apocalyptic myth, like the syndi-
calists' myth of the "general strike." It is not a rational programme so
much as a glowing symbol for the purpose of focusing belief, of setting
enthusiasm on fire for international order. As far as it does this it has

pragmatic value, but as far as it provides a certain radiant mirage of idealism for this war and for a world-order founded on mutual fear, it is dangerous and obnoxious. Idealism should be kept for what is ideal. It is depressing to think that the prospect of a world so strong that none dare challenge it should be the immediate ideal of the American intellectual. If the League is only a makeshift, a coalition into which we enter to restore order, then it is only a description of existing fact, and the idea should be treated as such. But if it is an actually prospective outcome of the settlement, the keystone of American policy, it is neither realizable nor desirable. For the programme of such a League contains no provision for dynamic national growth or for international economic justice. In a world which requires recognition of economic internationalism far more than of political internationalism, an idea is reactionary which proposes to petrify and federate the nations as political and economic units. Such a scheme for international order is a dubious justification for American policy. And if American policy had been sincere in its belief that our participation would achieve international beatitude, would we not have made our entrance into the war conditional upon a solemn general agreement to respect in the final settlement these principles of international order? Could we have afforded, if our war was to end war by the establishment of a league of honor, to risk the defeat of our vision and our betrayal in the settlement? Yet we are in the war, and no such solemn agreement was made, nor has it even been suggested.

The case of the intellectuals seems, therefore, only very speciously rational. They could have used their energy to force a just peace or at least to devise other means than war for carrying through American policy. They could have used their intellectual energy to ensure that our participation in the war meant the international order which they wish. Intellect was not so used. It was used to lead an apathetic nation into an irresponsible war, without guarantees from those belligerents whose cause we were saving. The American intellectual, therefore, has been rational neither in his hindsight nor his foresight. To explain him we must look beneath the intellectual reasons to the emotional disposition. It is not so much what they thought as how they felt that explains our intellectual class. Allowing for colonial sympathy, there was still the personal shock in a world-war which outraged all our preconceived notions of the way the world was tending. It reduced to rubbish most of the humanitarian internationalism and democratic nationalism which had been the emotional thread of our intellectuals' life. We had suddenly to make a new orientation. There were mental conflicts. Our latent colonialism strove with our longing for American unity. Our desire for peace strove with our desire for national responsibility in the world. That first lofty and remote and not altogether unsound feeling of our spiritual isolation from the conflict could not last. There was the itch to be in the great experience which the rest of the world was having. Numbers of intelligent people who had never been stirred by the horrors of capitalistic peace at home were shaken out of their slumber by the horrors of war in Belgium. Never having felt responsibility for labor wars and oppressed masses and excluded races at home, they had a large fund of idle emotional capital to invest in the oppressed nationalities and ravaged villages of Europe. Hearts that had felt only ugly contempt for democratic strivings at home beat in tune with the struggle for freedom abroad. All this was natural, but it tended to over-emphasize our responsibility. And it threw our thinking out of gear. The task of making our own country detailedly fit for peace was abandoned in favor of a feverish concern for the management of the war, advice to the fighting governments on all matters, military, social and political, and a gradual working up of the conviction that we were ordained as a nation to lead all erring brothers towards the light of liberty and democracy. The failure of the American intellectual class to erect a creative attitude toward the war can be explained by these sterile mental conflicts which the shock to our ideals sent raging through us.

Mental conflicts end either in a new and higher synthesis or adjustment, or else in a reversion to more primitive ideas which have been outgrown but to which we drop when jolted out of our attained position. The war caused in America a recrudescence of nebulous ideals which a younger generation was fast outgrowing because it had passed the wistful stage and was discovering concrete ways of getting them incarnated in actual institutions. The shock of the war threw us back from this pragmatic work into an emotional bath of these old ideals. There was even a somewhat rarefied revival of our primitive Yankee boastfulness, the reversion of senility to that republican childhood when we expected the whole world to copy our republican institutions. We amusingly ignored the fact that it was just that Imperial German regime, to whom we are to teach the art of self-government, which our own Federal structure, with its executive irresponsible in foreign policy and with its absence of parliamentary control, most resembles. And we are missing the exquisite irony of the unaffected homage paid by the American democratic intellectuals to the last and most detested of Britain's tory premiers as the representative of a "liberal" ally, as well as the irony of the selection of the best hated of America's bourbon "old guard" as the missionary of American democracy to Russia.

The intellectual state that could produce such things is one where reversion has taken place to more primitive ways of thinking. Simple syllogisms are substituted for analysis, things are known by their labels, our heart's desire dictates what we shall see. The American intellectual class, having failed to make the higher syntheses, regresses to ideas that can issue in quick, simplified action. Thought becomes any easy rationalization of what is actually going on or what is to happen inevitably tomorrow. It is true that certain groups did rationalize their colonialism and attach the doctrine of the inviolability of British sea-power to the doctrine of a League of Peace. But this agile resolution of the mental conflict did not become a higher synthesis, to be creatively developed. It gradually merged into a justification for our going to war. It petrified into a dogma to be propagated. Criticism flagged and emotional propaganda began. Most of the socialists, the college professors and the practitioners of literature, however, have not even reached this high-water mark of synthesis. Their mental conflicts have been resolved much more simply. War in the interests of democracy! This was almost the sum of their philosophy. The primitive idea to which they regressed became almost insensibly translated into a craving for action. War was seen as the crowning relief of their indecision. At last action, irresponsibility, the end of anxious and torturing attempts to reconcile peace-ideals with the drag of the world towards Hell. An end to the pain of trying to adjust the facts to what they ought to be! Let us consecrate the facts as ideal! Let us join the greased slide towards war! The momentum increased. Hesitations, ironies, consciences, considerations,—all were drowned in the elemental blare of doing something aggressive, colossal. The new-found Sabbath "peacefulness of being at war"! The thankfulness with which so many intellectuals lay down and floated with the current betrays the hesitation and suspense through which they had been. The American university is a brisk and happy place these days. Simple, unquestioning action has superseded the knots of thought. The thinker dances with reality.

With how many of the acceptors of war has it been mostly a dread of intellectual suspense? It is a mistake to suppose that intellectuality necessarily makes for suspended judgments. The intellect craves certitude. It takes effort to keep it supple and pliable. In a time of danger and disaster we jump desperately for some dogma to cling to. The time comes, if we try to hold out, when our nerves are sick with fatigue, and we seize in a great healing wave of release some doctrine that can be immediately translated into action. Neutrality meant suspense, and so it became the object of loathing to frayed nerves. The vital myth of the League of Peace provides a dogma to jump to. With war the world becomes motor again and speculation is brushed aside like cobwebs. The blessed emotion of self-defence intervenes too, which focused millions in Europe. A few keep up a critical pose after war is begun, but since they usually advise action which is in one-to-one correspondence with what the mass is already doing, their criticism is little more than a rationalization of the common emotional drive.

The results of war on the intellectual class are already apparent. Their thought becomes little more than a description and justification of what is going on. They turn upon any rash one who continues idly to speculate. Once the war is on, the conviction spreads that individual thought is helpless, that the only way one can count is as a cog in the great wheel. There is no good holding back. We are told to dry our unnoticed and ineffective tears and plunge into the great work. Not only is everyone forced into line, but the new certitude becomes idealized. It is a noble realism which opposes itself to futile obstruction and the cowardly refusal to face facts. This realistic boast is so loud and sonorous that one wonders whether realism is always a stern and intelligent grappling with realities. May it not be sometimes a mere surrender to the actual, an abdication of the ideal through a sheer fatigue from intellectual suspense? The pacifist is roundly scolded for refusing to face the facts, and for retiring into his own world of sentimental desire. But is the realist, who refuses to challenge or criticise facts, entitled to any more credit than that which comes from following the line of least resistance? The realist thinks he at least can control events by linking himself to the forces that are moving. Perhaps he can. But if it is a question of controlling war, it is difficult to see how the child on the back of a mad elephant is to be any more effective in stopping the beast than is the child who tries to stop him from the ground. The ex-humanitarian, turned realist, sneers at the snobbish neutrality, colossal conceit, crooked thinking, dazed sensibilities, of those who are still unable to find any balm of consolation for this war. We manufacture consolations here in America while there are probably not a dozen men fighting in Europe who did not long ago give up every reason for their being there except that nobody knew how to get them away.

But the intellectuals whom the crisis has crystallized into an acceptance of war have put themselves into terrifyingly strategic position. It is only on the craft, in the stream, they say, that one has any chance of controlling the current forces for liberal purposes. If we obstruct, we surrender all power for influence. If we responsibly approve, we then retain our power for guiding. We will be listened to as responsible thinkers, while those who obstructed the coming of war have committed intellectual suicide and shall be cast into outer darkness. Criticism by the ruling powers will only be accepted from those intellectuals who are in sympathy with the general tendency of the war. Well, it is true that they may guide, but if their stream leads to disaster and the frustration of national life, is their guiding any more than a preference whether they shall go over the right-hand or the left-hand side of the precipice? Meanwhile, however, there is comfort on board. Be with us, they call, or be negligible, irrelevant. Dissenters are already excommunicated. Irreconcilable radicals, wringing their hands among the debris, become the most despicable and impotent of men. There seems no choice for the intellectual but to join the mass of acceptance. But again the terrible dilemma arises,—either support what is going on, in which case you count for nothing because you are swallowed in the mass and great incalculable forces bear you on; or remain aloof, passively resistant, in which case you count for nothing because you are outside the machinery of reality.

Is there no place left, then, for the intellectual who cannot yet crystallize, who does not dread suspense, and is not yet drugged with fatigue? The American intellectuals, in their preoccupation with reality, seem to have forgotten that the real enemy is War rather than imperial Germany. There is work to be done to prevent this war of ours from passing into popular mythology as a holy crusade. What shall we do with leaders who tell us that we go to war in moral spotlessness, or who make "democracy" synonymous with a republican form of government? There is work to be done in still shouting that all the revolutionary byproducts will not justify the war, or make war anything else than the noxious complex of all the evils that afflict men. There must be some to find no consolation whatever, and some to sneer at those who buy the cheap emotion of sacrifice. There must be some irreconcilables left who will not even accept the war with walrus tears. There must be some to call unceasingly for peace, and some to insist that the terms of settlement shall be not only liberal but democratic. There must be some intellectuals who are not willing to use the old discredited counters again and to support a peace which would leave all the old inflammable materials of armament lying about the world. There must still be opposition to any contemplated "liberal" world-order founded on military coalitions. The "irreconcilable" need not be disloyal. He need not even be "impossibilist." His apathy towards war should take the form of a heightened energy and enthusiasm for the education, the art, the interpretation that make for life in the midst of the world of death. The intellectual who retains his animus against war will push out more boldly than ever to make his case solid against it. The old ideals crumble; new ideals must be forged. His mind will continue to roam widely and ceaselessly. The thing he will fear most is premature crystallization. If the American intellectual class rivets itself to a "liberal" philosophy that perpetuates the old errors, there will then be need for "democrats" whose task will be to divide, confuse, disturb, keep the intellectual waters constantly in motion to prevent any such ice from ever forming.

10. A Première in Paris

After the war the new generation of young writers and literary intellectuals forgot the cultural nationalism of the prewar critics and replaced it with another cultural goal—to be accepted within the modernist movement in the arts. Since Paris was the capital of the international literary world, it was there that American writers wanted to go. They went to stay or to visit, to write or to drink in cafes. They all went to share in the atmosphere of aesthetic seriousness that America seemed so woefully to lack.

It was possible, of course, for American writers to be in Paris but not of it. If they were writing in English and sending their manuscripts back home to be published, making their friendships among fellow expatriates, or working for one of the American newspapers in Paris—all practices that were common—they might not take part in French culture at all. But such isolation would have been self-defeating for a composer like George Antheil (1900–1959). He needed a conductor and musicians to play his music, a hall, an audience, publicity. Thus he tried to forge a more intimate relation with Parisian cultural life, especially in preparation for the world première in June, 1926, of his controversial *Ballet Mécanique,* scored for mechanical pianos, automobile horns, electric bells, and airplane propellers. Ezra Pound had written a book on the composer, *Antheil and the Treatise on Harmony* (1924), but Antheil did not fulfill the high hopes of the Paris *avant-garde.* Later he worked in Hollywood and published an autobiography, *Bad Boy of Music* (1945).

Bravig Imbs (1904–1946), who describes the first performance of the *Ballet Mécanique* in his *Confessions of Another Young Man,* was a Midwesterner who left Dartmouth after two years, got a job selling ads for an American newspaper in Paris, studied music with Antheil, and mingled with writers at Gertrude Stein's salon. During the Second World War Imbs was assigned to the Office of War Information, and in June, 1944, he began broadcasting from Cherbourg on the first Allied radio station in France. He became a widely known and popular figure in postwar France, before his death in an automobile accident in 1946.

Confessions of Another Young Man
BRAVIG IMBS

It seemed curious to me at that time and curious still, that the preoccupation of talented people in America, and those who surround them, should be the fear that their talent might fail them. Instead of forgetting that they have a gift, and settling down to work, they worry their inspiration with critical questioning until, indeed, what light is left is cold and sterile. I suppose the atmosphere of the country is largely to blame. America is a wonderfully deadly place to work in; the critical spirit which rules there, manifested so often in mere carping, is an unendurable force. It has not the advantage of a frank obstacle, because it is too insidious to incite one to rebellion, but its chilling finger is on the creative pulse wherever it beats. In France, where the major virtue is not economy, as is generally believed, but the generous spending of one's self in almost ceaseless industry, the question of failing talent does not find the hot-house atmosphere of tired conjecture which it requires.

It was this feeling of freedom, more than any other, which buoyed me up that day. I arose late and shaved leisurely, preoccupied as to what I should wear. Not that I had any embarrassment of choice. Both of my two suits were shabby and shiny at the knee, and my one good shirt had not come back from the laundry. I did want to wear something especial for the occasion, and fortunately the weather came to my aid. It was cold as a Fall day and the skies were grey. The temperature was low enough to permit me to wear my Mackinaw. This coat, which had been a sensation in Dartmouth, was certain to seem special in Paris. It was checquered black and orange in four-inch squares, and the orange was a particularly violent shade and the black particularly sable. It seemed to me quite in keeping with the *Ballet Mécanique* and I felt that choosing to wear it was a good omen.

About three, I went to call for Sylvia and if she were taken aback by the coat, she hid her feelings, for I remember her saying I looked festive.

Bravig Imbs, *Confessions of Another Young Man* (New York, 1936), pp. 52–58, 78–81, 96–103.

We went together in a taxi to fetch Joyce, and all the way along she talked about music and George and my fiddling and it was very pleasant.

Mr. Joyce lived just off the rue de Grenelle then, in a tiny square near the École Militaire. "You wait here while I go for him," said Sylvia.

It seemed hours before she reappeared because I was so impatient to see the great man. Of course, I was disappointed at first sight. I had pictured him as a vigorous, rather assertive figure with a full beard. Instead, I saw a tall stooped thin man, whose clothes hung loosely on him and who moved with a languid, almost faltering step. He had no beard, but a wisp of goatee and mustache, and his face was sunburned a bright red. He was wearing a very elegant Panama hat, and a large dull silver ring quietly called attention to his very beautiful hands. But his whole demeanor was so grave and reserved that all I had saved up to say to him vanished in the air, and after our brief introduction I remained tongue-tied, almost oppressed by his silence, until we arrived at the Concert Hall.

In those days, Pleyel's was located in the rue Rochechouart and a pleasant old-fashioned place it was. There were innumerable corridors with two steps up and three steps down, vast rooms that seemed to contain acres of pianos without a soul in sight, and a kind of half-light everywhere, grey and mysterious. Our voices in that muffled place seemed like echoes of the past and we threaded our way down the dim halls, Joyce's stick occasionally tapping the floor, until finally we arrived at the room in back, where the performance was to be held. It was a room where Chopin had played, and one of his pianos stood at the far end, a neglected haughty instrument. In the other corner of the room, there was a little knot of people which disintegrated at Joyce's arrival, and while Sylvia introduced him, an almost funereal silence hovered over us all.

I knew everyone there with the exception of Elliot Paul, so it was easy to single out the timid slightly corpulent man who seemed to be trying to hide behind some chairs. I ferretted him out forthwith and took advantage of his obvious malaise to be suave and disarming.

"I have so enjoyed your work," I told him, measuring him with my eyes. Another disappointment. His face was pale, the color of a grub, and the features were either flabby or receding. He was bald and wore a scrubby brown mustache. But his eyes were very strange and comprehending, a dark hazel color, large and limpid.

"I do want you to enjoy George Antheil," I continued, "but remember you must listen to modern music with an open mind."

Later on, when we were friends, Elliot would tease me by repeating this phrase. It was, of course, too absurd, for if anyone was open to modern music, indeed, strongly in favor of it, that one was Elliot Paul.

In answer to his teasing, I would ask why he had taken any notice of me at all. "That coat," he answered, "I thought anyone who could wear a coat like that was worth knowing." But that was years later, when the reserves of mere acquaintanceship had broken down, and he was his natural loquacious self.

The day of the concert, he was as New England as you please and I found my one-sided conversation something of a strain. I left him to greet Fraser, who, out of sheer arrogance, refused to be impressed by Mr. Joyce. He was chaffing about the lateness of the hour and I was surprised to see by his watch that the concert should have started fifteen minutes before. I went to look for the young lady who was to play the pianola and eventually found her. The rolls had been finished just that minute, she assured me, and they were the dickens to play; sometimes half the keys went down at once.

When we returned to the room, we found the group scattered in expectant attitudes. Mr. Joyce was draped loosely over one chair, Sylvia was seated near him, with her friend Adrienne Monnier, moonfaced, flushed and beaming, obviously having arrived but a moment before, Elliot Paul was at the window looking at the roofs below with apparent interest, a nondescript newspaperman from the *New York Herald* sat, pad and pencil in hand (Mr. Schwerke, I noted with mixed pleasure and annoyance had ignored my invitation). Fraser leaned against the wall, skeptical but keen, and I took my place near the pianola to be of assistance to the girl if any necessity should arise.

All I remember of her is that she was very polite and had brightly rouged cheeks which became redder still as she pumped out that mastodon of music, the *Ballet Mécanique*. The terrific thumping—it was a new idea then to employ the piano as a percussive instrument—and wild chords which seemed to be torn alive and bleeding from the maws of machines, electrified the audience. Joyce seemed gripped in spite of himself, Fraser was suffering from unpleasant shock, Elliot Paul was deeply absorbed, Sylvia enthralled. The relentless outpouring of the composer's tumultuous emotion, accompanied by a fundamental rhythm which had the harrowing persistence of a tom-tom, was overwhelming. I had heard snatches of the *Ballet* before, but now that coherence was established its force was centupled. Time and again the music would surge to an impossible peak, and then break with a despairing cry, falling to a turgid swirl of muttering bass notes. The Ballet was so intense and concentrated, so strange and even irritating to the ear, that there was a gasp of audible relief when the first roll abruptly finished. There was that curious unpleasant flapping sound as the roll was unreeled rapidly, and then as the second roll was adjusted, the various people shifted their positions and became tense, as though they were to enter a long, dangerous tunnel.

But now the sweetness of Antheil began to tell and without restraining the impetuosity of the first rapture, the music became richer, less strident and there was a succession of passages, poignant and all but lyrical. Nevertheless, the combination of sounds, the cadences, were so fresh that the series of new impressions became fatiguing and exalting to a degree.

The third roll was mercifully short and rapid, a brilliant paroxysm of sound, as close to chaos as it was possible to be and still remain music. I felt so enthusiastic and exhausted that I could scarcely listen to it.

I had sense enough to thank the girl for pumping so diligently and she rewarded me with a weary smile. I imagine playing those three rolls was like running three miles. And then Mr. Joyce asked to hear a part of the second roll again!

The chattering which had broken out like fireworks as soon as the music stopped, subsided as the girl, with admirable docility, pumped now and again, making little spurts of sound until she found the measures which had interested Joyce. Heard away from their context, these few bars lost none of their peculiar vitality. Mr. Joyce was highly satisfied. "That's like Mozart," he said.

Elliot Paul was as excited as I; he came up to say goodbye and his hand trembled as he shook mine. "Wonderful," he said, his eyes shining, "so different from Vareze. I admire Vareze extremely, but this, this sweeps one off his feet."

"Do you know, young man," said Fraser, interrupting in a slightly bad humour, "your friend repeated one measure forty-five times. That's unpardonable."

"Not at all," I said, "that's where the pianola accompanies the drums and airplane propellers. It stops being the solo instrument for a while."

"Perhaps, perhaps," said Fraser, still disgruntled, "I never heard anything like it."

"Did you say seventeen pianolas?" queried the reporter with an anxious air, "I am writing an article and I want it to be right."

"It was a good idea of George to have you arrange this afternoon," said Sylvia.

"*Magnifique, splendide, ravissante,*" murmured Adrienne, wreathed in smiles.

I shook hands and shook hands. What a letter I would write to George that evening! There was no doubt about it, the *Ballet* would be a success, a huge success.

* * *

"My goodness," said Sylvia, waving a blue telegram at me, "George's father is all upset."

I had just stopped by to pass the time of day—it was twilight and the shop looked so cool and inviting—and I was delighted to hear that George's father was upset. That meant that my little publicity story had been travelling. George's father was the proprietor of the Friendly Shoe Store in Trenton, N. J., and if my little story of George's disappearance in the Sahara desert had reached there, it must have been printed throughout the States.

It was George's idea, of course. "The *Ballet* is the *pièce de résistance,*" he said to me before leaving for Tunis, "but it needs some sauce if it's going to get any attention in the newspapers. What do you think if, in the search of new rhythms, I allowed my enthusiasm to carry me too far—and I became lost in the desert? Can't you see the headline, 'American Composer Menaced by Desert Tribes, No Trace Found of George Antheil' something like that . . . what do you think?"

"If you weren't such a good composer" I said, "I would say you had missed your vocation."

"I've got it all worked out," said George, "I'll send you letters telling you how I am always getting further South—and some photographs too,—then when I send you a telegram from my comfortable hotel in Tunis, you start the story. Of course, reporters will come to interview you because you are one of my closest friends, and then you can fork out your letters and tell them how intrepid and reckless I am."

"I'm sure it will go over very well," I said, "I'll talk it over with Fraser."

George hadn't been in Tunis but a day or so before I received a very strange letter, telling me how his guides had deserted him, leaving him to push on further South, where music became "just sticks."

This was followed by two others, equally picturesque, as well as photographs of George resting from his rhythm-hunting under a palm-tree.

A few days after the papers in Paris had published an account of the private performance of the *Ballet Mécanique,* Fraser released the lost-in-the-desert story in the *Tribune,* taking care to have the news cabled to

Chicago as well. He did it all in a very pretty way, typing out the story on a yellow piece of paper with the name of a fictitious news agency on top.

"We might pass this for what it is worth," he said lightly, tossing it over to Ragnar (it was Darrah's night off) and Ragnar without any more ado sent it down to the composing room.

The very next day I received the visit of newspapermen, just as George had imagined, and the letters seemed convincing enough. The story of George's disappearance was re-told with lurid touches.

"A number of people have come to the shop," said Sylvia to me, "quite worried and wondering if I had any news. Personally, I think this little wave of excitement is going to help George."

"Of course, it will," I answered, "but I think we can run another little story, saying that George has been rescued by the Foreign Legion."

"Splendid," said Sylvia.

But that story never did appear. Darrah quietly killed it, smelling a rat, and it was so condensed and reduced in the Paris *Times* that I doubt if anybody saw it.

However, a ripple of excitement had been caused, and it was not long after George returned that a wealthy American woman found him and became his patron. I can remember with what delight George showed me his little bank-book. "Look, one quarter of a million francs, that's *something*." Böske became haughty with all the people she did not like; a two room apartment on the same floor was added to their one room, and the whole redecorated by a Russian artist, with whom George had a proper outburst of temper over the extortionate charges; a few tailors and dressmakers worked overtime for a week or so, and then all the excitement was over. The money did not make George lose his head in the least; on the contrary, he soberly set to work on a Symphony, indulged his whim for the Bal Tabarin more frequently than formerly, and began making preparations for a grand concert in the Spring.

❊ ❊ ❊

The climax of the season was George's concert at the Theatre des Champs Elysées. I had scarcely seen George, he was so suddenly caught up in a whirl of managers and printers and important American dowagers. The concert had been decided on hurriedly, and as George staked a great deal on it, he wanted to have it perfect, and that meant work. One of the best conductors in town, Golschmann, was engaged. He had a matinee-idol face, lustrous black curls, a distinguished limp and considerable musical ability. I had tea with him at that little shop on the Place de la Madeleine where American layer cakes are sold. Böske was with us, very elegant in a misty blue tweed *tailleur*, and between bites of luscious coconut cake, Golschmann was already lamenting about the seventeen pianolas.

"We tried and tried, but it was impossible to have them play absolutely together," he said, "only one was needed to put the other sixteen off."

"Couldn't they be operated electrically?" I suggested thinking of the exertion of the pretty girl at Pleyel's.

"Goodness, no," said Mr. Golschmann, "there isn't a hall in town with enough power for that!"

I don't remember exactly how the matter was finally arranged, except that real pianists were used along with a few pianolas.

Allen Tanner was among the pianists chosen and as it was to be his first appearance before a Parisian public, he was so nervous he could scarcely sleep and practised those blind blundering chords and breakneck runs hours a day. His great preoccupation, though, was whether at the moment of the concert the *Ballet* would still be dedicated to him.

"It's been dedicated to me and undedicated so many times," he said one afternoon when I came to visit him, "that I can't say it's officially dedicated to me. But, if it's printed on the programme, there'll be no doubt about the matter."

George came bursting in on us at that moment, red faced and excited. He was living in a continual state of agitation in that feverish week.

"The posters are up," he announced gleefully, "and they're all right," he said. "The printers had added an 'S' to my first name, and it was only by a miracle that Böske saw it just before the printers went to press."

"Oh, I don't know," said Allen, "Georges Antheil sounds very distinguished."

"But I don't want to pose as a frog," protested George.

"Even though you pose very well," said Allen, (he could not resist that remark) "no one could ever mistake you for a Frenchman."

Needless to say the *Ballet* was again undedicated.

The crushing blow, however, was delivered the day before the concert. George told Allen that, after all, they would not need him. I was waiting with Pavlik when Allen came in, looking as if he had been through the Hundred Years War. He was looking for comfort, but received only derision.

"Look at him," said Pavlik, "as pale as a ghost and so romantic, it's disgusting. If it continues, I shall have to leave the apartment. Just allowing himself to be influenced by that fidgetty foolish Chopin."

"I stopped on the way back at Gertrude's," said Allen, "she said right away she wouldn't come if I were not to play. George will be frightfully annoyed because he reserved a box for her.

Allen, of course, thought too highly of George's music not to attend the concert—he would have been spiting his face if he had stayed at home —and he showed real nobility by turning up at George's apartment before the concert, to see if there was anything he could do.

Was there! George was frantic. Böske had already gone off to the concert hall with Sylvia and Adrienne and he had just discovered that moths had damaged his afternoon trousers with signally malign intent.

"That they had to choose that part of all places!" exclaimed George, stamping about with impatience, and otherwise perfectly dressed.

"Keep calm for your concert," said Allen, "I can sew."

And then, while George sat fuming on a couch, exasperated beyond endurance, Allen silently and dexterously repaired the grey striped trousers. It took him some time but he did a good job.

"Thanks awfully!" said George, with one of his adorable boyish grins, "I'll dedicate the *Ballet Mécanique* to you!"

But, alas, it was too late for the programme!

Meanwhile, the fashionable and near-fashionable audience at the Champs-Elysées was becoming restive. It was perfectly all right for an artist to be late, but to be *so* late was exaggerating. Mr. Ezra Pound was much in evidence, jumping up from his seat in the parterre like a jack-in-the-box. He was wearing a bright blue shirt, open at the neck, and waggled his red beard at everyone he knew. The aisles were cluttered with various Montparnasse celebrities: Lincoln Gillespie, who scared Böske by telling her one day she was "butter mumbled on velvet wings"; Eugene Jolas, stalwart, dark and defiant; Zadkine, with his dog; Pierre Minet, who was the wonder boy of the moment; Mr. Derain, bulky and forbidding; Kiki, the mad queen of the quarter with her eyes painted in triangles to match her triangular earrings . . . oh, there was a host of them, milling about, wondering what they were going to hear and when the conductor would emerge from the non-committal door.

Finally, I caught a glimpse of George in Sylvia's box, blushing with embarrassment, his hair slicked back so straight and shiny that he looked like a scared rabbit. I knew then that the concert was to begin. Mr. Golschmann appeared on the stage and seemed impressed by the applause which was not for him, but just the audience letting off steam, and the concert began with much éclat.

First, there was the "Concerto Grosso" by Handel, so that those who did not like Antheil would have something for their money, and then George's "First Symphony."

I became exceedingly nervous listening to it, fearing that people might object to it, and little by little this fear turned into belligerency, for I could not understand why they should. The Symphony was a very special piece, dry but not dull, and the machinery that made it go was all of silver mincing precision. Toward the end, George added some almost sentimental effects with the tuba but they did not fool anyone. The audience had the preconceived idea that George was a harsh, brutal composer and they were not going to be belied. The Symphony received a wave of polite attentive applause. The *Ballet* was what the audience was after.

There was a great deal of fuss while the orchestra arranged itself for this event. George appeared on the stage, pale and nervous, giving crisp directions to the movers who were pushing five pianos into place, and to the electricians who were arranging a loud-speaker to amplify the small electric fans that took the place of the airplane propellers. All these operations variously provoked fear, pity and amusement in the audience. Finally, George nodded his head, as a cue to Golschmann that everything was ready, and sat down at his piano with a grim expression on his face.

Within a few minutes, the concert became sheer bedlam. Above the mighty noise of the pianos and drums arose cat-calls and booing, shrieking and whistling, shouts of "thief" mixed with "bravo." People began to call each other names and to forget that there was any music going on at all. I suffered with George, wishing that people would have at least the courtesy to stay quiet, but Golschmann was so furious he would not give up his baton, and continued to conduct imperturbably as though he were the dead centre of a whirlpool.

I caught the general fever of unrest myself.

"Do keep quiet, please," I said to some of my particularly noisy neighbours.

"Shut your face, yourself," they answered, and then started whistling, which is the supreme form of contempt in France.

Then, for an instant, there was a curious lull in the clamor and Ezra Pound took advantage of it to jump to his feet and yell, "*Vous etes tous des imbéciles!*"

He was shouted down from the gallery, of course, with many vulgar epithets, and the music continued monotonously and determinedly.

The *Ballet* began to seem to me like some monstrous abstract beast, battling with the nerves of the audience, and I began to wonder which would win out. Some of the listeners were in obvious ecstasy, others were worn out and resigned, others snobbishly indifferent, others openly aggressive.

The opposition reached its climax, though, when the loud-speaker began to function. It made as much noise as a dozen airplanes, and no amount of shouting could drown it completely. One fat bald old gentleman who had been particularly disagreeable would not be balked by this, however, and to the glee of the audience, lashed out his umbrella, opened it and pretended to be struggling against the imaginary gale of wind from the electric fans. His gesture was immediately copied by many more people in the audience until the theatre seemed decked with quite a sprinkling of black mushrooms.

Of course, when the *Ballet* was over, George got an ovation which was greater than the cat-calls, for everyone was willing to applaud a man who had at least accomplished something. He bowed and blushed and blushed and bowed and all his friends were very proud of him.

"Gentle Georgie, meek and mild," said a *Tribune* man near me, "I haven't come to my senses yet."

Jean Aron came up to me and said, "If you can sincerely say you like that 'music' all I can say is that you are a fearful snob."

"You came of your own free will," I answered him, irritated, "and it's your funeral if you can't appreciate such a wonderful programme." That was the beginning of a *brouille* which lasted several years.

The crowd left the theatre slowly, gathering in excited little knots which would suddenly undo at the explosion of some statement. Whether people liked the *Ballet* or not, no one could deny that it was a stirring composition.

11. The Aesthetics of Industry

For painters and sculptors the symbolic moment of aesthetic liberation came not with the war but at the Armory Show of 1913, which introduced modern art to America, scandalizing the genteel arbiters of taste. The prewar years became a time of exceptional creativity for American artists, and their achievements inspired the young literary and social critics who hoped for an artistic renaissance in America and were striving to build a national culture. But the cultural milieu of international modernism in painting disintegrated in the war. To painters and sculptors, as to the critics, the Twenties turned into a period of dispersion and fragmentation, rather than the decade of fulfillment it became for novelists and poets. Nevertheless, significant young painters like Charles Burchfield and Stuart Davis did emerge in the Twenties, and the promising artists of the Armory Show days—John Marin, Marsden Hartley, Charles Demuth, Edward Hopper, Charles Sheeler, and others—continued to advance or transform their individual styles.

Though every artist's career follows its own arc, the case of Charles Sheeler (1883–1965) is a particularly interesting one. In the Armory Show Sheeler exhibited several still lifes and landscapes done in an idiom strongly influenced by Cezanne and the Cubists. Before the war he continued to paint in the international style and also took up commercial photography, not—in the beginning at least—as a means of artistic expression, but of financial support. Yet during the Twenties Sheeler's reputation as a photographer for *Vogue and Vanity Fair* nearly surpassed his fame as a painter, and in 1927 he was commissioned to make a photographic record of the Ford Motor Company's River Rouge Plant. The six weeks he spent at River Rouge marked a turning point in his career, leading him to develop his "immaculate" style of heightened realism and geometrical form in such widely known paintings of modern industrial scenes as "American Landscape" (1930), "Classic Landscape" (1931), and "City Interior" (1936)—all strikingly similar to his River Rouge photographs. The poet William Carlos Williams recognized in Sheeler's art an aesthetic like his own, aimed at concentrating on particulars, on things in themselves. For many critics, Sheeler's River Rouge photographs particularize the object more powerfully and more successfully than his famous paintings of the same scenes. Nine of Sheeler's River Rouge photographs are reproduced here.

1. *The Foundry*

2. *Ore Docks.*

3. *Coke Conveyors.*

4. *The Pit of the Open Hearth Building.*

5. *Hot Metal Train.*

6. *Blast Furnace.*

7. *Hydraulic Shear.*

8. *Hot Metal Ladle.*

9. *Steam Forging Hammer.*

12. A Show of One-Man Acts

Midway through the Twenties many writers and critics began to feel that the energy of aesthetic liberation had been spent, and none too wisely. In May, 1926, F. Scott Fitzgerald published an essay called "How to Waste Material—a Note on My Generation," introducing Ernest Hemingway to readers of The Bookman. Of the prose works written by the young generation since the war, Fitzgerald said, only E. E. Cummings' The Enormous Room would survive. To Cummings' work Fitzgerald then added Hemingway's early In Our Time short stories, and we, of course, would add Fitzgerald's own The Great Gatsby.

A month later The New Republic printed an anonymous essay, "The All-Star Literary Vaudeville." Written in much the same tone as Fitzgerald's, the essay was more comprehensive in its range, covering works by novelists of all ages as well as criticism, nonfiction prose, and poetry, and if anything it was more generous in giving praise than was Fitzgerald. One reason for these expressions of discontent was a dislike of the overblown publicity given to many undistinguished works in a period of real creativity and unusual public interest in good writing. Another reason was the pervasive feeling among writers that they had estranged themselves from American society, thus forfeiting their power to describe the evils of American life and to imagine ways· of social improvement. For many the execution of Sacco and Vanzetti in 1927 crystallized their unease. Even before the Great Crash of 1929 writers had begun seeking new ideas for social change in America.

Many readers of "The All-Star Literary Vaudeville" must have recognized the distinctive style of Edmund Wilson (1895–   ), then an editor and regular reviewer for The New Republic. Wilson later revised the essay for his collection The Shores of Light (the version reprinted here), but his changes were directed more to improving the style than toning down harsh judgments of individuals, as he suggests in an added footnote. Wilson's literary criticism in the Twenties culminated in Axel's Castle: A Study in the Imaginative Literature of 1870 to 1930 (1931). Like many other writers, he devoted much of his energy in the Thirties to social questions, as a political journalist and in his study on the origins of socialism, To the Finland Station (1940).

The All-Star Literary Vaudeville
EDMUND WILSON

The writer of this article is a journalist whose professional activities have been chiefly concerned with the American literary movement of the last fifteen years. He has written reviews of the productions of that movement and worked on magazines which were identified with it; he has lived constantly in its atmosphere. And he feels a certain human sympathy with all of its manifestations, even with those of which, artistically, he disapproves. It is to him a source of deep gratification that literature has been "sold" to the American public, and, on principle, in the face of alien attack, he will stand by even the least intelligent, the least disinterested, of its salesmen: he has served in that army himself. But it has recently occurred to him that, when he comes to take stock and is perfectly honest with himself, he must admit to feeling only the mildest interest in most of the contemporary literary goods which now find so wide a market, and that he is disaffected to the point of disgust with the publicity service which has grown up in connection with them. He has to take account of the fact that it is scarcely possible nowadays to tell the reviews from the advertising: both tend to convey the impression that masterpieces are being manufactured as regularly as new models of motor-cars. In the early days of the present era, the reviews of H. L. Mencken, Francis Hackett, Floyd Dell and Louis Untermeyer set an example of honesty and boldness. Today these journalist critics, having got the kind of literature they want, are apparently quite content; and most of the reviews are now written by people who do not try to go beyond them. The present writers on American literature all have interests in one phase or another of it: either the authors know one another personally or they owe one another debts of gratitude or they are bound together by their loyalty to some stimulating common cause. And almost all forget critical standards in their devotion to the great common causes: the cause of an American national literature in independence of English literature, and the cause

Edmund Wilson, "The All-Star Literary Vaudeville," *The Shores of Light: A Literary Chronicle of the Twenties and Thirties* (New York, 1952), pp. 229–247. Originally published in *The New Republic*, vol. 47, June 30, 1926, pp. 158–163.

of contemporary American ideas as against the ideas of the last generation. Even Stuart P. Sherman, once so savage in the opposite camp, has become as benevolent as Carl Van Doren and now occupies what has perhaps become, from the popular point of view, the central desk of authority, to which each of the performers in the all-star circus, from Ben Hecht to Ring Lardner, steps up to receive his endorsement. The present writer has, therefore, for his own satisfaction, for the appeasement of his own conscience, made an attempt to draw up a balance-sheet of his opinions in regard to his contemporaries, not merely in disparagement of those whom he considers rather overrated but in justice to those he admires. If he succeeds in disturbing one editor or reviewer, in an atmosphere where now for some time politeness and complacency have reigned, he will feel that he has not written in vain.

To begin with the contemporary American novel—which is commonly assumed to be our principal glory—I must confess that I have difficulty in reading our novelists. We compare our fiction with English fiction and conclude that we have been brilliantly successful in this field; but the truth is merely that the English novel is just now at a particularly low ebb. We have no novelist of the first importance, of the importance of James, Joyce or Proust; or of that of Balzac or Dostoevsky. Dreiser commands our respect; but the truth is he writes so badly that it is almost impossible to read him, and, for this reason, I find it hard to believe in his literary permanence. To follow the moral disintegration of Hurstwood in *Sister Carrie* is to suffer all the agonies of being out of work without being rewarded by the aesthetic pleasure which art is supposed to supply. Sinclair Lewis, with a vigorous satiric humor, has brought against certain aspects of American civilization an indictment that has its local importance, but, when one has been through *Main Street* and *Babbitt*, amusing though they certainly are, one is not left with any appetite to read further novels by Lewis: they have beauty neither of style nor of form and they tell us nothing new about life. Joseph Hergesheimer, though he knows how to tell a story, writes nearly as badly in a fancy way as Dreiser does in a crude one: the judgment of him that I most agree with is the remark attributed to Max Beerbohm: "Poor Mr. Hergesheimer, he wants so much to be an artist." Cabell, though a man of real parts, is, at his worst, a case of the same kind: *Beyond Life* I regard as one of the most obnoxiously written books I have ever read. *Jurgen* certainly had its merits: it was well-planned and curiously successful in the artificial evocation of the atmosphere of primitive folklore. But, except at Cabell's moments of highest imaginative intensity, which are neither very frequent nor very intense, he is likely to be simply insipid. His genealogies and maps of Poictesme bore me beyond description, and the whole Poictesme business strikes me as the sort of thing with which ingenious literary school-boys sometimes amuse themselves. I dislike also Cabell's Southern sentimentality, which leaves him soft when he thinks he is most cynical. One cannot help feeling that, in the impression he gives of living and working in a vacuum, he furnishes a depressing illustration of the decay of the South since the Civil War. Willa Cather is a good craftsman, but she is usually rather dull. In spite of a few distinguished stories, she suffers from an anemia of the imagination and, like that other rather distinguished novelist, Zona Gale, is given to terrible lapses into feminine melodrama. As for Waldo Frank, he writes in a style—to me, never quite satisfactory—that combines James Joyce with the Hebrew prophets. At his best, he touches tragedy and, at his worst, embraces melodrama. He possesses a real poetic sensibility and is refreshing in so far as his vision is different from that of any one else; but, in his novels, where we hope to see him stage a drama, he is usually content to invoke an apocalypse. I consider Jean Toomer's *Cane* rather better in literary quality than Frank's somewhat similar *Holiday*. I feel more interest in John Dos Passos and F. Scott Fitzgerald than in any of the writers mentioned above: they are younger than the others, and one does not feel as yet that one knows exactly what to expect of them. Dos Passos is ridden by adolescent resentments and seems given to documenting life from the outside rather than knowing it by intimate experience; but, though, like Lewis, that other documentator, he is far too much addicted to making out cases against society, he is a better artist than Lewis and has steadily progressed in his art. Scott Fitzgerald, possessing from the first, not merely cleverness, but something of inspired imagination and poetic literary brilliance, has not until recently given the impression of precisely knowing what he was about; but with *The Great Gatsby* and some of his recent short stories, he seems to be entering upon a development in the course of which he may come to equal in mastery of his material those novelists whom he began by surpassing by vividness in investing it with glamor. Besides these, there are the other fabricators of fantasy and the realists, satiric and plain; but the former, so far as I have read them, are either tawdry, like Ben Hecht, or awfully mild, like Carl Van Vechten; and the latter, though both in novel and drama they have learned to apply the formulas of naturalism to almost every phase of American life and have, therefore, a certain interest in the history of American culture, are otherwise especially uninteresting at a time when naturalism has run its course and everywhere except in America is either being transformed or discarded. And we have also had the Wellsian social novel, at various levels of mediocrity.

Sherwood Anderson is a different matter. In his novels, despite excellent pages, I invariably become exasperated, before I have got to the end of them, by the vagueness of the characters and the constant repetitiousness of the form. But his short stories and his symbolist prose-poems have a kind of artistic authenticity that neither Lewis's richer resources nor Miss Cather's technical efforts have been able to win for those writers. Without ever having learned the tricks of his trade, Sherwood Anderson, in the best of his stories, has shown an almost perfect instinct that fashions, from what seems a more intimate stratum of feeling and imagination than our novelists usually explore, visions at once fresh and naïve and of a slightly discomfiting strangeness. He could stand to learn something, however, from the methods both of Miss Cather and of Lewis: too much of his material has evaporated in his hands from his not knowing how to deal with it. It can probably be said that, in general, the newer American writers have so far been distinguishing themselves in the short story rather than the novel. The short stories of Sherwood Anderson, Ernest Hemingway's *In Our Time* and Gertrude Stein's early *Three Lives*, to which should be added the best of Ring Lardner, constitute an impressive group and one quite free from the outworn conventions and the suggestion of second-rate imitation that make many of the novels unsatisfactory. It is interesting to note that all four of these writers have certain characteristics in common, that they may almost be said to form a school, and that, remote though they may seem from one another, there is a fairly close relationship between them. Thus, Anderson has read Gertrude Stein and seems to have been influenced by *Three Lives;* and Hemingway has evidently read and been influenced by all three of the others. Each of these four writers has developed what seems only a special branch of the same simple colloquial language, based directly on the vocabulary and rhythm of ordinary American speech; and, if there can be said to be an American school of writing, aside from American journalese or from the use of American slang in otherwise conventional English prose, these writers would seem to represent it. It is a genre that has already produced one masterpiece in Mark Twain's *Huckleberry Finn,* a work to which Anderson, Hemingway and Lardner are probably all indebted.

As for the dramatists, there is still only O'Neill, who, for all his efforts to break away from naturalism, remains a typical naturalistic dramatist of something under the very first rank. He is a writer of the same school as

Hauptmann, with much the same kind of merits; but, where Hauptmann is as steady as Shakespeare, O'Neill is hysterically embittered. He forces his tragic catastrophes and, at the same time, fails to prepare them; and despite the magnificent eloquence of which he is sometimes capable, especially when handling some form of the vernacular, he has grave deficiencies of literary taste which allow him to leave great areas of his dialogue either banal or bald. John H. Lawson has a wit and a fancy which have found their proper vehicle in the theater; but, even more than his ally, Dos Passos, he is given to adolescent grievances and adolescent enthusiasms.

We come now to literary criticism. In my opinion, H. L. Mencken (who is perhaps a prophet rather than a critic) is ordinarily underrated as a writer of English prose. Belonging himself to the line of Butler and Swift rather than to that of Pater and De Quincey, he cherishes a rustic reverence for the more "aesthetic" branch and is never tired of celebrating the elegances of such provincial fops as Lord Dunsany, Hergesheimer and Cabell, who have announced—it is, I think, Mr. Cabell's phrase—that they aim to "write beautifully about beautiful things." But although it is true that Mencken's style lends itself to excesses and vulgarities, especially in the hands of his imitators, who have taken over the Master's jargon without possessing his admirable literary sense, I believe that his prose is more successful in its way than that of these devotees of beauty usually is in theirs. The ideas themselves behind Mencken's writing are neither many nor subtle and, even in his most serious productions, even in *The American Language,* he overindulges an appetite for paradox. But some strain of the musician and poet has made it possible for Mencken to turn these ideas into literature: it is precisely through the color and rhythm of a highly personal prose that Mencken's opinions have become so infectious. He has now been repeating these opinions with the same pugnacious emphasis for fifteen or twenty years, and one has become rather tired of hearing them; yet he sustains a certain distinction and affords a certain satisfaction. Consider, for example, the leaflet he recently circulated on the adventures of the *American Mercury* with the Boston Watch and Ward Society: this statement, of no literary pretensions, in which he appears without war-paint or feathers, displays most attractive eighteenth-century qualities of lucidity, order and force, for lack of which the youngest of the younger literary generation, who have thrown Mencken overboard, have proved so far rather ineffective.

Paul Rosenfeld is another critic very unpopular with this youngest generation who seems to me an excellent writer. Though he, too, has his faults of style, which include a confusing weakness for writing French and German locutions in English, his command of a rich English vocabulary is one of the things that make him exceptional among recent American writers—who are not infrequently handicapped by not having at their disposal a large enough variety of English words, or, if they have them, by not knowing what they mean. Mr. Rosenfeld, at his worst, is given to overwriting: receiving in his soul the seed of a work by some such writer as Sherwood Anderson, himself one of the tenderer plants, he will cause it to shoot up and exfloreate into an enormous and rather rank "Mystic Cabbage-Rose." On these occasions, his prose seems sometimes rather coarse in quality and his colors a little muddy; but, at his best, Mr. Rosenfeld's writing is certainly among our soundest and his colors are both brilliant and true. He is sensitive, intelligent, well-educated and incorruptibly serious; and he is perhaps the only American critic of the generation since that of James Huneker who has written anything of any real value on the current artistic life of Europe. Van Wyck Brooks, who also writes excellent prose, though of quite a different sort, I propose to discuss in another connection.

George Jean Nathan is a wonderful humorous writer and a better critic of the theater than A. B. Walkley, in a recent article, gave him credit for being; but his writing, which superficially resembles Mencken's, is usually lacking in the qualities that give Mencken's its durable texture. Willard Huntington Wright, some years ago, gave the impression of being some one important; and Lewis Mumford now gives the impression of some one perhaps about to be. Gilbert Seldes, through his activities as an editor of the *Dial* and his cultivation of the popular arts, has filled a role of considerable importance; but his principal literary quality is a kind of undisciplined wit which figures too often in his writings at the expense of lucidity and taste. He has lately become addicted to aesthetic editorial writing, a department for which his alert and vivid but glancing and volatile mind, is perhaps not very well adapted. In my opinion, he is seen at his best in passages of straight description of some movie or vaudeville act which has aroused his imagination. Burton Rascoe has performed the astonishing and probably unprecedented feat of making literature into news. A master of all the tricks of newspaper journalism, which he has introduced into the Sacred Grove to the horror of some of its high priests, his career has yet been singularly honorable in its disregard of popular values; and the cause of letters has profited more from his activities than the proprietors of popular newspapers who have inevitably discovered in the long run that they would feel more comfortable with a literary editor who did not find books so exciting. Mr. Rascoe has always written respectably and, at his best, with much ease and point. Most of the younger generation of critics either are badly educated or have never learned to write, and many suffer from both disabilities. At best, we have produced no literary critic of the full European stature. The much-abused Paul Elmer More still figures as our only professional critic whose learning is really considerable and whose efforts are ambitious and serious. His prose is quite graceless and charmless, but always precise and clear; his point of view, though the Puritan rationalism of which it is a late product has imposed on it some rigid limitations, has the force of a deep conviction and the advantage of a definite formulation. Mr. More, although hopelessly inhibited in the exercise of his aesthetic sensibility, has become, insofar as is possible without the free range of this, a real master of ideas.

The new post-war method of biography, based on Strachey and psychoanalysis, has had many practitioners in America: Katherine Anthony, Van Wyck Brooks, Thomas Beer, M. R. Werner and others; but, though it has turned out a number of agreeable books, I have not seen any except Brooks's *Mark Twain* that seemed of first-rate importance. In the special departments of scholarly and expository writing, the general inferiority of the level of our culture to that of Great Britain or France becomes inescapably plain. There are not many of our college professors who can command the attention of the reading public. Professor John Dewey writes much and his influence has been considerable, but he has not inherited with pragmatism William James's literary gift. Professor Morris Cohen, who does possess a literary gift, has so far published nothing but reviews, and not very many of them. In the classics, Professor Tenney Frank seems the only representative of a new generation; but Professor Frank, although competent in a literary way and bold in interpretation, appears to be rather indifferent to the literary interest of the classics. Professor Paul Shorey of Chicago is perhaps the only other scholar who writes readable books in this field. We have, in short, no university professor with a literary reputation equal to that of Garrod, of Gilbert Murray, of Mackail, of A. E. Housman, or of Whitehead or Bertrand Russell or Lowes Dickinson. I can remember no recent book by an American professor which has been widely read on its literary merits, except Professor Warner Fite's *Moral Philosophy* and Professor Samuel Morison's *Maritime History of Massachusetts*. In science, we have some readable popularizers in the rousing modern manner, but they are mostly undistinguished writers: Doctor Fishbein, Doctor De Kruif and Doctor Dorsey.

Edwin Slosson is rapidly becoming a sort of William Lyon Phelps of scientific culture. The zoölogist William Beebe writes a prose that is shamelessly journalistic; but he is a man of some literary ability, who deserves to be read by writers. One of his assets is an extraordinary vocabulary, which blends scientific with literary language in such a way that his scientific words are imbued with a new life and color. I doubt, however, whether the cable to the *New York Times* is a very good school of writing. I am sorry not to be able to do justice to our recent political writers. I believe that in this department we are somewhat better off than elsewhere; but it is the one in which I have lately read least.

As for poetry, the new movement of twelve years ago seemed at the time to assume impressive proportions. But who can believe in its heroes now? Edgar Lee Masters did one creditable thing: *The Spoon River Anthology;* but, except for a single fine poem called *Silence,* I have seen nothing by him since that I could read. Vachel Lindsay's best poems, such as his *Bryan,* are spoiled by the incurable cheapness and looseness which are rampant in the rest of his work. Carl Sandburg, unlike Masters and Lindsay, has a genuine talent for language; with a hard-boiled vocabulary and reputation, he offers what is perhaps the most attractive surface of any of the men of the group. But, when we come to read him in quantity, we are disappointed to find him less interesting than we had hoped; his ideas seem rather obvious, his emotions rather meager. The work of Amy Lowell is like a great empty cloisonné jar; that of John Gould Fletcher a great wall of hard descriptive prose mistakenly presented as poetry. Conrad Aiken, except in a few of his lyrics, is one of those curious people, like William Vaughn Moody, who can turn out a rich-looking texture of words and who can make at first glance the impression of being true and highly gifted inheritors of the English tradition of the nineteenth century, but who leave us, on closer reading, with a feeling that they have not quite got the "afflatus" that their themes and their style imply. Robert Frost has a thin but authentic vein of poetic sensibility; but I find him excessively dull, and he certainly writes very poor verse. He is, in my opinion, the most generally overrated of all this group of poets. Ezra Pound, who deserves all honor as a champion and pioneer, has worked conscientiously and stubbornly as one who understands very well, and as few of his contemporaries do, in what the highest poetry consists, but who has rarely been able to affect us as the highest poets do. His cantos of a "poem of considerable length," so ambitious and so full of fine passages, passages that, standing by themselves, might lead us to believe them mere ornaments from a masterpiece on the great scale, seem entirely composed of such fragments; a mosaic which fails to reveal a pattern, a monument, in its lack of cohesion, its lack of driving force or a center, to a kind of poetic bankruptcy. The other poets of the literary Left, though, like Pound, they can often write, seem to suffer from a similar sterility. Marianne Moore, for example, is sometimes very fine; but, as she herself has shrewdly noted in choosing a title for her collected verse, the bulk of her work answers better to the description of "Observations," than to that of poetry. From a slag of intellectual processes that has only a viscous flow, there emerge intense and vivid images that seem to have been invested with a sharp emotional meaning but that are rarely precipitated out in such a way as to make the piece a poem. H. D., like Carl Sandburg, writes well; but, like Sandburg, there is not much in her. Wallace Stevens has a fascinating gift of words that is not far from a gift of nonsense, rather like that of Edith Sitwell, and he is a charming decorative artist. Alfred Kreymborg has his dry distinction, but he tends fatally toward insipidity. I think I prefer the oddity of his early work, frankly prosaic and dry, to his later more pretentious sonnets. E. E. Cummings possesses, in some respects, a more remarkable lyric gift than any of the poets reviewed above; his feeling is always spontaneous, and his words run naturally into music. But, as in his rather limp line-drawings, the hand does not seem very firm: all sorts of ideas and images have come streaming into his head, and he doesn't know how to manipulate them to make them artistically effective. W. C. Williams and Maxwell Bodenheim I have tried my best to admire, but I have never been able to believe in them.*

Since these poets made their first reputations, the general appetite for poetry seems to have somewhat abated. Among the younger poets, for example, even those of most brilliant promise are having difficulty in getting their poems printed, not by the publishers only, who have evidently come to the conclusion that poetry is bound to be unprofitable, but even by the magazines. The editors of the magazines, who have brought out, since the poetic revival, two or three crops of poets, seem content now to close the canon, and have no place for the poetry of unknown men— even if so obviously gifted as Phelps Putnam or Allen Tate—who cannot be found in Mr. Untermeyer's anthologies or among the original contributors of the *Dial*.

---

* It was at about this time that Maxwell Bodenheim described me in some such phrase as "a fatuous policeman, menacingly swinging his club." In rereading this essay—in which I have qualified or softened some of the original judgments—I have sometimes been reminded of this.

I have left aside the women lyric poets in order to discuss them as a group by themselves. On the average, though less pretentious, I think I find them more rewarding than the men: their emotion is likely to be more genuine and their literary instinct surer. Miss Lizette Woodworth Reese, the dean of the guild, astonishes one by continuing to write, not only with the same fine quality, but almost with the same freshness, as forty years ago. Sara Teasdale, the monotony of whose sobbing note caused her to become rather unfashionable when a more arrogant race of young women appeared, has made definite progress in her art since her earlier books of poems and has recently written some of her most charming lyrics. Miss Edna St. Vincent Millay has now, in turn, grown so popular that she, too, is in danger of becoming unfashionable; but she remains the most important of the group and perhaps one of the most important of our poets. Like Mencken, the prophet of a point of view, she has, like him, become a national figure; nor, as in the case of some other prophets, is her literary reputation undeserved. With little color, meager ornament and images often commonplace, she is yet mistress of deeply moving rhythms, of a music which makes up for the ear what her page seems to lack for the eye; and, above all, she has that singular boldness, which she shares with the greatest poets and which consists in taking just that one step beyond where one's fellows stop that, by making a new contact with moral reality, has the effect of causing other productions to take on an aspect of literary convention. Elinor Wylie, in the best of her verse and her novel *Jennifer Lorn,* gives expression to a set of emotions quite different from those of Miss Millay, but one which has also its typical interest and its own kind of intensity. Her literary proficiency is immense: she is never at a loss for a clever rhyme, a witty reference or a brilliant image; she can command all the finest fabrics, the choicest works of art, the most luxurious sensations, the most amusing historical allusions and the most delicious things to eat. And, as a consequence, her inferior work is almost as well-written as her best; and her best work has both a style and a splendor of a kind very rare in America—where, even when these qualities do appear together, as they did to some extent in Amy Lowell, they too often remain hollow and metallic from the lack of a heart at the core. Edna Millay's inferior work has no such embroidery to deck it; and, save in her vein of classical austerity, she has for her best but the imagery of the sorrel or mullein stalk of the barren and rocky pastures, the purple wild sweetpea dragging driftwood across the sand, the dead leaves in the city gutters, the gray snow in the city street, the kettle, the broom, the uncarpeted stairs and the dead father's old clothes—grown strange and disturbing now, to this reader's sense, at least, as the prison cell of Verlaine or Catullus's common crossroads. Louise Bogan plucked one low resounding theme on tensely strung steel strings, but it is now the vibrations of this rather than a further development that are ringing still in the air. Léonie Adams's *Those Not Elect* is a very remarkable book, of which the language, which seems to branch straight from the richest seventeenth-century tradition, strikes music from the calm summer starbreak, the brightwashed night after rain or the blue translucence of evening, where a gull or a pigeon that flies alone, seeking freedom in that space and clarity, is lost in a confusion of cloud and light. An anthology of these women poets should include, besides those named above, the *Cinquains* of the late Adelaide Crapsey and the best of Miss Genevieve Taggard, Miss Babette Deutsch and several others, of whom the younger Laura Gottschalk may turn out to be one of the most interesting and in whose company Dorothy Parker, long known as a humorous writer, has recently, it seems to me, fully proved her right to belong.

I have left to the last two poets whom, among the men, I admire most: T. S. Eliot and E. A. Robinson. T. S. Eliot, though heavily infected with the Alexandrianism of the Left, has been able to imbue with a personal emotion, not only his inveterate literary allusions and his echoes of other poets, but even the lines that he has borrowed from them. He deserves, both as critic and as poet, his present position of influence. I deplore the fatigued and despondent mood that seems lately to have been drying up both his criticism and his poety; but I cannot believe that a passion for poetry so serious and so intense can be permanently stifled or numbed. E. A. Robinson is the last and, artistically (leaving the happiest flashes of Emerson aside), the most important of the New England poets. Though he has recently run much into the sands of long and arid blank-verse narratives, I believe that he is one of the poets of our time most likely to survive as an American classic. He and Eliot both, though there are times when they disappoint us by the tendency of their motors to stall and times when they get on our nerves by a kind of hypochondria of the soul, have possessed the poetic gift and the artist's mastery of it.

The subject of Mr. Robinson may lead us to some more general observations. I have said that E. A. Robinson is the last of the New England poets, and it is true that he really belongs to an earlier period than the present and has little in common with the writers in whose company the anthologists now place him. (He is closer to Hawthorne and Henry James.) When we look back on the literary era which preceded the recent renascence, we are surprised, after all that has been written about its paleness, its tameness and its sterility, to take account of the high standard of excellence to which its best writers attained. When we consider Henry James, Stephen Crane and even such novelists of the second rank as George W. Cable and William Dean Howells, with such critics as Irving Babbitt, W. C. Brownell and Paul Elmer More, who belong essentially to the same era, we are struck with certain superiorities over our race of writers today. It may be said of these men, in general, that, though their ideas were less "emancipated," they possessed a sounder culture than we; and that, though less lively, they were better craftsmen. They were professional men of letters, and they had thoroughly learned their trade. Note the intense concentration, the incapacity for careless writing, of even Stephen Crane, who passed for a clever newspaper man and an outlaw to repectable literature, but whose work astonishes us now by an excellence of quality by no means incomparable—as how much of our present fiction is?—to the best European work in the same kind.

Another writer who, like Mr. Robinson, is bound closely, through her craftsmanship and her culture, to this earlier American tradition, but who, by reason of her critical point of view, makes a connecting link with our own, is Edith Wharton. Often described as an imitator of Henry James, she was really, in her important novels, a writer of a different kind. Henry James, except at very rare moments, was never a preacher or a bitter social satirist; but Mrs. Wharton was perhaps the first American to write with indignant passion *against* American values as they had come to present themselves by the end of the last century. Her recent books, since *The Age of Innocence,* have been of rather inferior interest; but, in her prime, she produced what I strongly believe are the best examples of this kind of fiction that we have had in the United States. She was soon followed by Van Wyck Brooks, who represented a similar reaction against a world either brutal and commercial or moribund and genteel. One of the prophets of the present generation, he belongs to the older and more sober tradition and has never, for better or for worse, learned any of the methods of the new.

Join these writers with the others I have mentioned and it will be seen that they make a remarkable group. They have provided both a picture and a criticism of one period of American life. The writing of our own age will hardly, I fear, present so dignified or so firm a front. We have the illusion of a stronger vitality and of a greater intellectual freedom but we are polygot, parvenu, hysterical and often only semi-literate. When time shall have weeded out our less important writers, it is probable that those who remain will give the impression of a literary vaudeville: H. L. Mencken hoarse with preaching in his act making fun of preachers; Edna St. Vincent Millay, the soloist, a contralto with deep notes of pathos; Sherwood Anderson holding his audience with naïve but disquieting bedtime stories; Theodore Dreiser with his newspaper narrative of commonplace scandals and crimes and obituaries of millionaires, in which the reporter astonishes the readers by being rash enough to try to tell the truth; T. S. Eliot patching from many cultures a dazzling and variegated disguise for the shrinking and scrupulous soul of a hero out of Henry James. Let us remember, however, that vaudeville has always been an American specialty; and that the writers we value most highly in the pre-Civil War period have not in general been such as I have mentioned above as typical of the generation just before our own. Emerson, Whitman, Poe; *Walden* and *Moby Dick:* they are all independent one-man turns, and who can say that we may not find their peers among our present bill of comic monologuists, sentimental songsters and performers of one-act melodramas?

13. No Ideas But in Things

Unquestionably the greatest artistic achievements of the Twenties came in poetry. T. S. Eliot, Wallace Stevens, Robert Frost, all major poets in the Twenties, were recognized within their lifetimes as modern masters of English poetry, along with William Butler Yeats; the reputation and influence of William Carlos Williams have grown since his death; and though Ezra Pound's name has suffered from his war-time propaganda broadcasts and subsequent indictment for treason, his significance as a poet, critic, and entrepreneur for modern poetry can only be enhanced by historical perspective. Alongside these poets are others of considerable importance, Marianne Moore, Hart Crane, E. E. Cummings, and more.

How does one account for the extraordinary power of American poetry during the first half of the twentieth century? Some of the credit must go to Pound, for his encouragement and criticism of nearly all the emerging young poets, for his efforts to define a new aesthetic, for his role as publicist and ambassador for poetry to the outside world. It was also important that the young American poets discovered the French symbolist aesthetic, with its emphasis on the individuality of the artist and the separate integrity of his work, at the very moment—the decade 1912 to 1922—when it was of most use. As Louis Zukofsky remarks in his essay, "American Poetry 1920–1930," they developed "literary mechanisms for expressing the movements of individual brains." Nevertheless, the literary achievements of poetic individualism did not long satisfy. By the late Twenties many of the poets discarded the masks of their private identities and began to promote political solutions for society's ills. Eliot's Anglo-royalism and Pound's support for fascism paradoxically contributed to a public reaction against the power of poetry.

Louis Zukofsky (1904–   ), himself a distinguished modernist poet, published "American Poetry 1920–1930" in *The Symposium,* one of the new critical quarterlies beginning to appear in the late Twenties. The essay reprinted here is a revised and slightly condensed version which appeared in *Prepositions: The Collected Critical Essays of Louis Zukofsky* (New York, 1967). In his revision Zukofsky eliminated his references to several minor poets, and also his unfavorable opinion of Robert Frost: "He is just too cutely pastoral, too cutely rampant to be alive, to be true."

American Poetry 1920-1930
LOUIS ZUKOFSKY

The brain and conscience of Joyce are that of his literary generation. After him: his visible influence on Cummings (of course, Cummings might have existed of himself)—'mil(lions of aflickf) litter ing brightmillion of S hurl; edindodg:ing'; on what is fairly readable in Hart Cane—*smithereens;* on the newest generation of *Blues* (edited by C. H. Ford, Columbus, Miss., 1929), mainly via Cummings.

Cummings' Elizabethan *in american* became Chaucerian *in american* in Ernest Walsh's Poems (*This Quarter*, No. 3): at times curious amoretti, at times poetry. The influence of Joyce is again evident, but Walsh too was Irish. Joyce's sense of simultaneity carries over in Williams, whose work shows also a kinship with the work of Gertrude Stein, in its analytical aspects Joyce's opposite. New writers had perhaps better be given a chance to find their own forbears. Varying from possibly evolutionary implications of statement one may study the progress of individual work rather than its use in an 'evolution' of poetry.

'No man ever writes much poetry that matters.' Yet if a man once does, one likes to see him continue for at least twenty years.

The first generation developed, after 1920 or shortly before, as did Joyce, literary mechanisms for expressing the movements of individual brains. An accurate consideration of the matter of influence may have to deal with the relation of Pound's *First Canto,* opening with the voyage of Ulysses, and the process of immediately shifting from one fact to the next in the other *Cantos,* to Joyce. Pound's first three *Cantos* preceded Joyce's *Ulysses* by some years.

Pound, Williams, Eliot, Marianne Moore, H. D. (when she does not suffer from an Anglicized dilution of metric and speech, defeating her

Louis Zukofsky, "American Poetry 1920–1930," *Prepositions: The Collected Critical Essays of Louis Zukofsky* (New York, 1967), pp. 129–143. Originally published in *The Symposium,* vol. 2, January, 1931, pp. 60–84.

double effort towards emotional expanse and condensation) did not stop with the monolinear image; they extended it to include 'a greater accessibility to experience' (Marianne Moore, 'N. Y.'). For that matter, they never started merely with the image (1913). They are thus not a gang-plank for a younger generation to step onto. Or if they are, their individual rungs matter, and Cummings is maybe on shore or sometimes certainly on board.

Robert McAlmon in *Unfinished Poem* has recalled in the inclusiveness of his American mock-historical, geographical scene, the scope of Marianne Moore's 'An Octopus,' retained an isolate individualism similar to hers while communizing quotation, hardly ever reached her incisiveness— the definite hardness of Whitman when he writes of a stallion 'Head high in the forehead, wide between the ears'—and added the indigenous cynicism of American song blues. Ezra Pound's conversation of American personae in the *Cantos* is much better than the conversation of similar personae in McAlmon's *Portrait of a Generation* (1926) and *Unfinished Poem* (1929).

The principle of varying the stress of a regular meter and counting the same number of syllables to the line was transferred from 'traditional' to cadenced verse in Williams' *Spring and All*. Not that he made each line of a stanza or printed division carry absolutely the same number of syllables, but there seems to have been a decided awareness of the printed as well as quantitative looseness of vers libre. Obviously, what counts is quantity; print only emphasizes—yet printing correctly a poet shows his salutary gift of quantity.

New work by Wallace Stevens, with the exception of *Academic Discourse at Havana* (1929), has not appeared since 1924. He returns with the same resonant elegance of precision—at least with 'Jehovah and the great sea-worm,' 'a peanut parody for peanut people,' 'the thickest man on thickest stallion-back,' and 'How full of exhalations of the sea.' His return, however, is marked by an attenuated 'accessibility to experience' characteristic of the latest Eliot (*Animula, A Song for Simeon, Ash Wednesday*), perhaps because, like Eliot, he has purposely led his rather submerged intellectual excellences (as contrasted with Pound's rebelliousness) to a versification clambering the stiles of English influence. Stevens'

> Speak and the sleepers in their sleep shall move,
> Waken, and watch the moonlight on their floors. . .

is good, but is too obviously Milton:

> That sing, and singing in their glory move
> And wipe the tears forever from his eyes.

The work of other 'formalists' seems also to droop from the stem of English influence; perhaps via Eliot. In any case, their linear and stanzaic impalings do not possess Eliot's spark of craftsman's accomplishment. Their steadiness is that of truncated emotions. Their poems are not *metaphysical*, as they intend perhaps, in the seventeenth century sense of emotional constructions mentally alive, precise, ramified and sub-ramified in their meaning. The poetic emotion is lacking, and the product is 'intellectual' rhetoric: blurred disjointed tangibilities.

The work of Hart Crane (including *The Bridge*), whose technical regularities tend to place him in class with this last 'group,' is emotionally preferable. He has energy. Yet it is an energy too often pseudo-musical and amorphous in its conflation of sense values. His single words are hardly ever alone, they are rarely absolute symbols for the things they represent, e.g.

The incunabula of the divine grotesque.

The result is an aura—a doubtful, subtle exhalation—a haze. All of which is more to the bad than the good, unless a kind of 'heat proper' gets across:

Take this sea, whose diapason knolls
On scrolls of silver snowy sentences

❀   ❀   ❀

Mark how her turning shoulders wind the hours,
And hasten while her penniless rich palms
Pass superscription of bent foam and wave.

'*Snowy* sentences' are not 'knolled.' Ezra Pound with reference to the Wagnerian ideal might be quoted: 'You confuse the spectator by smacking as many of his senses as possible at every possible moment, this prevents his noting anything with unusual lucidity, but you may fluster or excite him to the point of making him receptive.' The lines have interesting anthropomorphic feelings, but for this reason they are not the latest word in 'modern' writing, and they are too much of a metrical rocker to be 'primitive.'

To what extent Crane's music which is often Elizabethan in drive—iambic in the grand manner—helps an indefinite language and prolongs verbal indecision past the useful necessity of meaning is indicated by the poverty of his unrhymed work in recent numbers of *transition*. In these poems his words are obviously ineffectual. Their spirals of conceit are difficult to no good purpose, and the musical twisters of his metrical form are not present to carry them.

These strictures do not apply to Crane's 'O Carib Isle' which, but for a minimum of haze and a melody drummed by a kind of linguistic pedal, leaves the sensationally 'classic' and is, with distinction, of the senses. His other poems are mystical, filmy. If fish were a dead metaphor, the sea-film they wear is the logic surrounding these poems: the result is rhetoric— 'noon's tyranny,' 'sulphur dreams.'

Crane errs on the side of mysticism—to a recurrent shifting from one feeling-tone (one kind of ecstasy) to another. That there is a pseudo-substratum of idea contrasting with the feeling-tone is unfortunate in the first place. In Donne, the idea was also his feeling-tone and was also a particular metaphysical concept of his time—emotion propelling the crowding on of metaphysical things:

> For, nor in nothing, nor in things
> Extreme, and scatt'ring bright, can love inhere;
> Then as an Angell, face, and wings
> Of aire, not pure as it, yet pure doth weare,
> So thy love may be my love's spheare;

Strangely enough, the criticism of dialecticians inclined to think of Wm. Carlos Williams as a mountain goat butting among crags, has never stopped to analyse the metaphysical concept behind his improvisations. But it is a definite metaphysical concept: the thought is the thing which, in turn, produces the thought. Williams' feeling-tone, as Donne's, groups an order of tangible objects:

> Say it! No ideas but in things. Mr.
> Paterson has gone away
> to rest and write. Inside the bus one sees
> his thoughts sitting and standing. His thoughts
> alight and scatter—
> who are these people (how complex
> their mathematic) among whom I see myself
> in the regular ordered plateglass of
> his thoughts, glimmering before shoes and bicycles—?
> They walk incommunicado, the
> equation is beyond solution, yet
> its sense is clear—that they may live
> his thought is listed in the Telephone
> Directory—
>
>   (*Paterson*)

Of its time, but definitely the rare inheritance of metaphysical poetry. It is obvious why Williams should prefer the intellectual specifications, even dryness, of Mina Loy (*Contact Anthology*) to the pseudoecstatic work of a half dozen accepted lyricists or as many anthologized lyrics.

II

It is in the nature of things that poets should want to live; and ethically living cannot be a Wordsworthian dilution.

For exactness one goes back to Herrick's 'Divination':

> When a Daffadill I see
> Hanging down his head t'wards me
> Guess I may, what I must be:
> First, I shall decline my head;
> Secondly, I shall be dead;
> Lastly, safely buryed.

This is not death, or if it is 'we do not sell and buy things so necessary' (Cummings).

Ultimately, poetry is a question of natures, of constitutions, of mental colorings. But it is understood that if the author of 'Canto XXX' were incapable of the distinction of an ethical commonplace by Spinoza, it is not likely that he would have written the composite of internal rhyme, repetition of word, repetition of line with one word altered, delayed and rapidly extended cadence, and tendency towards wrenching of accent:

> Now if no fayre creature followeth me
> It is on account of Pity,
> It is on account that Pity forbideth them slaye.
> All things are made foul in this season,
> This is the reason, none may seek purity
> Having for foulnesse pity
> And things growne awry;
> No more do my shaftes fly
> To slay. Nothing is now clean slayne
> But rotteth away.

For bearings this essay returns to the several poets it started with. Its portmanteau bibliography of poetry after 1920 is brief: Pound's *Cantos;* Eliot's *The Waste Land;* Marianne Moore's *Observations;* Williams' *Spring and All,* 'Primavera' (the edition in the new *Imagist Anthology* is incomplete, yet anything but the fiasco which the rest of this anthology is); Cummings' *Is 5;* references to earlier volumes by Cummings, Stevens' *Harmonium; Exile* 3 and 4. Traditions and influences of one upon the other side, it is to be noted that these poets come out of a country which after a great deal of versified mess produced Emily Dickinson and the raw Whitman who giving 'the soul of literature' the cold shoulder 'descended upon things to arrest them all' and 'arrested' them 'all faithful solids and fluids.'

One proceeds with useful principle (Ezra Pound's *Pavannes and Divisions*, or *Instigations*, or *How to Read*, or all three). 'Emotion is an organizer of forms.' The image is at the basis of poetic form. In the last ten years Pound has not concerned himself merely with isolation of the image—a cross-breeding between single words which are absolute symbols for things and textures—

> The sand that night like a seal's back
> Glossy

—but with the poetic locus produced by the passage from one image to another. His *Cantos* are, in this sense, one extended image. One cannot pick from them a solitary poetic idea or a dozen variations of it, as out of Eliot's *Waste Land*, and say this is the substance out of which this single atmosphere emanates. The *Cantos* cannot be described as a sequence. A synopsis may no more be given of them than of a box, a leaf, a chair, a picture: they are an image of his world, 'an intellectual and emotional complex in an instant of time.'

In Williams, the advance in the use of image has been from a word structure paralleling French painting (Cézanne) to the same structure in movement—'Della Primavera Transportata Al Morale.'

Marianne Moore has allowed the 'neatness of finish' of her 'octopus of ice' to clarify ubiquitously the texture of at least a hundred images with a capacity for fact. Cummings is more sensuously evocative, sometimes fanciful ('after all white horses are in bed') but continually interested in something like capillaries, 'everything which we really are and never quite live,' the sources where images begin—

> if scarcely the somewhat city
> . . . . . . in considerable twilight

and are known perhaps only negatively—

> touch (now) with a suddenly unsaid
> gesture lightly my eyes?

His typography, illustrated by the use of the parenthesis around 'now' also suggests the image, by doubting it.

> 'A new cadence means a new idea' (Pound).

Naturally in a poem image, cadence, and idea are inseparable. The passage from Pound on Pity, quoted above, is effective because the cadence of the word 'pity' itself is never perfectly expected. The versification is not a matter of each syllable finding its usual place in an iambic pentameter, as in Frost's

> One bird begins to close a faded eye

whose drawback is submission to accent. Pound's contribution is quantity, and stock and trade sonnets and iambs have never taken up his challenge. It is time someone resurrected the sonnet from a form that has become an exercise. Cummings has partly done so in those attempts in which he is not palpably Shakespearean—with lines like

> moon's bright third tumbling slowly
> (sonnet IV—*Is* 5)

Occasionally his music has recalled Pound's with a difference in print and somewhat loosely:

> Cats which move smoothly from neck to neck of bottles, cats
> smoothly willowing out and in
> (Three—III—*Is* 5)

But for the most part, excepting a quatrain now and then in the manner of Eliot, he has been himself, the cadence approximating the actuality:

> the very swift and
> invisibly living
> rhythm of your Heart possibly
> (Four—XVII—*Is* 5)

and—

> bring on your fireworks, which are a mixed
> splendor of piston and of pistil; very well
> provided an instant may be fixed
> so that it will not rub, like any other pastel
> (One—XXXIX—*Is* 5)

Eliot has always been more interesting in his effects with quantity than in his effects with accent:

> Lord, the Roman hyacinths are blooming in bowls and

as against

> Kept faith and fast, provided for the poor

—both lines from *A Song for Simeon*.

The music of Marianne Moore's *Observations* varies from the quantitative couplets in 'An Egyptian Pulled Glass Bottle in the Shape of a Fish' to the complex stanza of 'Those Various Scalpels' (compared to which Donne's 'A Valediction of Weeping' seems easy), to the energy of her longer poems:

in which action perpetuates action and angle is at variance
    with angle
till submerged by the general action;
obscured by 'fathomless suggestions of color,'

       ✿   ✿   ✿

               ocean of hurrying
consonants

       ✿   ✿   ✿

crashing itself out in one long hiss of spray.
                       ('Novices')

The resonance of her 'Fear is Hope,' the length of its rhetorical periods
carried over despite the fall of the rhymes, are worthy of Donne:

>   . . . round glasses spun
> To flame as hemispheres of one
>   Great hourglass dwindling to a stem.

Williams' extremely important revisions and condensations of vers libre,
his contribution to an emphasis of word and stress in *Spring and All* and
'Primavera,' have already been discussed. 'Primavera' contains this perfect
lyric:

> as love
>   newborn
> each day upon the twig
>   which may die
>   springs your love
> fresh up
>   lusty for the sun
> the bird's companion

also this original stanzaic pattern with effective stress variations:

> Trundled from
> the strangeness of the sea—
> a kind of
> heaven—
>
> Ladies and Gentlemen!
> the greatest
> sea monster ever exhibited
> alive
>
> the gigantic
> sea-elephant—O wallow
> of flesh where
> are

> there fish enough for
> that
> appetite stupidity
> cannot lessen?

Music of word in a poem is to a great extent a matter of diction. The sedate will likely reject the last quotation from Williams and will admire the uncertain Elizabethan virtues of Cummings' 'my very lady,' or an extension of it, 'your crisp eyes actually,' rather than his 'why are these pipples taking their hets off?' (One—XVIII—*Is* 5), or the straightforward diction of

> And send life out of me and the night
> absolutely into me
>
> (Five—I—*Is* 5)

Whatever one's preferences, the diction of these poets remains their fully varied material, which includes quotations from sources apparently useful to an interest in preserving poetry wherever it is found. Pound's 'Canto XXVIII' contains:

> Joe hittin' the gob at 25 feet
> Every time, ping on the metal
> (Az ole man Comley wd. say: Boys! . . .
> Never cherr terbakker! Hrwwkke tth!
> Never cherr terbakker!

also—

> If thou wilt go to Chiaso wilt find that indestructible female
> As if waiting for the train to Topeka

'Canto XXIX':

> ❁   ❁   ❁
>
> narrow thighs,
> The cut cool of the air.

The diction which is dead today is that of poets who, as someone said of Matthew Arnold, have put on singing robes to lose themselves in the universal. Anent this matter, a paragraph from Roger Kaigh's *Paper* (still unpublished) is not inappropriate:

> The bias of paper, to this day, most radically affects logicians and philosophers. Logicians will admit that a word may have more than one meaning, but each must be definite and thus distinct. Infinite shades of meaning cannot be recognized, for the instrument of formal logic depends upon static or categorical meanings, that is, definitions, for its operation. Otherwise the logician detects the fallacy of four terms. But categories which appear distinct upon paper derive an infinity of variations in speech. 'Yes' and 'No' are categorically distinct upon paper, but

either may mean anything from emphatic 'Yes' to emphatic 'No' when spoken. For the context, gesture, intonation and pronunciation give words a stamp of meaning which a written form will lack.

The diction employed by Pound, Eliot, Williams, Marianne Moore and Cummings has always tended towards precise intension and to varied play of connotation. The devices of emphasizing cadence by arrangement of line and typography have been those which clarify and render the meaning of the spoken word specific. The things these poets deal with are of their world and time, but they are 'modern' only because their words are energies which make for meaning.

III

The Work of William Carlos Williams

He is of rare importance in the last decade (1920–1930), for whatever he has written the direction of it has been poetry—and, in a special sense, history. History, or the attractions of living recorded—the words a shining transcript.

> On the oak-leaves the light snow lay encrusted till the wind turned
> , a leaf over.
> No use, no use. The banality wins, is rather increased by the attempt to reduce it. Better to learn to write and to make a smooth page no matter what the incoherence of the day, no matter what erasures must be sacrificed to improve a lying appearance to keep ordered the disorder of the pageless actual.
> *A Novelette* (1929)

He has looked around—the dimensions of writing like those of music continually audible to him (somehow in a discussion of writing today, after his discussions, the word 'dimension' gets in): 'I think these days when there is so little to believe in—when the old loyalties—god, country, and the ·hope of Heaven—aren't very real, we are more dependent than we should be on our friends.' Isolation. Yet he has imagined 'each step enlarged to a plain'—known, in fact, 'his intimate, his musician, his servant.'

The aesthetics of his material is a living one, a continual beginning, a vision amid pressure; *The Great American Novel* (1923), the only one because it is the product of the scene given its parallel in words. America, the shifting, as one hurriedly thinks of it or sees it perhaps as one changes from street car to street car, resulted in this book in the swift hold of art on things seen, in the sudden completeness of the words envisioning them. 'He could see the red tail-light still burning brightly with the electricity that came from the battery under the floor boards. No one had stolen the spare tire.' (Chapter II). 'Corners of rooms sacred to so many deeds. Here he had said so and so, done so and so.' (Chapter XIII). Such things are seen and recorded not as notes, but as finished, swiftly trained deliberations of the mind between leaps to other work or the multiplicity of living scenes.

Therefore, his exclusion of sentimentalisms, extraneous comparisons, similes, overweening autobiographies of the heart, of all which permits factitious "reflection about," of sequence, of all but the full sight of the immediate, in *Spring and All* (1923). A collection of his works should contain only *the facts of his words*, even those which jar as they brighten in the composition—for these, too, illuminate, as against the personally lyric padding, the idly discursive depressing stages of writing not the product swift out of the material. In this he is almost unrelated: in a kind of morality which is his visioned impact against the environment, in a complete awareness of values in the living broken down for others by sentimentalisms.

In *The Tempers* (1913), *Al Que Quiere* (1917) and *Sour Grapes* (1922) there are poems that will stay though many lines are invalidated by his subsequent criticism. It is salutary that these lines may be omitted and still leave a number of structures. The process of rehabilitating the good to its rightful structure is always possible with writing in which something was seen, a quantity heard, an emotion apprehended to begin with.

One is faced with the same difficulties in the *Improvisations* (1920), and the same outlet: what he learned later to exclude may be omitted in the reading. The element is often not seen from the emanation, or as he has said, the paper is not felt from the glaze. But at best the writing in the *Improvisations* attains a Shakespearean verbalism:

> When beldams dig claims their fat hams (it's always beldams) balanced near Tellus' hide, this rhinoceros pelt, these lumped stones—buffoonery of midges on a bull's thigh—invoke, what you will: birth's glut, awe at God's craft, youth's poverty, evolution of a child's caper, man's poor inconsequence. Eclipse of all things; sun's self turned hen's rump. (XI, 2).

At best, there is a continual friskiness, the writing is a fugue, comparable to the scene in *Twelfth Night* in which the Clown proves Olivia a fool. (In 'The Descent of Winter' (1928) and in a few other scattered notes, he has written about the best Shakespearean criticism there is—at least, it is no more nor less serious than the incidental.)

> Porpoises risen in a green sea, the wind at nightfall bending the rose-red grass and you—in your apron running to catch—say it seems to you

to be your son. How ridiculous! You will pass up into a cloud and look back at me, not count the scribbling foolish that put wings to your heels, at your knees.' (1920). [To prove:] there is no thing that with a twist of the imagination cannot be something else. (*Improvisations, XXVII, 2*)

He has, since 1923, printed his poems differently—used print as a guide to the voice and the eye. His line sense is not only a music heard, but seen, printed as bars, printed (or cut as it were) for the reading—the sentimentalisms which might possibly have encroached brushed off like flies as at those clear times when the dynamic feeling of a person is not disturbed. One does not think of line-ends in him but of essential rhythm, each cadence emphasized, the rhythm breaking and beginning again, an action, each action deserving a line:

> the harried
> earth is swept.
> The trees
> the tulip's bright
> tips
>   sidle and
> toss

nouns: acts as much as verbs.

He has apparently broken with his own stylistic standards when the power behind the words demanded it. Thus, the conceit of his 'Botticellian Trees': but one feels 'the alphabet of the trees' identified with roots and growths which make the alphabet of his actual writing. The conceit does not stick out of the verse, but builds it: his kinship with Donne, with Shakespearean metaphor.

For these attainments, he has no need to make concessions to the 'obstinate rationalists.' Yet he has come across, and retained, more learning than he himself may be satisfied to allow he has: *In the American Grain* (1925) and *A Voyage to Pagany* (1929).

History is in these pages and in the poems—history defined as the facts about us, their chronological enlivening for the present set down as art, and so good for the next age and the next. *The pure products of America go crazy* is the poem it is through its realization of aesthetic, living values, social determinism of American suburbs in the first thirty years of the twentieth century. The poem could perhaps be realised only by one who has vicariously written, rather than painted as he has always wished to do, but in any event it has been realized by one vitally of his time.

No outside program has influenced his social awareness. It is the product of the singular creature living in society and expressing in spite of the numb terror around him the awareness which after a while cannot help be but general. It is the living creature becoming conscious of his own needs through the destruction of the various isolated around him, and till his day comes continuing unwitnessed to work, no one but himself to drive the car through the suburbs, till they too become conscious of demands unsatisfied by the routine senseless repetition of events.

PART THREE

THE CULTURAL
PROSPECT

14. The Black Migration Northward

The outbreak of war in Europe placed heavy demands on American industrial production, yet it cut off the vast migration of European peoples to the United States. The factories of the industrial North needed to find a new source for their labor, especially when American entry into the war in 1917 drained part of their work force into the Army. In their extreme need, industries turned to the large pool of native manpower they had previously neglected, except to use in breaking strikes—the Negro population of the South. Manufacturers' agents toured the South, promising jobs and good pay, giving away train tickets, refurbishing an old pre-Civil War slaves' dream that the Promised Land lay at the North. Thus was begun the great twentieth-century exodus of black people from the rural South to the urban North.

From the very beginning the movement was marked by strife as well as hope. Black workers immediately came in conflict with native whites and immigrant ethnic groups—over jobs, union rights, housing, and other economic and social issues. White grievances were heightened by the ethnic and national divisions created by the war. Though whites might quarrel with each other, they could unite against the threat of the Negro. In 1919 serious racial incidents—strikes, riots, lynchings—took place all over the United States. The worst violence occurred at Chicago. There thirty-eight persons were killed and 537 injured in a week-long riot.

Still, the promise remained, of a good job, money, dignity, urban pleasures, and all through the Twenties blacks moved North. The significance of this mass migration was the subject Charles S. Johnson (1893–1956) took up in his essay, "The New Frontage on American Life," for the famous anthology, *The New Negro: An Interpretation* (New York, 1925), edited by Alain Locke. Johnson was an outstanding social scientist and Negro intellectual of his day. From 1923 to 1929 he served as editor of *Opportunity,* the journal of the National Urban League, an organization founded in 1910 for the purpose of improving conditions of housing and employment for blacks in the urban North. In 1928 Johnson joined Fisk University as director of the Department of Social Science, and from 1946 until his death he served as president of Fisk.

The New Frontage on American Life

CHARLES S. JOHNSON

I

The cities of the North, stern, impersonal and enchanting, needed men of the brawny muscles, which Europe, suddenly flaming with war, had ceased to supply, when the black hordes came on from the South like a silent, encroaching shadow. Five hundred thousand there were in the first three-year period. These had yielded with an almost uncanny unanimity of triumphant approval to this urge to migration, closing in first upon the little towns of the South, then upon the cities near the towns, and, with an unfailing consistency, sooner or later they boarded a *Special* bound North, to close in upon these cities which lured them, with an ultimate appeal, to their gay lights and high wages, unoppressive anonymity, crowds, excitement, and feverish struggle for life.

There was Chicago in the West, known far and wide for its colossal abattoirs, whose placarded warehouses, set close by the railroad, dotted every sizable town of the South, calling for men; Chicago, remembered for the fairyland wonders of the World's Fair; home of the fearless, taunting "race paper," and above all things, of mills clamoring for men.

And there was Pittsburgh, gloomy, cheerless—bereft of the Poles and Lithuanians, Croatians and Austrians, who had trucked and smelted its steel. And along with Pittsburgh, the brilliant satellite towns of Bethlehem and Duquesne and Homestead. The solid but alert Europeans in 1916 had deserted the lower bases of industry and gone after munitions money, or home to fight. Creeping out, they left a void, which, to fill, tempted industry to desperate measures. One railroad line brought in 12,000 of these new laborers graciously and gratuitously. The road-beds and immense construction projects of the State were in straits and the great mills wanted men.

And there was New York City with its polite personal service and its

Charles S. Johnson, "The New Frontage on American Life," from *The New Negro: An Interpretation*, Alain Locke, ed. (New York, 1925), pp. 278–298.

Harlem—the Mecca of the Negroes the country over. Delightful Harlem of the effete East! Old families, brownstone mansions, a step from worshipful Broadway, the end of the rainbow for early relatives drifting from home into the exciting world; the factories and the docks, the stupendous clothing industries, and buildings to be "superintended," a land of opportunity for musicians, actors and those who wanted to be, the national headquarters of everything but the government.

And there was Cleveland with a faint Southern exposé but with iron mills; and St. Louis, one of the first cities of the North, a city of mixed traditions but with great foundries, brick and terra-cotta works; Detroit, the automobile center, with its sophistication of skill and fancy wages reflecting the daring economic policies of Henry Ford; Hartford, Connecticut, where, indeed, the first experiment with southern labor, was tried on the tobacco plantations skirting the city; Akron and its rubber; Philadelphia, with its comfortable old traditions; and the innumerable little industrial towns where fabulous wages were paid.

White and black these cities lured, but the blacks they lured with a demoniac appeal.

II

Migrations, thinks Professor Carr-Saunders—and he is confirmed by history—are nearly always due to the influence of an idea. Population crowding, and economic debasement, are, by their nature, more or less constant. In the case of the Negroes, it was not exclusively an idea, but an idea brought within the pale of possibility. By tradition and probably by temperament the Negro is a rural type. His metier is agriculture. To this economy his mental and social habits have been adjusted. In exact contrast to him is the Jew, who by every aptitude and economic attachment is a city dweller, and in whom modern students of racial behavior are discovering a neurotic constitution traceable to the emotional strain of peculiar racial status and to the terrific pressure of city life.

South, there are few cities. The life of the section is not manufacture but the soil—and more than anything else, the fluffy white bolls of cotton. There is Mississippi where 56 per cent of the population are Negroes and 88 per cent of the Negroes are farmers. Cotton is King. When it lives and grows and escapes the destroying weevil and the droughts and the floods, there is comfort for the owners. When it fails, as is most often, want stalks, and a hobbed heel twists on the neck of the black tenant. The iniquitous credit system breeding dishonesty and holding the Negroes perpetually in debt and virtually enslaved; the fierce hatred of poor whites in frightened and desperate competition; cruelty of the masters who reverently thanked God for the inferior blacks who could labor happily in the sun, with all the unfeeling complaisance of oxen; the barrenness and monotony of rural life; the dawn of hope for something better; distant flashes of a new country, beckoning—these were the soil in which the idea took root—and flowered. There was no slow, deliberate sifting of plans, or measurement of conduct, or inspired leadership, or forces dark and mysterious. To each in his setting came an impulse and an opportunity.

There was Jeremiah Taylor, of Bobo, Mississippi, long since at the age of discretion, gnarled and resigned to his farm, one of whose sons came down one day from the "yellow dog road" with the report that folks were leaving "like Judgment day"; that he had seen a labor man who promised a free ticket to a railroad camp up North. Jeremiah went to town, half doubting and came back aflush and decided. His son left, he followed and in four months his wife and two daughters bundled their possessions, sold their chickens and joined them.

Into George Horton's barber shop in Hattiesburg, Mississippi, came a white man of the North. Said he: "The colored folks are obligated to the North because it freed them. The North is obligated to the colored folks because after freeing them it separated them from their livelihood. Now, this living is offered with interest and a new birth of liberty. Will the colored man live up to his side of the bargain?" The clinching argument was free transportation. George Horton's grievance was in politics. He already earned a comfortable living and could decline the free ride as a needless charity. But his place contributed forty men. The next year the Hattiesburg settlement in Chicago brought up their pastor.

And there was Joshua Ward, who had prayed for these times and now saw God cursing the land and stirring up his people. He would invoke his wrath no longer.

Rosena Shephard's neighbor's daughter, with a savoury record at home, went away. Silence, for the space of six weeks. Then she wrote that she was earning $2 a day packing sausages. "If that lazy, good-for-nothing gal kin make $2 a day, I kin make four," and Mrs. Shephard left.

Clem Woods could not tolerate any fellow's getting ahead of him. He did not want to leave his job and couldn't explain why he wanted to go North and his boss *proved* to him that his chances were better at home. But every departure added to his restlessness. One night a train passed with two coaches of men from New Orleans. Said one of them: "Good-by bo, I'm bound for the promised land," and Clem got aboard.

Jefferson Clemons in De Ridder, Louisiana, was one of "1,800 of the colored race" who paid $2 to a "white gentleman" to get to Chicago on the 15th of March. By July he had saved enough to pay his fare and left "bee cars," as he confided, "he was tired of bein' dog and beast."

Mrs. Selina Lennox was slow to do anything, but she was by nature a social creature. The desolation of her street wore upon her. No more screaming, darting children, no more bustle of men going to work or coming home. The familiar shuffle and loud greetings of shopping matrons, the scent of boiled food—all these were gone. Mobile Street, the noisy, was clothed in an ominous quiet, as if some disaster impended. Now and then the Italian storekeeper, bewildered and forlorn, would walk to the middle of the street and look first up and then down and walk back into his store again. Mrs. Lennox left.

George Scott wanted more "free liberty" and accepted a proffered railroad ticket from a stranger who always talked in whispers and seemed to have plenty of money.

Dr. Alexander H. Booth's practice declined, but some of his departed patients, long in his debt paid up with an infuriating air of superiority, adding in their letters such taunts as "home ain't nothing like this" or "nobody what has any grit in his craw would stay," and the Doctor left.

John Felts of Macon was making $1.25 when flour went up to $12 a barrel and the New York *Age* was advertising cheap jobs at $2.50 a day. He had a wife and six children.

Jim Casson in Grabor, Louisiana, had paid his poll taxes, his state and parish taxes and yet children could not get a school.

Miss Jamesie Towns taught fifty children four months for the colored tenants, out near Fort Valley, Georgia. Her salary was reduced from $16.80 to $14.40 a month.

Enoch Scott was living in Hollywood, Mississippi, when the white physician and one of the Negro leaders disputed a small account. The Negro was shot three times in the back and his head battered—all this in front of the high sheriff's office. Enoch says he left because the doctor might sometime take a dislike to him.

When cotton was selling for forty cents a point, Joshua Johnson was offered twenty and was dared to try to sell it anywhere else. Said Joshua: "Next year, I won't have no such trouble," and he didn't.

Chicago's Negro population had dragged along by decades until the upheaval, when suddenly it leaped from 44,000 to 109,000. In a slice of the city between nineteen blocks, 92,000 of them crowded: on the east the waters of Lake Michigan; on the west the great nauseous stretch of the stockyards and the reeking little unpainted dwellings of foreigners; on the north the business district, and on the south the scowling and self-conscious remnant of the whites left behind in the rush of fashion to the North Shore.

Fifteen years ago over 60 per cent of all these working Negroes were engaged in domestic and personal service. There was nothing else to do. Then the fashion had changed in servants as Irish and Swedish and German tides came on. An unfortunate experience with the unions lost for Negroes the best positions in their traditional strongholds as waiters and poisoned their minds against organized labor. Racial exclusiveness, tradition, and inexperience, kept them out of industry. Then a strike at the stockyards and the employers miraculously and suddenly discovered their untried genius, while the unions elected to regard them as deliberate miscreants lowering wage standards by design and taking white men's jobs. Smoldering resentment. But with the war and its labor shortage, they came on in torrents. They overran the confines of the old area and spread south in spite of the organized opposition of Hyde Park and Kenwood, where objection was registered with sixty bombs in a period of two years. Passions flamed and broke in a race riot unprecedented for its list of murders and counter-murders, its mutilations and rampant savagery; for the bold resistance of the Negroes to violence. Then gradually passions fired by the first encounter subsided into calm and the industries absorbed 80 per cent of the working members.

Before the deluge, New York City, too, lacked that lusty vigor of increase, apart from migration, which characterized the Negro population as a whole. In sixty years, its increase had been negligible. Time was when that small cluster of descendants of the benevolent old Dutch masters and of the free Negroes moved with freedom and complacent importance about the intimate fringe of the city's active life. These Negroes were the barbers, caterers, bakers, restaurateurs, coachmen—all highly elaborated personal service positions. The crafts had permitted them wide freedom; they were skilled artisans. They owned businesses which were independent of Negro patronage. But that was long ago. This group in 1917 was rapidly passing, its splendor shorn. The rapid evolution of business, blind to the amenities on which they flourished, had devoured their establishments, unsupported and weak in capital resources; the incoming hordes of Europeans had edged them out of their inheritance of personal service businesses, clashed with them in competition for the rough muscle jobs and driven them back into the obscurity of individual personal service.

For forty years, moreover, there have been dribbling in from the South, the West Indies and South America, small increments of population which through imperceptible gradations had changed the whole complexion and outlook of the Negro New Yorker. New blood and diverse cultures these brought—and each a separate problem of assimilation. As the years passed, the old migrants "rubbed off the green," adopted the slant and sophistication of the city, mingled and married, and their children are now the native-born New Yorkers. For fifty years scattered families have been uniting in the hectic metropolis from every state in the union and every province of the West Indies. There have always been undigested colonies —the Sons and Daughters of North Carolina, the Virginia Society, the Southern Beneficial League—these are survivals of self-conscious, intimate bodies. But the mass is in the melting pot of the city.

There were in New York City in 1920, by the census count, 152,467 Negroes. Of these 39,233 were reported as born in New York State, 30,436 in foreign countries, principally the West Indies, and 78,242 in other states, principally the South. Since 1920 about 50,000 more Southerners have been added to the population, bulging the narrow strip of Harlem in which it had lived and spilling over the old boundaries. There are no less than 25,000 Virginians in New York City, more than 20,000 North and South Carolinians, and 10,000 Georgians. Every Southern state has contributed its quota to a heterogeneity which matches that of cosmopolitan New York. If the present Negro New Yorker were analyzed, he would be found to be composed of one part native, one part West Indian and about three parts Southern. If the tests of the army psychologists could work with the precision and certainty with which they are accredited, the Negroes who make up the present population of New York City would be declared to represent different races, for the differences between South and North by actual measurement are greater than the difference between whites and Negroes.

III

A new type of Negro is evolving—a city Negro. He is being evolved out of those strangely divergent elements of the general background. And this is a fact overlooked by those students of human behavior, who with such quick comprehension detect the influence of the city in the nervousness of the Jew, the growing nervous disorders of city dwellers in general to the tension of city life. In ten years, Negroes have been actually transplanted from one culture to another.

Where once there were personal and intimate relations, in which individuals were in contact at practically all points of their lives, there are now group relations in which the whole structure is broken up and reassorted, casting them in contact at only one or two points of their lives. The old controls are no longer expected to operate. Whether apparent or not, the newcomers are forced to reorganize their lives, to enter a new status and adjust to it that eager restlessness which prompted them to leave home. Church, lodge, gossip, respect of friends, established customs, social and racial, exercise controls in the small Southern community. The church is the center for face-to-face relations. The pastor is the leader. The rôle of the pastor and the social utility of the church are obvious in this letter sent home:

"Dear pastor: I find it my duty to write you my whereabouts, also family . . . I shall send my church money in a few days. I am trying to influence our members here to do the same. I received notice printed in a R.R. car (Get right with God). O, I had nothing so striking as the above mottoe. Let me no how is our church I am so anxious to no. My wife always talking about her seat in the church want to no who occupies it. Yours in Christ."

Religion affords an outlet for the emotional energies thwarted in other directions. The psychologists will find rich material for speculation on the emotional nature of some of the Negroes set into the New York pattern in this confession:

"I got here in time to attend one of the greatest revivals in the history of my life—over 500 people join the church. We had a Holy Ghost shower. You know I like to have run wild."

In the new environment there are many and varied substitutes which answer more or less directly the myriad desires indiscriminately comprehended by the church. The complaint of the ministers that these "emancipated" souls "stray away from God" when they reach the city is perhaps warranted on the basis of the fixed status of the church in the South, but it is not an accurate interpretation of what has happened. When the old ties are broken new satisfactions are sought. Sometimes the Young Men's Christian Association functions. This has in some cities made rivalry between the churches and Associations. More often the demands of the young exceed the "sterilized" amusements of Christian organizations. It is not uncommon to find groups who faithfully attend church Sunday evenings and as faithfully seek further stimulation in a cabaret afterwards. Many have been helped to find themselves, no doubt, by having their old churches and pastors reappear in the new home and resume control. But too often, as with European immigrants, the family loses control over the children who become assimilated more rapidly than their parents. Tragic evidences of this appear coldly detailed in the records of delinquency.

Social customs must change slowly if excesses and waste would be avoided. Growth of a new custom on a town will be slow; introduction of a foreigner to a new custom in its maturity necessitates rapid accommodation. It cannot be fully comprehended at first sight. The innumerable safeguards which surround these departures from social customs are lacking. There is a different social meaning in Ophelia, Mississippi, when one does not go to church, or a woman smokes or bobs her hair; Palatka's star elocutionist does not always take Chicago's dramatic circles by storm; neither does Noah Brown, the local potentate of fraternal circles wield the same influence in New York. There are new leaders and new objectives, which for many moons remain incomprehensible to the newcomer.

There is a reorganization of attitudes. There is a racial as well as a social disorientation. For those who fed their hopes and expectations on a new status which would afford an escape from unrighteous and oppressive limitations of the South, there is a sensitiveness about any reminder of the station from which they have been so recently emancipated—a hair-trigger resentment, a furious revolt against the years of training in the precise boundaries of their place, a fear of disclosing the weakness of submission where it is not expected, an expansiveness and pretense at ease in unaccustomed situations. Exact balance is difficult. Here are some of the things that register: John Diggs writes home to his friend this letter:

"Dear Partner: . . . I am all fixed now and living well, I don't have to work hard. Don't have to mister every little boy comes along. I haven't heard a white man call a colored a nigger you know how— since I been here. I can ride in the street or steam car anywhere I get a seat. I don't care to mix with white what I mean I am not crazy about being with white folks, but if I have to pay the same fare I have learn to want the same acomidation and if you are first in a place here shoping you don't have to wait till all the white folks get thro tradeing yet amid all this I love the good old south and am praying that God may give every well wisher a chance to be a man regardless of color . . ."

If the Negroes in Harlem show at times less courtesy toward white visitors than is required by the canons of good taste, this is bad, but understandable. It was remarked shortly after the first migration that the newcomers on boarding street cars invariably strode to the front even if there were seats in the rear. This is, perhaps, a mild example of tendencies expressed more strikingly in other directions, for with but few exceptions they are forced to sit in the rear of street cars throughout the South.

The difference between the background of northern and southern Negroes is even wider than it seems. In the two there are utterly different packets of stored up memories marking out channels of conduct. The southern Negro directs his ambitions at those amenities of which the northern Negro boasts and, until the first wonderment and envy subside, ignores his reservations. This is the hectic period of transition, so noticeable after huge accessions—inevitably in the wake of the newcomers north, whether the numbers are large or small. There comes the testing of long cherished desires, the thirst for forbidden fruit—and disillusionment, partial or complete, almost as inevitably.

IV

Cities have personalities. Their chief industries are likely to determine not only their respective characters, but the type of persons they attract and hold. Detroit manufactures automobiles, Chicago slaughters cattle, Pittsburgh smelts iron and steel—these three communities draw different types of workers whose industrial habits are interlaced with correspondingly different cultural backgrounds. One might look to this factor as having significance in the selection of Negro workers and indeed in the relations of the Negro population with the community. The technical intricacy of the automobile industry, like the army intelligence tests, sifts out the heavy-handed worker who fits admirably into the economy of the steel industries, where 80 per cent of the operations are unskilled. A temperamental equipment easily adapted to the knife-play and stench of killing and preserving cattle is not readily interchangeable either with the elaborated technique of the factory or the sheer muscle play and endurance required by the mill. These communities draw different types of workers.

Similar differences between cities account for the curiously varied directions of growth which the Negro populations take. They help to explain the furious striving after commercial glory in Chicago, and the chasing of the will-o'-the-wisp of culture in New York; the objective of an unshakable berth in a skilled job at $10 a day in Detroit, and a near future of benign comfort in Philadelphia. The Negro workers can no more become a fixed racial concept than can white workers. Conceived in terms either of capacity or opportunity, their employment gives rise to the most perplexing paradoxes. If it is a question of what Negroes are mentally or physically able to do, there are as many affirmations of competence as denials of it.

In skilled work requiring membership in unions they are employed only in small numbers, and membership is rarely encouraged unless the union is threatened. Since the apprentice-recruits for these jobs are discouraged, and the numbers sparse, the safety of the union is rarely threatened by an unorganized Negro minority. In certain responsible skilled positions, such as locomotive engineers, street cars and subway motormen, Negroes are never employed.

The distinctions are irrational. A Negro worker may not be a street or subway conductor because of the possibility of public objection to contact —but he may be a ticket chopper. He may not be a money changer in a subway station because honesty is required—yet he may be entrusted, as a messenger, with thousands of dollars daily. He may not sell goods over a counter—but he may deliver the goods after they have been sold. He may be a porter in charge of a sleeping car without a conductor, but never a conductor; he may be a policeman but not a fireman; a linotyper, but not a motion picture operator; a glass annealer, but not a glass blower, a deck hand, but not a sailor. The list could be continued indefinitely.

Between the principal northern cities there is a simple but vital difference to be observed. While New York City, for example, offers a diversity of employment, the city has not such basic industries as may be found in the automobile plants of Detroit, or the iron and steel works and gigantic meat slaughtering industries of Chicago. In Chicago, there is diversified employment, to be sure, but there is a significantly heavier concentration in the basic industries; more than that, there are gradations of work from unskilled to skilled. In certain plants skilled workers increased from 3.5 per cent of the Negro working population in 1910 to 13.5 per cent in 1920 in Chicago. In the slaughtering houses there are actually more semi-skilled Negro workers than laborers. The number of iron molders increased from 31 in 1910 to 520 in 1920 and this latter number represents 10 per cent of all the iron molders.

In the working age groups of New York there are more women than men. For every hundred Negro men there are 110 Negro women. This is abnormal and would be a distinct anomaly in an industrial center. The surplus women are doubtless the residue from the general wash and ebb of migrants who found a demand for their services. The city actually attracts more women than men. But surplus women bring on other problems, as the social agencies will testify. "Where women preponderate in large numbers there is proportionate increase in immorality because women are cheap." . . . The situation does not permit normal relations. What is most likely to happen, and does happen, is that women soon find it an added personal attraction to contribute to the support of a man. Demoralization may follow this—and does. Moreover, the proportion of Negro women at work in Manhattan (60.6) is twice that of any corresponding group, and one of the highest proportions registered anywhere.

The nature of the work of at least 40 per cent of the men suggests a relationship, even if indirectly, with the tensely active night life by which Harlem is known. The dull, unarduous routine of a porter's job or that of an elevator tender, does not provide enough stimulation to consume the normal supply of nervous energy. It is unthinkable that the restlessness which drove migrants to New York from dull small towns would allow them to be content with the same dullness in the new environment, when a supply of garish excitements is so richly available.

With all the "front" of pretending to live, the aspect of complacent wantlessness, it is clear that the Negroes are in a predicament. The moment holds tolerance but no great promise. Just as the wave of immigration once swept these Negroes out of old strongholds, a change of circumstances may disrupt them again. The slow moving black masses, with their assorted heritages and old loyalties, face the same stern barriers in the new environment. They are the black workers.

V

Entering gradually an era of industrial contact and competition with white workers of greater experience and numerical superiority, antagonisms loom up. Emotions have a way of re-enforcing themselves. The fierce economic fears of men in competition can supplement or be supplemented by the sentiments engendered by racial difference. Beneath the disastrous East St. Louis conflict was a boiling anger toward southern Negroes coming in to "take white men's jobs." The same antagonisms, first provoked sixty years ago in the draft riots of New York during the Civil War, flared again in the shameful battle of "San Juan Hill" in the Columbus Hill District. These outbreaks were distinctly more economic than racial.

Herein lies one of the points of highest tension in race relations. Negro workers potentially menace organized labor and the leaders of the movement recognize this. But racial sentiments are not easily destroyed by abstract principles. The white workers have not, except in few instances, conquered the antagonisms founded on race to the extent of accepting the rights of Negro workers to the privileges which they enjoy. While denying them admission to their crafts, they grow furious over their dangerous borings from the outside. "The Negroes are scabs." "They hold down the living standards of workers by cutting under!" "Negroes are professional strike breakers!" These sentiments are a good nucleus for elaboration into the most furious fears and hatreds.

It is believed variously that Negro workers are as a matter of policy opposed to unions or as a matter of ignorance incapable of appreciating them. From some unions they are definitely barred; some insist on separate Negro locals; some limit them to qualified membership; some accept them freely with white workers. The situation of the Negroes, on the surface, is, to say the least, compromising. Their shorter industrial experience and almost complete isolation from the educative influence of organized trade unions contribute to some of the inertia encountered in organizing them. Their traditional positions have been those of personal loyalty, and this has aided the habit of individual bargaining for jobs in industry. They have been, as was pointed out, under the comprehensive leadership of the church in practically all aspects of their lives including their labor. No effective new leadership has developed to supplant this old fealty. The attitude of white workers has sternly opposed the use of Negroes as apprentices through fear of subsequent competition in the skilled trades. This has limited the number of skilled Negroes trained on the job. But despite this denial, Negroes have gained skill.

This disposition violently to protest the employment of Negroes in certain lines because they are not members of the union and the equally violent protest against the admission of Negroes to the unions, created in the Negroes, desperate for work, an attitude of indifference to abstract pleas. In 1910 they were used in New York City to break the teamsters' strike and six years later they were organized. In 1919 they were used in a strike of the building trades. Strained feelings resulted, but they were finally included in the unions of this trade. During the outlaw strike of the railway and steamship clerks, freight handlers, expressmen and station employees, they were used to replace the striking whites and were given preference over the men whose places they had taken. During the shopmen's strike they were promoted into new positions and thus made themselves eligible for skilled jobs as machinists. In fact, their most definite gains have been at the hands of employers and over the tactics of labor union exclusionists.

Where the crafts are freely open to them they have joined with the general movement of the workers. Of the 5,386 Negro longshoremen, about 5,000 are organized. Of the 735 Negro carpenters, 400 are members of the United Brotherhood of Carpenters and Joiners. Of the 2,275 semi-skilled clothing workers practically all are members of the International Ladies Garment Workers Union. The musicians are 50 per cent organized. The difficulty is that the great preponderance of Negro jobs is still in lines which are not organized. The porters, laundresses (outside of laundries) and servants have no organization. The Negroes listed as painters are not in the painters' union, many of them being merely whitewashers. The tailors are in large part cleaners and pressers. The waiters, elevator tenders (except female) are poorly organized.

The end of the Negro's troubles, however, does not come with organization. There is still the question of employers, for it is a certain fact that preference is frequently given white workers when they can be secured, if high wages are to be paid. A vicious circle indeed! One Negro editor has suggested a United Negro Trades Union built on the plan of the United Hebrew Trades and the Italian Chamber of Labor. The unions are lethargic; the Negroes skeptical, untrained and individualistic. Meanwhile they drift, a disordered mass, self-conscious, but with their aims unrationalized, into the face of new problems.

Out of this medley of strains in reaction to totally new experiences, a strange product is evolving, and with it new wishes, habits and expectations. Negro workers have discovered an unsuspected strength even though they are as yet incapable of integrating it. Black labor, now sensitive and insistent, will have the protection of workers' organizations or by the strength of their menace keep these organizations futile and ineffective.

With the shift toward industry now beginning, and a subsequent new status already foreshadowed, some sounder economic policy is imperative. The traditional hold of domestic service vocations is already broken: witness the sudden halt in the increase of Negro male servants and elevator men. The enormous growth of certain New York industries has been out of proportion to the normal native production of workers. The immigration on which these formerly depended has been cut down and the prospects are that this curtailment will continue. For the first time, as a result of promotion, retirement and death, gaps are appearing which the limited recruits cannot fill. Note the clothing industry, one of the largest in New York. There is a persistent lament that the second generation of immigrants do not continue in the trade. Already Negro workers have been sought to supplement the deficiencies in the first generation recruits. This sort of thing will certainly be felt in other lines. The black masses are on the verge of induction from their unenviable status as servants into the forces of the industrial workers, a more arduous, but less dependent rank. They require a new leadership, training in the principles of collective action, a new orientation with their white fellow workers for the sake of a future peace, a reorganization of the physical and mental habits which are a legacy of their old experiences, and deliberate training for the new work to come. It is this rehabilitation of the worker that the Urban Leagues have tried to accomplish, accompanying this effort with a campaign against the barriers to the entrance of Negro workers into industry. Conceiving these workers as inherently capable of an infinite range of employment, this organization insists merely upon an openness which permits opportunity, an objective experiment uncluttered by old theories of racial incompetence and racial dogmas.

The workers of the South and the West Indies who have come to the cities of the North with vagrant desires and impulses, their endowments of skill and strength, their repressions and the telltale marks of backward cultures, with all the human wastes of the process, have directed shafts of their native energy into the cities' life and growth. They are becoming a part of it. The restive spirit which brought them has been neither all absorbed nor wasted. Over two-thirds of all the businesses operated by Negroes in New York are conducted by migrant Negroes. They are in the schools—they are the radicals and this is hopeful. The city Negro—an unpredictable mixture of all possible temperaments—is yet in evolution.

VI

The violent sub-currents of recent years, which have shifted the economic base of Negro life—as indeed they have affected all other groups— have brought about a new orientation throughout, and have accentuated group attitudes among both black and white, sometimes favorably, sometimes unfavorably; here in a spurt of progress, there in a backwash of reaction.

Take the case of Negro business. It is only within recent years that a coldly practical eye has been turned to the capital created by that body of black workers; to the very obvious fact that a certain affluence breeds a certain respect; that where the pressure is heaviest, and unjust restrictions imposed, there is a politely effective boycott possible in "racial solidarity" which diverts Negro capital from disinterested hands into the coffers of "race institutions." Instance the Negro insurance companies, of which there are now sixty-seven, with over $250,000,000 worth of insurance in force, flourishing out of the situation of special premium rates for Negroes instituted by some companies, and a policy of total exclusion practiced by others. No work for young Negro men and women in general business? Then they will establish their own businesses and borrow from the sentimental doctrine of "race pride" enough propulsion to compensate for the initial deficiences of capital. But is this entirely representative of the new Negro thought? It is not. This increased activity is largely an opportunistic policy, with its firmest foothold in the South. Where it exists in the North it has been almost wholly transplanted by southern Negroes. The cities of the North where conditions tend most, in special instances to approach the restrictions of the South, become the most active business centers. The greater the isolation, the more pronounced and successful this intensive group commercialism.

Or, to take another angle of this picture: Mr. Marcus Garvey has been accused of inspiring and leading a movement for the "re-exaltation" of things black, for the exploitation of Negro resources for the profit of Negroes, and for the re-establishment of prestige to things Negro. As a fact, he has merely had the clairvoyance to place himself at the head of a docile sector of a whole population which, in different degrees, has been expressing an indefinable restlessness and broadening of spirit. The Garvey movement itself is an exaggeration of this current mood which attempts to reduce these vague longings to concrete symbols of faith. In this great sweep of the Negro population are comprehended the awkward gestures of the awakening black peasantry, the new desire of Negroes for an independent status, the revolt against a culture which has but partially (and again unevenly) digested the Negro masses—the black peasants least of all. It finds a middle ground in the feelings of kinship with all oppressed dark peoples, as articulated so forcefully by the Negro press, and takes, perhaps, its highest expression in the objectives of the Pan-African Congress.

New emotions accompany these new objectives. Where there is ferment and unrest, there is change. Old traditions are being shaken and rooted up by the percussion of new ideas. In this the year of our Lord, 1925, extending across the entire country are seventeen cities in violent agitation over Negro residence areas, and where once there was acquiescence, silent or ineffectually grumbly, there are now in evidence new convictions which more often prompt to resistance. It is this spirit, aided by increased living standards and refined tastes, that has resulted in actual housing clashes, the most notorious of which have been occurring in Detroit, Michigan, where, with a Negro population increase of more than 500 per cent in the past ten years, this new resistance has clashed with the spirit of the South, likewise drawn there by the same economic forces luring and pushing the Negroes. This same spirit was evidenced in the serious racial clashes which flared up in a dozen cities after the first huge migration of Negroes northward, and which took a sad toll in lives. Claude McKay, the young Negro poet, caught the mood of the new Negro in this, and molded it into fiery verse which Negro newspapers copied and recopied:

> If we must die, let it not be like hogs,
> Hunted and penned in an inglorious spot . . .

Nor does this embrace all of the ragged pattern: Silently and yet with such steady persistence that it has the aspect of an utterly distinct movement, the newer spirits are beginning to free themselves from the slough of that servile feeling (now happily classified by the psychologists as the "inferiority complex") inherited from slavery and passed along with virulence for over fifty years. The generation in whom lingered memories of the painful degradation of slavery could not be expected to cherish even those pearls of song and poetry born of suffering. They would be expected to do just as they did: rule out the Sorrow Songs as the product of ignorant slaves, taboo dialect as incorrect English, and the priceless folk lore as the uncultured expression of illiterates,—an utterly conscious effort to forget the past, and take over, suddenly, the symbols of that culture which had so long ground their bodies and spirits in the dirt. The newer voices, at a more comfortable distance, are beginning to find a new beauty in these heritages, and new values in their own lives.

Less is heard of the two historic "schools of thought" clashing ceaselessly and loud over the question of industrial and higher education for the Negro. Both schools are, sensibly, now taken for granted as quite necessary. The new questions of the industrial schools are concerned with adjusting their curricula to the new fields of industry in which Negro workers will play an ever mounting rôle, and with expanding their academic and college courses; while the new question of the universities is that of meeting the demand for trained Negroes for business, the professions, and the arts. The level of education has been lifted through the work of both, and the new level, in itself, is taking care of the sentiment about the division.

Thus the new frontier of Negro life is flung out in a jagged, uneven but progressive pattern. For a group historically retarded and not readily assimilated, contact with its surrounding culture breeds quite uneven results. There is no fixed racial level of culture. The lines cut both vertically and horizontally. There are as great differences, with reference to culture, education, sophistication, among Negroes as between the races. (This overlapping is probably what the new psychologists have been trying to point out with their elaborately documented intelligence measurements.) And just as these currents move down and across and intersect, so may one find an utter maze of those rationalizations of attitudes of differently placed Negro groups toward life in general, and their status in particular. But a common purpose is integrating these energies born of new conflicts, and it is not at all improbable that the culture which has both nourished and abused these strivings will, in the end, be enriched by them.

15. Faces of Harlem

The New Negro: An Interpretation began as a special graphic number of *The Survey* magazine for March, 1925, on the theme, "Harlem: Mecca of the New Negro." The possibility of a "New Negro" was one of the most creative and fruitful cultural concepts to grow out of the ruins of genteel cultural control. Cultural changes brought about by the war liberated black writers and intellectuals both artistically and racially. No longer did they feel the need to accept identities or cultural constraints imposed by genteel editors and publishers. They could freely explore black cultural traits and values, and experiment and create on the foundation of their own separate identities.

Other racial and ethnic minorities also were freed artistically and culturally by the war, but Negroes possessed one major advantage: a vigorous national cultural center, black Harlem. Harlem gave black writers and intellectuals the same stimulation as midtown Manhattan or Greenwich Village gave to whites, with the added values of racial homogeneity, separate institutions, a congenial audience. Black writers could have access both uptown and downtown to publicity, theater, radio and recording companies, contact with white writers and intellectuals, and a rich and varied cultural life. Around them in Harlem flowed the many strands of black life in the Americas, people from the West Indies, from the South, from the small towns and cities of the midwest. In this environment the idea of the "New Negro" was nurtured.

The Survey's graphic number contained drawings and portraits of black people, famous and unknown, by the German-born artist and designer Winold Reiss (1886–   ). Reiss' drawings and designs, along with some new ones, then went into *The New Negro* as virtually its only illustrated material. Why did the anthology's editor, Alain Locke, feature a white artist's work so prominently as the visual counterpart to the prose and poetry of the Negro Renaissance? A note in the anthology suggests that Reiss and Locke worked closely together, conceiving the drawings in close collaboration. Reiss was known for his drawings of American Indians and Mexicans, and was considered especially good at depicting "folk character." Locke described the drawings as "revealing some of the rich and promising resources of Negro types." Thus they may be viewed as expressing an image of black people that interpreters of the "New Negro" wished to convey. The drawings reproduced here are taken from *The Survey* special graphic number of March, 1925.

Congo: a familiar of the New York studios

Harlem Types

PORTRAITS BY WINOLD REISS

HERE and elsewhere throughout this number, Winold Reiss presents us a graphic interpretation of Negro life, freshly conceived after its own patterns. Concretely in his portrait sketches, abstractly in his symbolic designs, he has aimed to portray the soul and spirit of a people. And by the simple but rare process of not setting up petty canons in the face of nature's own creative artistry, Winold Reiss has achieved what amounts to a revealing discovery of the significance, human and artistic, of one of the great dialects of human physiognomy, of some of the little understood but powerful idioms of nature's speech. Harlem, or any Negro community, spreads a rich and novel palette for the serious artist. It needs but enlightenment of mind and eye to make its intriguing problems and promising resources available for the stimulation and enrichment of American art.

1. *Congo: a familiar of the New York Studios.*

Mother and child

CONVENTIONS stand doubly in the way of artistic portrayal of Negro folk; certain narrowly arbitrary conventions of physical beauty, and as well, that inevitable inscrutability of things seen but not understood. Caricature has put upon the countenance of the Negro the mask of the comic and the grotesque, whereas in deeper truth and comprehension, nature or experience have put there the stamp of the very opposite, the serious, the tragic, the wistful. At times, too, there is a quality of soul that can only be called brooding and mystical. Here they are to be seen as we know them to be in fact. While it is a revealing interpretation for all, for the Negro artist, still for the most part confronting timidly his own material, there is certainly a particular stimulus and inspiration in this redeeming vision. Through it in all likelihood must come his best development in the field of the pictorial arts, for his capacity to express beauty depends vitally upon the capacity to see it in his own life and to generate it out of his own experience.

Young America: native-born

2. Mother and Child.

3. Young America: Native-born.

WINOLD REISS, son of Fritz Reiss, the landscape painter, pupil of Franz von Stuck of Munich, has become a master delineator of folk character by wide experience and definite specialization. With ever-ripening skill, he has studied and drawn the folk-types of Sweden, Holland, of the Black Forest and his own native Tyrol, and in America, the Black Foot Indians, the Pueblo people, the Mexicans, and now, the American Negro. His art owes its peculiar success as much to the philosophy of his approach as to his technical skill. He is a folk-lorist of the brush and palette, seeking always the folk character back of the individual, the psychology behind the physiognomy. In design also he looks not merely for decorative elements, but for the pattern of the culture from which it sprang. Without loss of naturalistic accuracy and individuality, he somehow subtly expresses the type, and without being any the less human, captures the racial and local. What Gauguin and his followers have done for the Far East, and the work of Ufer and Blumenschein and the Taos school for the Pueblo and Indian, seems about to be done for the Negro and Africa: in short, painting, the most local of arts, in terms of its own limitations even, is achieving universality.

A Boy Scout

A woman lawyer

Girl in the white blouse

4. A Boy Scout.

5. A Woman Lawyer.

6. Girl in the White Blouse.

A college lad

7. *A College Lad.*

Four Portraits of Negro Women

Drawn by Winold Reiss

A Woman from the Virgin Islands

8. *A Woman from the Virgin Islands.*

9. *The Librarian.*

10. *Two Public School Teachers.*

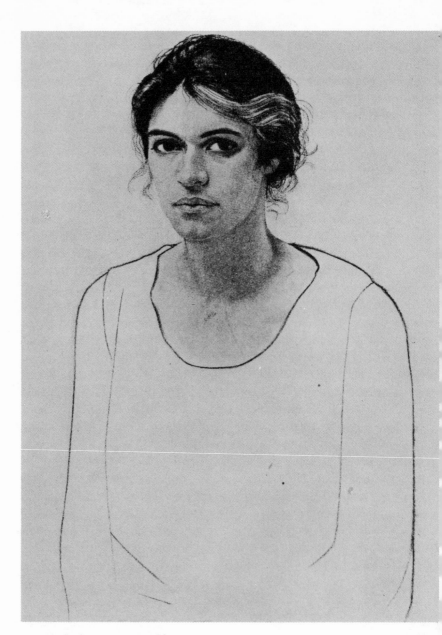

11. *Elise Johnson McDougald.*

16. The Fate of the Melting Pot

The war created a new and largely unfavorable setting for ethnic and nationality groups in American life during the Twenties. Over the previous generation the dominant native Anglo-Saxon Protestants had accepted millions of new immigrants from Southern and Central Europe, in the belief the newcomers could be "Americanized," their offensive traits sloughed off, the values of American culture—genteel middle class version—learned and internalized. Influential spokesmen for immigrant groups supported the idea that America was becoming a great melting pot, where a multitude of races and nationalities could be boiled down into one American type. Though agitation had been growing from some native Americans to stop the flow of immigration, the melting pot idea prevailed until the war.

With the war, however, genteel middle-class culture gave American loyalty a new definition. Loyalty was required as well to British civilization and Anglo-Saxon customs and values. Many new Americans, and considerable numbers of old ones, refused to be boiled down so far—Irish Catholics supporting Irish independence, Eastern Europeans from the disintegrating Austro-Hungarian empire, Socialists in the European tradition, and, of course, Americans of German descent. For both sides, the immigrant and the genteel, hostilities and disillusionment engendered by the war destroyed their tolerance for "Americanization," their faith in the melting pot idea.

Thus the Twenties became a period marked by intensified conflict along religious, ethnic, and nationality lines. Rural and small-town America, which had lost stature as guardians of moral wisdom in the aftermath of war, responded with hatred for the urban strongholds of the foreign-born, leading to an upsurge of Ku Klux Klan activity directed mainly against Catholics and Jews. Anglo-Saxon Americans, turning from persuasion to coercion and from culture to politics, put through Congress in 1924 a National Origins Act, limiting immigration from Europe on a quota system, and completely forbidding immigration from the Orient.

In the midst of the tide of nativist sentiment, one of the most clear and persuasive voices in defense of cultural diversity and pluralism belonged to Horace M. Kallen (1882–   ), the noted philosopher and professor at the

New School for Social Research. Here in a section from an essay, " 'Americanization' and the Cultural Prospect" (1924), he discusses problems of role and identity faced by ethnic and nationality groups after the war.

"Americanization" and the Cultural Prospect

HORACE M. KALLEN

I

Fear, unlike selfishness, can have no commerce with intelligence. Like love, it is blind. Although it rationalizes its behavior and justifies self-defeating action with wise cracks and sounding phrases, its conduct nullifies understanding. It moves legislatures and administrative officials more than plain citizens, for the fortune of these is made and unmade by the law of opinion and not by the laws of things. Its popular manifestation, therefore, has been the brute violence of the American Legion and the dressed-up violence of the Ku Klux Klan, both, on the whole, too intermittent and transitory, too interwoven with post-war depression to be of much significance. It is different with the state and national legislatures and the Department of Labor. These, responding to opinion, must enact laws and establish precedents that carry on when opinion has become indifferent, and only a violent and massive shift of it can disturb the inertia of established precedent. Already before the war the tendencies toward the current modes of repression and intimidation had become manifest. Since the Armistice, they have been developed into almost public policies. The instrument which renders them effectual is the formula "likely to become a public charge." Under this formula the unnaturalized immigrant lives in constant danger of deportation. He belongs just now to the "new" migration, that is, the places of his origin are central and eastern Europe. He works for the old migration. He is the miner, the mill-worker, the stockyards man, the roadmaker and the

Horace M. Kallen, *Culture and Democracy in the United States: Studies in the Group Psychology of the American People* (New York, 1924), pp. 150–172.

ditch-digger. His employers, afraid of his economic Americanization, attribute this inevitable change in his economic standards and associations to his ethnic and cultural difference. They call it radicalism, Bolshevism, criminal syndicalism, or whatever the current shibboleth is that gives articulation to their fear and direction to the conduct it motivates. They contrast his labor organization with the orthodox aggregation headed by Samuel Gompers, from which he is excluded, and they demand that every possible precaution shall be taken when he enters the land that he shall be safe for the democracy of which they are the palladia and beneficiaries. Thus, the scope of immigrant exclusion has within a generation been extended from health, to literacy, to opinion. Unorthodox economic opinion they regard as always an alien importation, never a home-grown product of the soil of exploitation they have themselves prepared and cultivated. When it occurs, therefore, the saving clause of the immigration law is invoked. The alien is arrested for his imputed political opinion, held without appeal or redress, tried in secret, without due process of law, by a prosecuting immigration inspector who has also been charged with the pleasure of his arrest. Now to make assurance doubly sure, the newest immigration laws passed by Congress have been so framed as to establish once more a preponderance in numbers among the immigrants of the north European stocks. In the light of the fact that of 39 or more persons deported between 1918 and 1920 for unorthodox economic and social opinions, 27 came from England, Scotland, Ireland, Denmark, Norway and Finland, the relation between fear and intelligence comes to a glare of significance.

Meanwhile, many of the non-British communities, native and naturalized as well as alien, have been in a state of panic. Their feeling of insecurity has necessarily drawn them more compactly together, consolidated their associations, closed their ranks and given their leaders an unprecedented importance in their lives. It has called the attention of the governments of the countries of their origin to the necessity of some sort of mass protection for them, to the desirability of maintaining with them a more than accidental cultural contact and interchange. The new countries particularly, whose creation has been in a large measure due to the interest of the government of the United States, are dependent not only culturally but economically and politically on a keen sensitiveness of their brethren in the North American enclaves to their hopes and needs. Such states as Poland, Czechoslovakia, Lithuania, Hungary, Jugo-Slavia, Ireland, would be bound, even if they had not before them the examples of Great Britain, Holland, Japan, France and the Scandinavian countries, to urge upon groups of their race and speech in the United States the desirability and value of the highest degree of ethno-cultural integration. Russians and Germans, of course, far more than the others, have been forced into such a conception by events.

II

Only in very rare instances did a disinterested patriotic or humanitarian concern set itself the task of neutralizing fear and greed, and of replacing them with vision regarding the nature, trend and future of group-adjustments in the United States. Such an instance was the Peoples of America Society, "an organization of Americans of all origins, which in the midst of a new wave of Know-Nothingism, is seeking through mutual knowledge to eliminate friction and promote good relations among the peoples of the United States." The immigrant and ethnic organizations themselves were, in their perplexity, overeager to justify themselves, and conceded more than was proper, necessary, or good. Labor unions became protagonists of "Americanization," and vied with the manufacturers' associations in appropriating the term to their special interests. Their positive achievements in "eliminating" friction and promoting good relations among the peoples of the United States were obscured in a fog of "labor-education" theory and a confusion of practice. That, in such a union as the Amalgamated Clothing Workers of America, Poles, Lithuanians, Jews, Italians, Czechs, Letts and Slovaks, the bitterest national feudists in the countries of their origin, could, without any surrender of their ethnic tradition and cultural integrity, but rather through the acknowledgment and utilization of these, develop a degree of solidarity, coöperation and moral enthusiasm unprecedented in American labor history, went unregarded. Individuals—Jews, Syrians, Dutchmen, and such —hurried to add their testimonials to the standard-giving supremacy of the *homo Americanus* in works that ranged from *The Making of an American*, by Max Ravage, to *The Americanization of Edward Bok*, by the subject himself. The last-named book may indeed be regarded as the climax of the wave of gratulatory exhibition which Mary Antin's *Promised Land* began. Now there are signs that the ebb is at hand, and that the doctrinal pattern of autobiography for the Americanized is likely to be more analytical, discriminative, and sad.[1]

---

[1] See *Up Stream*, by Ludwig Lewisohn. More recently there has appeared a pseudo-autobiography entitled *Haunch, Paunch and Jowl*, which gives vivid point to the character of the change. The book illuminates day-to-day realities of the Americanization process.

Indeed, analysis and discrimination have come more significantly to light in other forms. It is, of course, inevitable that the academic pursuit of material for a discipline looking toward a job in the gentle art of Americanization should, in some places, at some time, lead the more scholarly-minded and scientific among the professors of Americanization to forget the end in the means, and to replace racial anxiety, political expediency and moral fatuousness with a free curiosity about the patterns of group behavior under the conditions of life on the richest part of the North American continent. So far, however, the inevitable and the actual do not coincide. Ross is still the standard instance of the academic special pleader in this field, and the brilliant work of W. I. Thomas[2] and his associates still stands alone among academic productions. It is outside of the academies, among representatives of ethnic stocks disturbed about their status and anxious to envisage it in a coherent philosophy of the national life, that something approaching to free inquiry has been undertaken, partly in the attempt to find an intellectual way through the emotional turmoil about Americanization. One sought to discover how stable was the ethnic ground of cultural diversity;[3] another, to evaluate theories of Americanization through an analysis of their bearing on the lives of the smaller communities of which the life of the country is composed.[4] Still another, surveying the whole field, was initiated by the trustees of the Carnegie Corporation of New York and was designed "to set forth, not theories of social betterment, but a description of the methods of the various agencies engaged in such work." Its assumption—ironic, in view of its conclusion—was, however, that "Americanization is the uniting of new with native-born Americans in fuller common understanding and appreciation to secure by means of individual and collective self-direction the highest welfare of all. Such Americanization should perpetuate no unchangeable political, domestic and economic régime delivered once for all to the fathers, but a growing and broadening national life, inclusive of the best wherever found. With all rich heritages, Americanism will develop best through a mutual giving and taking of contributions from both newer and older Americans in the interest of the commonweal."[5]

The upshot of the first endeavor is a compromise between Democracy and the Melting Pot, a giving unto Cæsar what is Cæsar's so that God may keep his own. The philosophy of Messrs. Drachsler and Berkson is

---

[2] Cf., *The Polish Peasant in Europe and America.*
[3] Cf., J. Drachsler: *Democracy and Assimilation.*
[4] Cf., I. Berkson: *Theories of Americanization.*
[5] Cf., Parks and Miller: *Old World Traits Transplanted:* Publisher's Note.

identical. They believe that the American peoples, left to themselves, are likely to assimilate into a single stock. They believe that this blind, spontaneous assimilation is fraught with much pain and hardship, and that intelligent statesmanship would so direct it as to ease it. They also believe in democracy, and in the application of the terms of democracy to groups as well as to individuals. But they cannot stick having these groups called nationalities. They prefer to call them communities. They are plainly disturbed about the irrelevant political suggestion of the word "nationality" and are much exercised over the idea of race as an element in nationality. They show emotion about both things and are at pains to prove over again the well-known anthropological commonplaces that race is a concept the underlying facts of which are mutually contradictory, that races are indefinite and impermanent and that communities themselves dissolve. Messrs. Drachsler and Berkson believe that even if you can't change your own grandfather, you can modify your great-grandchild's, by choosing for a him a great-grandmother of another stock than your own. That people are hardly ever known to marry out of consideration for their great-grandchildren does not seem to have occurred to them. So Mr. Drachsler eloquently shows that in New York City, and by implication in the rest of the country, a great deal of such prospective grandpaternal modification does take place, at least from the first to the third immigrant generation. He has figured out that the largest number of intermarrying persons come from what he calls the "mediocre culture groups," by which he means, apparently, economic groupings bringing into the greatest degree of propinquity the largest number of persons of different ethnic stocks. "Amalgamation," Mr. Drachsler concludes, "of the European peoples in the United States is going on and gathering momentum on the way." Its tendency is to dilute the native stocks, as the direction of intermarriage is from the lower to the higher social classes, and the range of intermarriage narrows from twelve nationalities in the first generation to six in the second. The writer believes that the hardship which this "amalgamation" involves will be eased if the immigrant groups conserve for America "through voluntary cultural community organizations, the unique value of their heritage; while the state will find its proper function in the harmonization of these values through a synthetic cultural curriculum in its public educational system." The "voluntary cultural organizations" are to be called, not nationalities but "communities" and Mr. Berkson adds to the contentions of Mr. Drachsler some further observations about communities. He believes in the *status quo* and wants to leave well enough alone. He thinks the formula of the "community" is flexible and free. . . . "It leaves all the forces working . . . where its alternatives presume too much to 'fix' conditions." He wants "all forces to be given a just opportunity to exert their influence." Thereupon, "if the ethnic group perpetuates itself, reason accepts it," and "if the ethnic group finally disintegrates, the 'community' theory resolves itself into the 'Melting Pot' theory, accomplishing fusion without the evils of hasty assimilation." His panacea, in a word, is a sort of ethnic and cultural *laissez faire.*

Of a similar, more decisional character, is the conclusion of the Carnegie Americanization study. Its attitude toward the purely ethnic considerations of its problem is, however, one of pronounced skepticism. Though "the characteristics of the Swede, the Jew, the Italian, may be connected with their original inborn temperamental dispositions," they can never be discovered in their originality and purity. Circumstances modify them continually and the "primary group organization," that which persists as an element of all present society, and the home forms of which immigrants spontaneously reproduce and live in, is itself too much an interpenetration of heredity and environment to permit of successful analysis. The point of importance is that the immigrant penetrates the American scene from the springboard of these basic familial associations. His adjustments to the scene are facilitated by the institutions of his group, these being, first of all, his ethnic boarding-house, then the banks and employment agencies, then the mutual aid and benefit societies, finally the nationalistic societies, like the Sons of Italy with their 125,000 members distributed in 887 lodges through 24 States, or the Polish National Alliance with its 130,000 members and 1,700 lodges, or the Japanese Association of America, or the various French Canadian and Jewish societies. The existence of all these appears to be postulated upon the realization that "the individual will not be respected unless his group is respected." Many derive from a political idealism for the home-country and therefore resent and seek to avert Americanization—as for example, the Poles, some of whose leaders call them "a Polonia Americana, the fourth division of Poland"—and draw their intellectual sustenance entirely from the home country.

But regardless of whether their spirit is that of the colonist merely or of the settler come "to secure an existence," they automatically Americanize, and their own organizations are the chief instruments in the process. For without them the immigrant would be completely lost. They both ease his transition and speed it. Although he can swiftly change his clothes and his superficial manners, thus throwing off the external differences between himself and his new *milieu*, the inner change, the conversion of habit and attitude are another story, and it is in this story that the immigrant's institutions are the hero. In the new community his old habits and attitudes do not obtain the old results, and the old results are no longer successful adjustments in the situation. The immigrant's personality suffers attrition and dislocation. He doesn't belong, and so, cannot find himself. Disjoined from the old ways and values and not yet at home in the new, he becomes demoralized. Just in so far as he can live and move and have his being in the groupings of his own people he is saved, however, from the consequences of his demoralization. The groupings are his organs of contact with the new social *milieu*. They speak his language and convey his ideas; they speak the language of the land and communicate its moods. They are the intermediaries between him and it. They carry him over and ultimately they adjust him.

In this mediating relationship, language is perhaps the most important of all the elements. It is the intimate symbol of association; so far as the immigrant is concerned, its warmest and most significant base. Race, in fact, is often hardly more than a linguistic term. For this reason the immigrant or foreign-language press becomes one of the nodal immigrant institutions. Forty-three or forty-four dialects are spoken in the United States and more foreign journals are published and read in more languages per capita than in the whole of Europe. They serve their readers with news of the countries of their origin, and help adjust them to the country of their habitation; and they are used—in all cases except that of the Jews—for the purpose of preserving or aggrandizing one or another nationality abroad. They have a political import for foreign policy which the world war should have mitigated. Their cultural significance is low. As their readers are mostly peasants, they tend to stay upon the level of the American yellows. They print some poetry, much sentimental fiction, and they often come under the domination of advertisers —to say nothing of the politicians. There are exceptions, of course. The Yiddish press tends on the whole to maintain a superior intellectual level, and the "radical" press of all nationalities is filled with disquisitions beyond the mind of the average reader. But the literary quality of the foreign-language press has no particular influence upon its social function—the newcomer's graduation into American life. This it serves efficiently. The graduation takes place.

Mr. Gavit's study of naturalization shows[6] that the immigrant of the

---

[6] "Americans by Choice," *The Survey*, February 25, 1922.

new migration is as eager, and more eager, to enter into the fullness of American citizenship as the immigrant of the old. The inferences and conclusions which his comprehensive survey of all the available data has enabled him to draw are to the effect that the presumption that the later migration is of a worse character than the earlier is a pure myth; so is the notion current that the later migration is less amenable to citizenship; or that it differs from the older migration in anything but "the political, social and economic conditions at the time of migration in the country of origin." All that can be discovered as "the controlling factor in political absorption is length of residence." The process of naturalization is a phenomenon altogether independent of racial origin and altogether dependent on economic status: "the racial groups show a slower desire for citizenship and a slower rate of naturalization while they are employed in the more poorly paid industries; both the individual interest and the rate increase as the individuals toil upward in the social and economic scale. . . . Those from countries where at the time of their migration there was either autocratic government or political discontent or inferior economic opportunity, head the list of those who seek, and upon examination prove, their title to fellow-membership with us."

"Assimilation," Mr. Parks concludes,[7] and his conclusion is a fit summary for the study, "is as inevitable as it is desirable; it is impossible for the immigrants we receive to remain permanently in separate groups. Through point after point of contact, as they find situations in America intelligible to them in the light of the old knowledge and experience, they identify themselves with us. We can delay or hasten this development. We cannot stop it. If we give the immigrants a favorable *milieu*, if we tolerate their strangeness during their period of adjustment, if we give them freedom to make their own connections between old and new experiences, if we help them to find points of contact, then we hasten their assimilation. This is a process of growth, as against the 'ordering and forbidding' policy and the demand that the assimilation of the immigrant shall be "sudden, complete and bitter." And this is the completely democratic process, for we cannot have a political democracy unless we have a social democracy also."

III

That time—he, the notorious healer of all hurt—will put a period to the public sentiment underlying the Americanization hysteria and shift

[7] *Old World Traits Transplanted.*

the approval of public opinion from the coercive to the persuasive conception of public policy regarding the integration of immigrant groups and native society, is by no means a foregone conclusion. The causes of disturbance are as varied as they are lasting. Their repression on one side leads most of the time only to their protrusion on another. Alone the coincidence of ethnic differences with economic stratification is enough to exacerbate a condition which, with the pressure of immigration removed, must of necessity tend toward fixation. One need only cast an eye over the negro-white relations in the South to realize the limit that such a condition would, unchecked, engender. And even checked, with all the healing that time might bring, the current of public sentiment would still have left institutional deposits, have set up interests and organizations whose pattern of behavior and endeavor to survive would be postulated upon this sentiment. The Americanizers and the Americanization agencies are themselves such interests and organizations. Such, also, the immigrant institutions, now reënforced and sustained by the solicitude of the new and old governments abroad, have been compelled to become. These, and the protective reactions which they express against the assault of the public sentiment to which they are in part a reply, form the mutually sustaining halves of a circle; a complete, a closed circle. Only a stronger sentiment of another nature can break their circle, break it either by displacing the original mood as the power sustaining the interests and organizations, or by diverting the nourishing energy of opinion into the generation and sanction of other vocations and institutions. The likelihood of such an eventuality, however, seems at present too remote. Unless it happens soon, it will happen too late.

For the Americanization emotion of 1919 was no eccentric or isolated phenomenon, no idiosyncratic aspect of war-psychology. The moods of war were added unto it, but did not create it; they intensified it, but its original force did not come from them. Nor was its source—as some, following the current fashion of interpreters of social behavior, opine—in the conflict of economic interests. Organized labor's attitude toward immigration might be so envisaged, and the passing complication of the immigrant with economic radicalism might be so envisaged. But the classes in whom the Americanization psychosis was most compulsive and outstanding were the classes whose economic interests are most fully served by un-Americanized, that is, by cheap, ignorant and slavish immigrant labor, such as Judge Gary's liberalism toward the immigrant specifically calls for. The more intelligent among these classes, such as the Inter-Racial Council, recognized this, and set themselves hard at the task of persuading their peers of it—with doubtful success. The mood of 1919 has an authenticated ancestry in the story of the persistent temper of public sentiment in the United States. It is the old Know-Nothingism in contemporary dress. This Know-Nothingism was not postulated on either economic rivalry or war anxiety. It was postulated on something more protean and more enduring, on something taboo to law and intelligence, something that even derision strengthens and scorn confirms. The something is religious tradition, the prejudice of cultus. Its language is various, but its mood is the same. It is transmitted through one of the most basic and intimate of community groupings and it goes on, from the Massachusetts colonials to their offspring in the fourth, and even the forty and fourth, generation. It has, of course, its peaks and its valleys, its cycles of mania and depression. The post-armistice manifestations were a period of mania. The witch-hunting of the Quaker attorney-general, Palmer, the czaristically inspired Jew-baiting of the Baptist automobile maker, Ford, the malevolent mass-mummery of the Ku Klux Klan, the racial rumblings[8] of Mr. Madison Grant, Mrs. Gertrude Atherton, the *Saturday Evening Post,* are all, ultimately, manifestations of this Know-Nothingism. The economic process has, on the whole, tended to reënforce rather than to subdue it. There is the possibility that it might, by shifting the balance of social power, drain it, and finally dry it up. But this is only a possibility, and at best, a possibility of the far future. The testimony of history favors rather the cumulative integration and enhanced rate of explosion of the emotions underlying this Know-Nothingism.

Intellectuals dealing with the process and qualities of group-adjustment in the United States have altogether overlooked the psychological substructure of American Know-Nothingism, its patterns and periods. As it is the non-British, not the native community, that is being thereby challenged as a menace, the attention of the intellectuals has been devoted to the analysis and dissipation of this imputed menace, and to the restoration of that complacency of conduct which is the crown of unruffled feelings. They have been content to pass by the prior question regarding the specific nature and social significance of that which the non-British communities are said to be a menace to, and which would have to absorb them and digest them, converting them into flesh of its flesh and soul of its soul, if it is to be forever inviolate and safe. Assimilation, declares the Carnegie Study, is as inevitable as it is desirable. But of what, to

---

[8] Directly derivative from the race-mythology imagined in Germany and elaborated for pan-Germans by Houston Stewart Chamberlain, a renegade Englishman.

what? How is assimilation to be understood? As a coöperative harmony, which is the outcome of mutual respect, understanding and adjustment, on the rule of one for all and all for one, or as the dissolution and absorption of diversities, on the rule of all for one and all in one? The very language of the Study, written about "foreigners" from the standpoint of the American native insecure in their presence, shows how impossible it is for the best will in the world to avoid sharing the native emotion and the native assumption that alien heritages, which are "methods of valuation," are inferior to the native and must give way to the native. This assumption of superiority is, of course, automatic, universal, and endemic. It is to be found everywhere that individual or group diversities confront one another. It is everywhere a defense against and an evasion of the intolerable alternative which challenges every student of civilization—the alternative, namely, that the heritage which is his, is at least not better than and perhaps not as good as the heritage which confronts his. Yet intelligence cannot be honest or effective in this field, cannot *be* intelligence, until it has learned not only to tolerate but to feel at home with this intolerable thing. Until it does, it will at bottom, like the Carnegie Study, knowingly or unknowingly, condone conformity and approve submission.

And conformity and submission are what will seem to come. But only seem. For the adaptability of life is wonderful, and communities, like persons, suffer much and surrender more, only to save their souls alive. The compulsion of native *mores* is a stimulus to which the American of non-British stock makes appropriate response. But the response is far from determined by this stimulus alone. In one way or another, that inward half of his being, the "methods of valuation," the group patternings, the consuetudinous rhythms and symbols of custom and speech that are his heritage, the springs of his character, will color and direct his response. This inward half necessarily and automatically behaves in such a way as to maintain itself and grow, and if it is prevented from doing so directly, openly, in free interplay with its social *milieu*—then, necessarily and automatically, it will do so obliquely, hiddenly, in conflict with its *milieu*. The *milieu* may exterminate it, but the *milieu* will not assimilate it. It will fight like the Irish, or recede behind the church like the Poles, or intrench itself in cult like the Pennsylvania Dutch or generate protective adaptations like the Jews. But it will not of its own will give up the ghost. It will automatically defend itself from day to day, and to gain strength concede its own failure, justify itself by the ideology of its opponents, and carry on; all with the deepest, naïvest sincerity, the greatest piety, to the ineffables of the ruling society, the utmost deference toward this society's taboos.[9] All the valuations of the majority, its idols from cave, market place, forum, closet and altar, are automatically and unconsciously used as agencies to conserve the integrity of the minority's values; formulæ are confused with facts, events with appreciations, to the end that the assault upon the group's individuality may be relaxed and the group suffered to live for the present, even if eventually it must die a natural death. The sophism lies in the fact that every moment which is, is the present moment. The group changes, but it does not lose continuity, even if it loses memory; and where the continuity of life persists, the forgetting of past life may be overcome.

The treatment of such conceptions as *race, democracy,* and *culture* by the recent studies of group contacts in America mentioned earlier, is a sophism of this class. It is the argument of a foregone conclusion in the light of an immediate interest rather than an ultimate eventuality, a practical deduction from a mystic and ineffable premise, wherein the inalterable concept is invoked to justify the struggling and contrary fact. As if culture, race and democracy could have any meaning apart from the shifting constellations of men and events which they designate, or could serve as programs—programs are usually given an ineffable dimension by being called ideals—apart from the ungratified or obstructed wishes they are plans to gratify and to set free!

[9] Cf. Mr. Ludwig Lewisohn's "wealthy Jewish physician who had turned Methodist in his boyhood, avoided all questionable subjects, prayed at love feasts in the church, and, though he surreptitiously distributed alms among the poor Jews of the city, achieved a complete conformity of demeanor." He has his comrades in every race.

17. A Wet Nation with Dry Laws

Temperance had been a goal of reform movements associated with the genteel middle class since the mid-nineteenth century. After 1900, when the middle classes turned their energy to politics through the Progressive Movement, the drive against drink gained further impetus. And when the European War broke out, the struggle against intoxicating beverages reached its peak by merging with the dominant cultural temper of the time. Those who drank happened also to be people least likely to obey the dictates of genteel culture as it marched into war—city dwellers, immigrants, Germans, Catholics, Jews, workers and the poor, sybarites and the rich. After 1914, especially after 1917, the Great War to save civilization also became a lesser war to smash every liquor bottle in America.

The battle for temperance went through the same transformation as other genteel middle-class efforts at cultural control: coercion took the place of persuasion. Temperance, which stressed local option and personal changes of heart, was supplanted by Prohibition. Congress passed the Eighteenth Amendment to the Constitution in December, 1917, and the required number of states ratified it in January, 1919. The manufacture, sale, or transportation of intoxicating liquor within, into, or out of the United States was prohibited. The Volstead Act of 1919 provided the federal government some powers to enforce the Amendment. The Eighteenth Amendment and the Volstead Act were great victories for Prohibitionists, though flawed by compromise, and openly flouted by those against whom the laws were chiefly directed.

City dwellers, immigrants, rich, and poor had little desire to observe laws enshrining the hatreds and prejudices of a cultural group whose power was in decline. Contempt for the law was open, and it was circumvented in cities from the start, in small towns and on the farm, too, as the decade wore on. By the end of the Twenties congressmen flooded their committees with bills and constitutional amendments calling for repeal. A major hearing on the Prohibition Amendment was held by the House Judiciary Committee in February, 1930. The first witness called was Walter W. Liggett (1886–1935), a free-lance journalist, who had written a series of articles in *Plain Talk*

magazine describing illegal drinking in cities and states throughout the country. What follows is his testimony before the Committee, slightly abridged.

The Prohibition Amendment
WALTER W. LIGGETT

MR. LIGGETT. Mr. Chairman, and gentlemen of the House Judiciary
Committee, I would like to ask your indulgence for just a moment to
make a personal statement, and that is that I originally was a dry. In
1914, in the State of Washington, when a state-wide election was being
held on this question, I not only voted dry, but supported the dry cause.
I then owned my own newspaper, and I want to assure you gentlemen
of the committee that the support of the dry cause at that time cost me
considerable money.

I am merely making this statement, not to attempt in any way to throw
any high lights on my own motives, but only to indicate to you that I
was a dry, and that I was a sincere dry, and that I did believe at that
time that the passage of the state-wide dry act would immeasurably
improve conditions in the State of Washington.

Furthermore, gentlemen of the committee, I then believed, and still
believe, in the principle of local option. I believe that that is a democratic
method of handling the liquor-control situation.

I also want to say, Mr. Chairman and gentlemen of the committee, that
until comparatively recently, while I was not perfectly innocent of the
grave evils and the crime and corruption attendant upon the prohibition
law, I did, nevertheless, believe that it had probably decreased the actual
volume of drinking. I want to say, Mr. Chairman and members of the
committee, that for the last eight months I have been employed by a
New York magazine, called *Plain Talk*, to make a personal and detailed
investigation all over the United States. Of course, I have not quite
covered the United States as yet; we have to progress rather slowly, and

*The Prohibition Amendment. Hearings Before the Committee on the
Judiciary, House of Representatives, Seventy-First Congress, Second Session,
on H.J. Res. 11, 38, 99, 114, 219, and 246.* Serial 5, February 12, 13, 19, 20,
26, 27, March 4, 1930. Part 1 (Washington, 1930), pp. 12–19, 21–22,
24–25, 31.

I will take up a city and State at a time, but I have, however, in the last several months made a detailed personal investigation of the city of Washington in the District of Columbia, of the city of Boston, of the State of Kansas, and of the State of Michigan with particular reference to Detroit which might interest Mr. Michener.

MR. EARL C. MICHENER, *R–Mich.* I read your article last night.

MR. LIGGETT. Thank you; and I have also made a rather intimate survey of my own native State of Minnesota, where I not only had a chance to survey conditions as they are, but where I had an exceptional opportunity to compare the conditions as they used to be, because I will say that from 1906 until 1916 I worked as a newspaper reporter, police reporter, and rewrite man on all the newspapers in the three principal cities of Minnesota, and I visited every county in that State repeatedly and I think, with due deference to Mr. Volstead, that I know conditions in that State better than Mr. Volstead does. [Applause.]

Now, what have we to-day, gentlemen of the committee? Before the prohibition law was passed, you had in the District of Columbia 300 legally licensed saloons. Those saloons could only be kept open for certain limited hours, and the owners of those saloons had a considerable stock in their business. They not only had to pay for a license, and to pay a considerable sum for it, but they had to equip their places and take leases on the property, and in some cases they owned their own buildings. Those saloon keepers, while I am not offering any brief for them, and I do not want to see a return to the saloon—I will say that to you frankly—yet I will say that most of these saloon keepers did obey the laws as they then existed, and if you were a minor in the District of Columbia you would have found it difficult to get a drink in any of the saloons of the District of Columbia, and, if you were a girl of tender years, you would have found it practically impossible.

What do we have to-day? We have to-day, Mr. Chairman and gentlemen of the committee, not less than 700 speakeasies in the city of Washington, running day and night, right at the present time. We have at the present time not less than 4,000 bootleggers plying their trade daily and nightly in the District of Columbia.

From investigations which I have made, and I want to say that I did not confine my investigation to the bootleggers nor the police, but I conferred with the heads of the prohibition unit, with Sergeant Little and Sergeant Letterman of the vice squad, and also with every recognized antisaloon leader in this city, and, as a result of six weeks' investigation, I have absolutely come to the conclusion that to-day there is not less than 1,600,000 gallons of hard liquor alone being consumed in the District of Columbia every year.

I also checked up, members of the committee, the amount of home brew being made in the District of Columbia, and there I have an absolute check, because I went to individual grocers, I went to brokers, I went to the wholesale grocers, and I discovered, gentlemen of the committee, that to-day, at the very minimum, there are at least 6,000,000 gallons of home brew being made every year in the city of Washington. What have we in regard to conditions in the city of Washington? I went to Mr. Wilson, the head of the District of Columbia Anti-Saloon League. He is a very charming gentlemen. I have not the slightest doubt in the world that he is a perfectly honest gentlemen, and he impressed me as being a very lovable old man, who is sincerely desirous of improving conditions, and I respect him for that. I went to Mr. Wilson and I said, "Mr. Wilson, what do you think about conditions as compared to 10 years ago"?

"Why," he said, "there is no comparison; there is not one twenty-fifth of the drinking now that there was 10 years ago."

"Well," I said, "how do you account, then, for the fact that the arrests for drunkenness have practically trebled in the last 10 years?"

He answered that question by disputing my facts. He did it in a polite way; he was sure that I was mistaken, but he did dispute my facts. I had exactly the same experience with Judge Brott, of the Prohibition Unit, and with a number of other gentlemen; they all answered that question by disputing my facts.

Gentlemen, they can not dispute the facts. I got the facts off the records of the police department, as compiled by Lieutenant Edwards. I had the original documents in my possession for at least 10 days. Since then they have been printed in every paper in Washington.

The facts are, gentlemen, that now, 10 years after national prohibition, and 12 years after the Sheppard law was passed, the arrests for drunkenness alone in the city of Washington have trebled, have increased three times, and are constantly on the increase; and not only have the arrests for drunkenness trebled, but the arrests for murder, for embezzlement, for rape, for every kind of crime, have increased far beyond the natural increase of Washington's population.

Now, Washington is not alone in this condition. I made what I intended to be a very painstaking investigation of the city of Boston. Massachusetts, before prohibition, had practically just about 1,000 licensed saloons. Massachusetts to-day, gentlemen, has at least 4,000 speakeasies. There are at least 4,000 open speakeasies running in the city of Boston to-day, and there are at least 15,000 people who do nothing but purvey booze illegally in the city of Boston to-day.

How do you think they do it? They can only do it, gentlemen, under one condition, and that condition is the corruption of the police. I do not know whether any one of you gentlemen here to-day is from Massachusetts, but if he is I want to tell him that I reported these charges to the grand jury, and the grand jury listened to me, and, if I am not mistaken, the grand jury are going to return some indictments against corrupt police officials.

I want to say that the police of Boston and the State police of Massachusetts are very largely corrupted as a result of this prohibition act. I have positive evidence, in affidavit form, and affidavits substantiated by several persons in each case, that not only are the police corrupted, but State officials have been corrupted, and even ex-governors and their secretaries and commissioners of public safety have been illegally selling confiscated liquor on a wholesale scale.

Prostitution is absolutely rampant in the city of Boston. You have an organized white-slave ring of international scope, that operates not only in Massachusetts, but in Connecticut, Pennsylvania, and eastern Michigan, going into this criminal, nefarious, vile business on a wholesale scale, and I say to you that that question is a direct and immediate and inevitable concomitant of prohibition, or so-called prohibition as you have it to-day.

Now, as to the dope traffic. As you can easily ascertain by summoning or citing here the Federal officials charged with the suppression of narcotics, the dope traffic is on the increase in every city of the United States to-day. The chief of the Federal Bureau of Suppression in the city of Cleveland told me that not less than $22,000,000 a year is being spent in Detroit annually by drug addicts.

Now, I do not wish to say that I think that the fact that people are drug fiends is directly attributable to prohibition. I do not want to be so understood; but the growth of the drug traffic, this general disregard of law, this breakdown of morals, if not directly attributable to prohibition, at least came into being at the same time that prohibition was fastened upon this country.

I recently went out to the dry State of Kansas. Kansas, as you know, was the first State of the Union to adopt state-wide prohibition by a constitutional amendment. They recently—I think while I was in the State—celebrated the fiftieth anniversary of state-wide prohibition.

What conditions did I find in Kansas, a State that has been dry, or at least had dry laws, 50 years, a State that brags about its drastic, bone-dry law, where you can get three years for merely having possession of liquor? What did I find in Kansas, gentlemen? I will make the statement that there is not a town in Kansas where I can not go as a total stranger and get a drink of liquor, and very good liquor at that, within 15 minutes after my arrival.

While I was in the city of Topeka, I stopped at the best hotel in Topeka, and I had not been in the city five minutes before the bellboy who took me to my room asked me if I would like to have a pint of alcohol, and he also suggested that, if I wanted it, he could also provide a little indoor sport—this is the best hotel in Topeka, the capital of Kansas.

I went through 16 counties in the State of Kansas, and I found those conditions existing everywhere, bootlegging everywhere. Wichita is wide open. I went into one of the classiest roadhouses in Wichita; it compared very favorably indeed with the better class of roadhouses in New York, and it was running wide open; gambling going on upstairs, with the roof the limit, and 75 people were playing as I watched the game, and stacks high.

You can get liquor in any of the hotels at Topeka, and if you do not want to bother to register at a hotel, just step into a taxicab, and you get all you want in a short time.

I estimate from a close, detailed study of the conditions in Kansas, and I base my evidence on information given to me by State officials, by Federal officials, and by individuals who have lived in Kansas for years, that to-day not less than 6,000,000 gallons of hard liquor are being consumed in the State of Kansas alone; and, with the assistance of some friends who work for the Santa Fe Railroad, I have a very intimate close-up and accurate check of the amount of malt coming into the city of Topeka alone, and my facts, taken off the railroad records, showed me that in the city of Topeka alone, in the course of a year, some 600,000 gallons of home brew are being brewed; and Topeka, gentlemen, has a population of less than 60,000. That is a per capita consumption of 10 gallons of home brew per annum, and exceeds anything I know about before prohibition.

Let us go to Detroit. Detroit in some respects is one of our greatest, one of our most representative, one of our most typically modern of American cities. It is there where you have the principle of mass production. It was originated there; it was there it came into its fullest flower, and I want to state to the gentleman from Michigan that mass production in crime is also coming to its fullest flower in the city of Detroit, Mich.

I have it on the authority of the ex-mayor, and also the present chief of police, that there are to-day 20,000 speakeasies in the city of Detroit. Now, gentlemen, this is not a guess; this is not an estimate; it is the result of a careful census made by the police under the direction of the chief of police and the mayor, and two years ago the record showed that there were 20,000 speakeasies in the city of Detroit.

Arrests for drunkenness in Detroit in the last 10 years have practically almost doubled. Crime of every description in Detroit to-day has increased so fast that I do not want to arouse your incredibility by giving the exact statistics, but I wish to say, however, that to-day Detroit is in the grip of a bunch of gangsters, racketeers, crooked policemen, and grafting politicians, and I make that statement without claiming the right of privilege and I can prove everything I say. I have already made far more serious charges in my account in the magazine, *Plain Talk*.

I want to say furthermore that not only has this act resulted in wholesale crime, more drunkenness, more debauchery, disorder of every sort, but it is directly responsible, everywhere you go, for the corruption of high officials, for the hypocrisy of high officials.

There came to my attention in the city of Detroit—and this took place last November—a wild party given at a road house, and a very wild party, where the liquor was donated by one of the principal gamblers of Detroit—Denny Murphy, if you want his name—and there were at that drunken revel, at the Grand Avenue road house, the Governor of Michigan, the chief of police of Detroit, the chief of the State police, politicians, club men, gamblers, criminals, bootleggers, all there fraternizing in the spirit of the most perfect equality, under the god Bacchus, and I will also say that there were four judges of the circuit court of Michigan at that drunken revel, at which naked hoochy-koochy dancers appeared later in the evening, and I want to say that these officials of the city of Detroit and the judges of the Michigan bar and the Governor of the State of Michigan attended that drunken debauch and the next day they said that they would enforce the law and that they believed in the dry law.

Hypocrisy of that sort sickens any honest person; hypocrisy of that sort sickens any person, and yet you find that hypocrisy to-day all over the length and breadth of this land.

Mr. Leonidas C. Dyer, *R–Mo.* Will the gentleman state when that event took place?

Mr. Liggett. Yes, sir; on the evening of November 5 and the morning of November 6, 1929.

Mr. Henry St. George Tucker, *D–Va.* Were you there?

MR. LIGGETT. I was not. I am more careful of my associates. [Applause.]

MR. MICHENER. You, of course, have the proof, and when called upon to produce this proof, you will be in position and will, of course, gladly do that?

MR. LIGGETT. Mr. Michener, that statement I made here and the statement I made in my magazine are criminal libel unless proved.

MR. MICHENER. I appreciate that.

MR. LIGGETT. I can assure you that I have the proof, and I am perfectly willing to produce the proof, but that I will not be called upon to do so. [Applause.]

MR. GEORGE R. STOBBS, R–*Mass.* I happen to be a Representative from Massachusetts, and I am deeply interested and concerned in what the gentleman said as to the conditions existing there, and I assume that your reply will be the same as that which you made to Mr. Michener that, when you made this sweeping indictment of ex-governors and secretaries of governors and commissioners of public safety, as well as other high police officials in the State of Massachusetts, you had the evidence to substantiate that, and have submitted that evidence to the United States attorney in Boston?

MR. LIGGETT. The Federal grand jury in Boston already has my evidence.

I want to say in this connection that I am not a snooper or an informer or a spy. [Applause.]

MR. HATTON W. SUMNERS, D–*Tex.* Mr. Chairman, I can quite appreciate the emotions of the audience, but I hope the audience will appreciate that this is a serious hearing before a committee of Congress which is undertaking to determine its duty with regard to pending legislation, and this sort of applause on either side can not do anything at all except to disturb. We are not going to cast our votes by our estimate of the amount of applause that comes from the group here.

I hope you will not take that as a rebuke, because I know what I might want to do if I were out there on either side, but my suggestion is that you suppress your emotions.

MR. LIGGETT. I want to make my position clear——

MR. SUMNERS. I do not want the audience to think, however, that I am rebuking them.

MR. LIGGETT. I want to make my position clear to you, that I am not in the least interested in turning up some half-pint bootlegger, and I am not paid to collect evidence for the Government. They have a small army of under-cover men whose duty it is to get the evidence, and they have no scruples against drinking with a person and then turning informer, and all that; but I have not the slightest hesitancy, any place, any time, anywhere, in giving to the properly constituted authorities of law evidence of dereliction of duty on the part of high officials who are sworn to obey the law, and I did give it to the Massachusetts grand jury, and I will give it to the Detroit grand jury, Mr. Michener, if I am summoned back there, very gladly, and plenty, too.

I do not want to take up any more of your time. I could go on. I have at home almost a truck load of detail and explicit facts—and it is not all at home, either—but I do not care to take up any more of your time in going into these details, because I think that you, as men of sense, of sophistication, have yourselves seen these things and must know them if you will remove the prejudice from your eyes and really look about.

I merely want to conclude by saying this, that there is absolutely no doubt in the world that to-day, all over the length and breadth of this land, right out on your farms as well as in your cities, there is more hard liquor being drunk, and considerably more hard liquor being drunk, than there was in the days before prohibition.

I also want to say, gentlemen, that it is being drunk under more evil surroundings. After all, when men openly walked into a saloon and went up to the bar and named their poison, there was not anything inherently vicious or criminal about that. But what do we have to-day? We have in Minnesota, Mr. Volstead's own native State, where Mr. Volstead sits to-day as the counsellor for the dry administrator, so that the administration of the prohibition act in Minnesota to-day is under the personal supervision of Andrew Volstead, and I do not think that even Senator Borah would claim that Mr. Volstead is not interested in the enforcement of this act—I say, we have what conditions in Minnesota?

Your drinking in Minneapolis, gentlemen, is done there in unspeakably vile dives that cater to the itinerant lumberman, to the harvest hands, and to the itinerant workers there—brothels, practically, most of them. The drinking of that class is mostly done in these vile places, down in the old gateway district, where girls are sitting behind fake cigar stores and candy stores and fake soft-drink parlors and fake barber shops; and I want to speak very plainly about this, that most of these places are nothing but crib-houses. A man will go there to get a drink, and there is a wink and the front door is locked and the curtains are pulled down, and something else besides drinking goes on.

There is not a decent speakeasy in the city of Minneapolis. Most of the drinking there is done in beer flats. I know; I have it on the very best of authority. There are there at least 3,000 beer flats, in the city of Minneapolis. A beer flat is an apartment. A girl may work in the daytime, in which case the beer flat runs at night; or, if she does not work, she runs the beer flat 24 hours, and the business man or the professional man, the men about town, and the young men, will have a list in their little book of, say, 15 or 20 of these beer flats, and they will call up and ask "Is Clara home?" They get the answer "Yes," and "I am coming up with a friend."

You can get anything you want; hard liquor, home brew, some pretty vile wine, and, when the drinking has progressed to a certain stage, and there are two or three men there, for the girl will often go out and call in some of her friends, and there is more drinking, and your imagination can picture the rest.

That is what goes on very frequently in these beer flats. It is quite different from the days of the open saloon.

They also have beer farms in the State of Minnesota. That is one reason why you have not heard so much about farm relief. A good many of the farmers there are making home brew and a more excellent brand of bootleg booze, and a considerable proportion of them are throwing their houses open to men and women, and to boys and girls who drive out from the city because they think they are in no danger of arrest there. And while I was in the city of Minneapolis, a beer farm was flourishing at Lesueur Center, 50 miles south of Minneapolis, and boys and girls were motoring down there, going there after school, and sitting around the tables in dark rooms, having debauches on those farms. It also developed that upon occasion the woman who ran the beer farm was not averse to renting rooms, and when you get children of a tender age filling up with a bad brand of liquor, you can fill in the rest of the picture.

That is what is going on in Minnesota to-day, right under the nose of Andrew Volstead. That is the general testimony of everybody who has lived in the State, and, as I told you, I worked all over the State as police reporter, that there is far more drinking going on in Minnesota to-day than there was before prohibition. Minnesota, before prohibition, was almost dry. They had local option, and pretty nearly 90 per cent of the State was dry, and it was dry, then; but to-day the entire State is wet, and it is very wet indeed.

Now, gentlemen, I simply want to leave this thought with you. I believe in good government, and I believe in decency, and I believe in civic ideals and in temperance, but it is my honest opinion—borne upon me as a result of, you might say, a nation-wide investigation, because these places that I have already visited are widely scattered and they are representative—it is my firm conviction to-day that the Volstead Act, the national amendment for prohibition, has increased drunkenness, not only among men, but more especially among women and children. It has resulted in infinitely more debauchery; it has loosened our entire respect for the law, and, what more, even more serious, it has resulted in widespread corruption of police enforcement officials and even politicians higher up. I do not need to go into details as to that.

✿ ✿ ✿

MR. EMANUEL CELLER, D–N.Y. Have your investigations brought you into contact with facts like these: For example, the Department of Agriculture indicates that almost one billion gallons of corn sugar were manufactured in the United States in the last fiscal year, a tremendous increase in the manufacture of corn sugar.

MR. LIGGETT. Yes. There are stills being set up all through the rural regions in practically all the Middle Western States. I am only speaking of States I personally know about—Minnesota, North Dakota, Iowa, Kansas, and Wisconsin. It is a very common practice for a farmer to go into the bootlegging business, or else rent his premises to a gang of city people who come out to do it. You can build one of these stills for $10,000. They have a capacity of about 800 gallons a day, and you can pay for your still in five days and after that everything you turn out is absolutely clear profit. It is not amazing, then, that a great many farmers, and a great many others, are going on the farms and putting up their stills, and I think Doctor Doran is right in one particular, although I do not always agree with him, and that is that the still out on the farm to-day is to a great extent replacing the diverted alcohol. It is much easier and cheaper to make; costs 50 cents a gallon to make.

MR. CELLER. So you came to the conclusion in your investigations in those States that this tremendous increase in the manufacture of corn sugar is due to the increase in the manufacture of whisky in homes or on the farms?

MR. LIGGETT. No doubt about it at all.

MR. GORDON BROWNING, D–Tenn. Do you think that the condition that you have described in the State of Kansas is of recent growth?

MR. LIGGETT. Yes; within 10 years.

MR. BROWNING. You said that prohibition had been in effect out there and on the statute books for 50 years.

MR. LIGGETT. Yes, sir.

MR. BROWNING. Can you give us any idea why you think a change in the national prohibition law would remedy a situation like that, which has grown up 40 years after prohibition went into effect?

MR. LIGGETT. Well, there was not prohibition in Kansas. Prohibition laws in Kansas have always been notorious for their open violation. I do not think there was any real attempt to enforce prohibition in Kansas. For instance, in Wichita, in 1906, there were wide-open saloons, a row of them. That is about the time Carrie Nation started her crusade. About 1907 Governor Stubbs, I believe his name was, came along, and he did believe in prohibition, and he tried to enforce prohibition, and, if my memory serves me correctly, I think he was followed by Senator Capper, then governor, and I am willing to concede that Senator Capper is a perfectly honest and sincere prohibitionist, and he made an honest attempt to enforce prohibition, and it was in 1907, I think, that Kansas passed its State bone-dry-act.

Yes; I think I can tell you why conditions have changed, because it was easily possible then for any thirsty Kansan to go to the border line and get a drink. For instance, the people residing at Topeka were only about 80 miles east of the line, and if anybody got very thirsty they would drive over there. Liquor was also brought into Kansas, although not so much of it. Then, too, North Dakota was the third State in the Union to go dry, and it was very dry indeed under state-wide prohibition. You could get liquor in North Dakota, and I have been in every county and liquor was very difficult to get if you wanted it, and there did not seem to be a great desire for it, and it is the general testimony of everybody that there was not much liquor consumed in North Dakota, nor was there much consumed in the dry portions of Minnesota, which was largely dry, under local option.

But when this thing was imposed upon them, it seemed to create a revolt—you can see the marked tendency there—it seemed to create a desire for liquor on the part of people who had not drunk before. For a long time North Dakota was one of the most traveled thoroughfares in the United States for bringing in liquor from Canada. A good deal of liquor brought in from Canada in 1920, 1921, and 1922 came through North Dakota, and, of course, as long as the bootleggers were there and engaged in the business, they were going to develop side lines as they went along, and they did do that, and it is the general testimony of everybody that drinking in North Dakota has increased immeasurably since the passage of the national prohibition act.

I do not want to mention any names, because it may get him in bad, but a certain enforcement officer in that State told me that there was liquor to-day in 80 per cent of the farms in North Dakota.

MR. BROWNING. Do you think that forcing something on somebody that they had for years would cause a revolt?

MR. LIGGETT. It is hard to say, but it did have that effect. It probably was coupled with other conditions. A good many of the Dakota boys were taken off the farm and had been to "gay Paree," and the conditions were more or less unsettled, and there is a certain spiritual exhaustion that follows every war, but there was that marked tendency, and where in communities you could not previously get a drink, you now find a bootlegger in every section. One farmer, pretty nearly, in every four is making booze. That is not intended as an exaggeration; it is almost a literal truth.

*　*　*

MR. SUMNERS. Let me ask you this question: Do you think or not that the enactment of the national prohibition law had a tendency to relieve the people of the communities of a sense of local responsibility, which weakened the general situation?

MR. LIGGETT. Yes, I think so most emphatically, Mr. Sumners. For instance, there are only 59 enforcement officers in the fourteenth district; that is the district over which Mr. Volstead has virtual charge. They cover an area of about 200,000 square miles, and there are 5,000,000 people in that district. Well, at least 10 of them are in the office constantly, and others are taking vacations or sick leave, and I do not suppose that there are ever more than 35 men in those three States, 35 Federal field people. Of course, it is impossible for 35 men to cover a great inland empire of that size. There are in that same territory about 12,000 peace officers, possibly; that is, sheriffs, deputy sheriffs, constables, and police, and it is the consensus of opinion, Mr. Sumners, that with very few exceptions they pay no attention at all to the Federal act. In other words, you have in Minnesota a direct reversal of what you had before prohibition. Before prohibition you had local option, local dry option in Minnesota, and I can only say that to-day you have local wet option in Minnesota. The average peace officer there will say that he is dry around election time, when the church people are pretty well organized, but after that he forgets about it.

MR. SUMNERS. Why do not the people in those communities, if they are dry, elect dry officers and enforce their laws in their respective communities?

Mr. Liggett. The answer is very easy. The wets are not organized as yet. The drys are organized. I do not want you to think that I am casting any slurs at any member of the committee, but there is a certain fanaticism connected with dry men whereby if a man is dry—and he may be a yellow dog in other ways—the drys will go out and vote for him. That is not so true with the wets. There are other factors that determine it, but you have your drys absolutely 100 per cent organized. You have your antisaloon leagues, your churches, your local dry organizations, and they can sway the vote——

Mr. Sumners. I do not want to interrupt you, but if the drys are organized, why do they not elect dry officers who will enforce the laws in their respective communities?

Mr. Liggett. They all claim to be dry. They are dry around election time, and then they pass the wink to the boys that they won't be bothered.

Mr. Sumners. Do you mean that they are wets parading as drys?

Mr. Liggett. Yes; and periodically and professionally dry, but otherwise wet.

❋ ❋ ❋

Mr. William C. Hammer, D-N.C. It is an admitted thing that prohibition has not been enforced effectively, and the general opinion prevails that there has not been the interest manifested in it that there should have been by those whose duty it is to be enforcement officers. Whether that is true or not is another question, but the idea does prevail now that the President is in earnest and that he has appointed an Attorney General who seems to be—and I am not questioning his sincerity—making an honest effort to see if this law can be enforced. It looks like he is making more than a mere gesture, from the morning papers yesterday and of the last few days in connection with events in Chicago and New York.

What do you think about letting Mr. Hoover and his Attorney General have sway for a while, to give them encouragement in getting something done?

Mr. Liggett. What do I think about that? I think the law is essentially nonenforceable. I think that Mr. Hoover will give out statements that he is trying to enforce it; maybe he will try to enforce it, but I do not believe, human nature being as fallible as it is, and habits and desires and ideas of people being such as they are, that even if Mr. Hoover were the superman that he is in some quarters said to be, he could enforce it.

Mr. Hammer. I do not think he is.

Mr. Liggett. I do not, either.

MR. HAMMER. But I think he is trying to make some effort here.

MR. DYER. This prohibition enforcement act gives authority to all the States, does it not, as well as the Federal Government?

MR. LIGGETT. Yes, sir.

MR. DYER. And all of the States, with the exception of, I think, three, have State enforcement acts, have they not?

MR. LIGGETT. I think four.

MR. DYER. If there is any dereliction of duty, it can not be charged alone to the Federal Government, but to the States as well?

MR. LIGGETT. That is exactly my contention, that it is not only corrupting the Federal Government, but corrupting State governments. It is corrupting your county governments, city governments, and even corrupting your very small village governments, right down to common constables.

MR. HAMMER. You think really that this law is not worth the honest effort which a great many people think they are just now beginning to try to enforce?

MR. LIGGETT. It is my honest belief, Judge, as an American citizen and a man who loves his country, that if you have 10 more years of this law, you will have the United States of America ruled and dominated by a gang of underworld rats and crooked politicians. [Applause.]

18. Rule by the Underworld

The average American in the Twenties believed that organized crime got its start through Prohibition. But then the average American was probably making use of the services of criminals in the Twenties for the first time—to buy an illegal drink. In fact, criminal syndicates had begun to form at least two decades prior to the Twenties, as criminal gangs shifted from disorganized robbery to the more lucrative and steady task of providing the country with desired, but illegal, services, particularly prostitution and gambling. Criminal organizations believed just as fervently as legitimate businessmen in the value of efficiency and rationality in their operations. They supported political organizations and participated in the normal service and reward system of big city politics; they befriended and corrupted police, prosecutors, judges, and office holders; and, when all else failed, resorted to murder and terror.

What Prohibition did for organized crime was enormously to raise the stakes. The money in prostitution or gambling was small-time compared to the profits in bootleg liquor. Bootlegging, however, also required a more complex operation, international in scope, and with some form of control over breweries, fleets of trucks, speakeasies, and nightclubs. Such control was neither easy to come by nor to keep. Changes in political administrations would bring into office politicians who favored one gang over another. As enforcement waxed and waned in the cities, syndicate operations in the suburbs would profit or decline. Nowhere was competition keener and conditions more unstable than in Chicago. The struggle for control over Chicago bootlegging led to scores of gangland murders and earned Chicago a permanent place in world folklore.

Under such circumstances, the career of Chicago gangland boss John Torrio was an unusual one. Torrio ruled Chicago's underworld in the early Twenties and made enormous profits in the bootleg business. In 1925 he retired and made his way safely to Italy with a fortune estimated at between ten and thirty millions. In comparison, his predecessor, "Big Jim" Colosimo, was gunned down in 1920 as a result of a political feud, and his successor, Al Capone—who had come to Chicago with Torrio in 1918 from the Five-Point Gang in New York—was sent to Alcatraz in 1931 for income tax evasion. Torrio's role as overlord of Chicago vice, gambling, and liquor traffic was depicted by John Landesco, then research director of the American Institute of Criminal Law and Criminology, in his important study of the underworld, "Organized Crime in Chicago," published as part of *The Illinois Crime Survey* (Chicago, 1929).

Organized Crime in Chicago
JOHN LANDESCO

I. BREWING AND BEER RUNNING, THE GOLDEN FUTURE

John Torrio, the protege and successor of Colosimo was born in Italy, in 1877, and is now fifty-one years of age. The organization of large scale illegal business in vice, supported by political influence, bribery, and violence, had been a matter of lifelong training for Torrio when, upon the death of Colosimo, the mantle fell upon his shoulders.

Torrio already was known both by politicians and gangsters as safe and level headed. At the funeral of Colosimo, conspicuous in the throng, which included judges, politicians, city officials, cabaret singers, gamblers, and waiters, were members of the Colosimo vice ring, and Torrio was an honorary pall-bearer. At this time Torrio was known as boss of the suburban town of Burnham, where he owned the Burnham Inn in a community of resorts and gambling dens. Ike Bloom owned the Arrowhead Inn, a suburban resort which he later sold to Colosimo before the latter's death. Jakie Adler and the Cusicks, and others of the Twenty-second Street Levee had moved to the southern and western suburbs as early as 1916.

The death of Colosimo occurred in the same year that the Eighteenth Amendment and the Volstead Act came into effect; and Torrio turned his attention to the organization of the contraband business of manufacturing beer and of distributing it by convoy through the streets of

John Landesco, "Organized Crime in Chicago," *The Illinois Crime Survey* (Chicago, 1929), pp. 909–919.

the city. In connection with his organization of metropolitan beer running, he extended direct rulership over the other west suburban towns.

2. THE OCCUPATION OF CICERO

Torrio took possession of Cicero, a western suburb, in 1923.

In addition to the vice and gambling houses in Burnham he had established several resorts in Stickney. Then he originated the scheme of making the town of Cicero a base for the operations of beer distribution and gambling. In the fall of 1923 he installed a vice resort on Roosevelt Road in Cicero. But Torrio was not without competition in his occupation of Cicero. Eddie Tancl, a Bohemian who was born and bred in the old Pilsen district, had risen to popularity as a prize fighter and because of his many acts of charity among poor Bohemians was very popular in Cicero at this time, and was conducting a cafe there. Tancl was killed by James Doherty, a Torrio gangster.

Torrio opened his resort without protection. The Cicero police raided it. Torrio moved the same resort to Ogden and Fifty-second Avenues, and the police wrecked it.

Through the influence of Torrio, Sheriff Hoffman ordered a raid on all slot machines in the suburb. Thus Torrio made it known that if he couldn't import prostitutes others couldn't have slot machines. After a few days the slot machines started going again and Torrio, Capone, and their followers moved into Cicero. Somewhere an understanding had been reached. The "mob" came in strong. They opened gambling houses, peddled beer, but did not bring prostitutes into Cicero again. Stickney and Forest Park and other places in the county were utilized for vice operations which were developed on a large scale. In the suburbs, Torrio, Capone, his first lieutenant, La Cava brothers, and Mondi assisted by Frankie Pope, Joey Miller (Italian), Jimmie Murphy, the Cusicks, and Charlie Carr managed a business which included vice, beer, and gambling.

Torrio and his lieutenants used intrigue and bribery and succeeded in controlling elections. The officials were actually under their thumbs— not only the village president, but every official, including the chief of police. Lauterbach's "The Ship" and "The Hawthorne Smoke Shop" operated apparently without opposition from Joseph Klenha, the village president, or his police chief, Theodore Svoboda, Sheriff Hoffman, or State's Attorney Crowe.

Federal officials, intent upon raiding the saloon concessions, always found the places "tipped off."

3. THE METROPOLITAN OPERATIONS

The *Daily News,* commenting on this situation, said:

"Under the graft system that flourished while Thompson was mayor of Chicago, Torrio's power increased. He had a finger in the gambling pie and his beer running business was organized in those pleasant times. He was reputed owner of several breweries when Mayor Dever up-ended everything with his beer crusade."

In his city-wide operations in beer, Torrio is first heard of as the real beer boss of the south side. He took over the big West Hammond Brewery (known also as the Puro Products Company) and began running beer at regular rates of fifty dollars a barrel, including protection. He had a monopoly in Woodlawn and all precincts south to the Indiana State line, and enjoyed official favor in the Stockyards and the New City districts. In Englewood, where Captain Allman, Commander of the Police, did not touch graft, Torrio had an even chance. Allman could not be transferred because he was in high favor with the Englewood business men.

In Englewood, and to some extent the Stockyards and the New City districts, the O'Donnells were developing a small but growing beer running business. This is not the same family as the O'Donnells who figured in the McSwiggin killing in Cicero. For brevity we will designate this family of Steve, Walter, Thomas and Spike as the "South Side O'Donnells," and the others as the "West Side O'Donnells."

4. THE O'DONNELLS INTRUDE

The South Side O'Donnells were not, however, in a position to challenge Torrio successfully. Thus matters stood when the city administration changed and the old Thompson machine went out in 1923. The transfer of authority caused a revolution in the underworld; the old system of protection was destroyed. None could be sure he was "in" anywhere; therefore competition was free and easy.

The South Side O'Donnells made use of their opportunity. They sold a better beer than did Torrio and began to "cut in" heavily in the Stockyards and the New City districts. Torrio, seeing his business wane, retaliated by cutting prices. He put out his beer at ten dollars less a barrel. The O'Donnells retaliated by terrorizing saloon-keepers who bought other beer than theirs.

Torrio's rise invited envy and competition but he knew how to deal with them. On September 7, 1923, Jerry O'Connor, tough young south side gangster, was shot dead. O'Connor was a "pal" and agent of the four O'Donnells. On the fatal night he was with Steve, Walter, and Tommy O'Donnell threatening and slugging saloon-keepers for buying beer from John Torrio. At the saloon of Joseph Kepka, 5358 South Lincoln Street, they encountered a Torrio gang. The lights went out; pistols roared; everyone scattered. When police arrived they could find no one who knew about the shooting. Two were arrested, but lawyers started habeas corpus proceedings which were entirely unnecessary, because Chief Morgan Collins had no reason for holding them and freed them instantly. Many people knew the story, more especially the saloon-keepers and bartenders, but they would not tell.

On September 17, 1923, George Meegan, 5620 Laflin Street, and George Bucher, 5611 Marshfield Avenue, were killed. Both men were considered dangerous because they threatened to reveal the murderers of Jerry O'Connor. Crowe began a "relentless investigation of the beer war." Torrio was now reputed as the "brains" of the biggest beer running syndicate in the country. He surrendered, in company with his attorney, Michael Igoe, to the State's Attorney and was to be grilled concerning beer running in general.

5. "HI-JACKING" AND GANG WARFARE

Morrie Keane and William Egan, invaders of Torrio territory, one night in December, 1923, started from Joliet at midnight to drive three truck-loads of beer to Chicago. At a lonesome stretch of the road, called "The Sag," they were stopped, it was later charged, by McErlane, Torrio gunman, and his "hi-jackers." After the beer had been turned over to some highway policemen, Keane and Egan were forced into McErlane's car. Their bodies, filled with bullets, were later found by the road side.

McErlane was arrested, held by the state's attorney in the Sherman Hotel, and then released.

Under pressure, State's Attorney Crowe laid the case before the grand jury. An indictment was voted. Long delays followed. Months afterward, an assistant state's attorney went into court and nolle prossed the case. McErlane left town a free man.

In this investigation it emerged that Walter Stevens, Daniel McFall, and Frank McErlane were leading Torrio's armed forces in the disputed territory. Walter Stevens, the dean of Chicago gunmen, at this moment was wanted for the killing of an Aurora policeman. He had served time in Joliet. It was known that he was a favorite of Governor Small for services rendered to him in his trial at Waukegan. McFall and McErlane were indicted in 1923 for the double killing of gangsters Meegan and Bucher, but the indictments were later nolle prossed. McFall and Red Golden were associates of Stevens and were also wanted for the murder. Torrio had developed powerful influence, as illustrated by his success in securing the pardon from Governor Small of Harry Cusick and his wife, Alma, convicted panderers. He was high in the esteem of the Thompson-Lundin machine. Frank McErlane is still in power in that district and recently, with Joe Saltis and Tim Murphy,[1] succeeded in nominating John "Dingbat" Oberta state senator and electing him ward committeeman.

6. POLICE PERSECUTION OF THE ENEMIES OF TORRIO

Torrio's enemies, the O'Donnells, had all been jailed at one time or another during this beer investigation, and two of them were indicted. Torrio had been unmolested and the police professed to be unable to find Stevens. The O'Connor killing was laid to Dan McFall, a Torrio man. McFall was arrested, but released on bail and became a fugitive. Red Golden, named as McFall's accomplice, was released after questioning and disappeared.

7. BREWERY OWNERSHIP

Torrio, owner of the West Hammond Brewery, later purchased the Manhattan Brewery, and was said to be worth millions. He boasted that he "owned" police captains and other officials.

Harry Cusick was serving as downtown "pay-off" man for Torrio and had an office in the "Loop," where he paid Torrio money to police officials who were protecting the vice ring.

The operations of the Torrio syndicate on the south side were disclosed in the investigation into the deaths of Jerry O'Connor, Meegan, and Bucher, which showed the dealings with the retailer and the war for territory.

On October 19, 1923, just a few weeks after these killings, the Puro Products Company (The West Hammond Brewery) was on trial in the Federal Court in proceedings to close it for one year under injunction. From this trial we learn more about Torrio's expanding ownership of breweries. Testimony revealed W. R. Strook, a former United States Deputy Marshal, as one-half owner of the concern, and Timothy J. Mullen, an attorney, as holder of one share of the stock. Mullen, accord-

---

[1] Later killed by gangsters.

ing to the Federal agents, was attorney with an interest in the Bielfeldt Brewery at Thornton.

The Puro Products Company was bankrupt in 1915. Then came prohibition and a turn in its financial tide, when Joseph Stenson acquired it in October, 1920. In October, 1922, Torrio bought it, and seven days later turned the lease over to the Puro Products Company. The presence of Stenson, a brewer in the days before prohibition, and these transfers of ownership prior to the hearing on the injunction, should be noted as a feature in our examination of brewery ownership later. Torrio and Strook pleaded guilty and were fined $2,000 and $1,000, respectively; and the company $2,000.

Torrio departed with his family on a European sightseeing jaunt that was to end in Italy, where he had purchased a villa for his mother. It was intimated that he took with him more than a million dollars' worth of negotiable securities and letters of credit. He was reported to have the beer concession to all syndicate resorts; to own West Hammond, Manhattan, and Best Breweries; to be a silent partner in several others. His pay roll during the fall of 1923, when beer running was at its then zenith, was said to be twenty-five thousand dollars a week. He carried a gun when he felt like it, but never, as far as is known in Chicago, did Torrio use that gun. When trouble came, those who took care of Torrio were in turn taken care of when their cases came to court.

8. CONTROLLING OF ELECTIONS

Six months later Torrio came back to Chicago. He slipped unostentatiously into the city and summoned his veteran adherents to meet him in a south side rendezvous.

County Judge Edmund K. Jarecki, conducting an investigation of bloodshed and riots in the April, 1924, election in Cicero, was interested in Torrio's return. Up to the day of the election, 123 saloons in Cicero had been serving beer put out by Torrio's breweries. For six years the same faction had been in control of Cicero's politics and its saloons. The election brought no change in administration. Democrats charged that the breweries sent into Cicero scores of gunmen who cast ballots and manipulated revolvers. During one of the gun-play episodes, Frank Capone, one of Torrio's closest lieutenants, was shot to death by Sergeant William Cusick's squad from the detective bureau. The night before election there was a Torrio clan gathering. Frank Capone and his brother, Scarface Al, better known as Al Brown, owner of the notorious "Four Deuces" Saloon at 2222 South Wabash Avenue, were present. Judge

Jarecki thought that Torrio had instructed the Capone brothers to act as his emissaries in directing the riots in Cicero.

After Frank Capone's killing, Torrio met Scarface Al in the Capone home. Probably others of the gang were present. The meeting or sessions following the shooting of a Torrio lieutenant usually have to do with matters of vengeance. Every saloon in Cicero was directed to pull down the blinds and to remain in a quasi-closed condition until after the excitement had passed. At the inquest over the body of his brother, Scarface Al testified. After a glance had passed between Capone and Charles Frischetti, a companion of Frank when he was killed, Capone announced that he had nothing to say.

9. METROPOLITAN BEER KING

The Sieben Brewery raid, a month later, was the complete disclosure of Torrio's power as the metropolitan beer king, flanked on one side by the mobilized gangster chiefs of the entire city and on the other by business partners, who were pre-Volstead brewers, by public officials, and the police.

On the morning of May 19, 1924, after a carefully planned campaign, a police squad under the direct command of Chief Morgan Collins and Captain Matthew Zimmer (without a betrayal in advance of an intention of immediate action) swooped down upon the Sieben Brewery and found thirteen truckloads of beer ready to be convoyed through the streets of the city; the convoy, composed of gang leaders, was arriving in touring cars. As each car arrived the police placed the gangsters under arrest.

While all of the captured gave aliases, the leaders were recognized, of course. John Torrio, Dion O'Banion, and Louis Alterie were among them, and probably Hymie Weiss. Dion O'Banion was then prince of the north side gang, composed of safe-crackers and gunmen of note. Louie Alterie was the chief of the Valley Gang, which under the leadership of Paddy the Bear Ryan had thrived for a quarter of a century. Alterie had succeeded Terry Druggan and Frankie Lake, who were in turn the successors of Paddy the Bear Ryan.

Chief of Police Collins did not turn the prisoners over to Robert E. Crowe, Prosecutor. He announced that other raids would be made if this one failed to frighten the beer runners out of business. Asked why he turned these prisoners over to the Federal Government, he answered: "District Attorney Olson has promised us prompt cooperation. That is why the case was turned over to him for prosecution. It was a police raid, pure and simple, but the prosecution will be handled by the Government."

Torrio obtained freedom soon after his arrival at the Federal Building, by peeling $7,500 off a roll he carried. The same roll brought freedom, at five thousand dollars, for James Casey. O'Banion did not have the "five grand" demanded of him as bail, nor could Alterie produce one thousand dollars; the others, at one thousand dollars also, each had to wait for bondsmen to appear. Curiously enough, Torrio did not bail them out, but William Skidmore and Ike Roderick, professional bondsmen, whose names have been associated both with gambling and vice, came to release them.

At this time Thomas Nash was attorney for the O'Banion gang. Later he was attorney for its enemies, the Genna gang, in the memorable Anselmi-Scalise case.

The chief of police, himself, tore the insignia from officers who were supposed to have been on duty at the brewery beat and were absent during the raid.

O'Banion, lieutenant of Torrio, had proved his power when he wriggled out of three tight legal holes that same year, prior to the Sieben Brewery raid,—the shooting of Dave Miller, chief of the Jewish gangsters; the "hijacking" of a truck-load of whiskey with Dapper Dan McCarthy; and the Carmen Avenue murders in which Two Gun Doherty was killed. All these cases had been nolle prossed by the State's Attorney, Mr. Crowe.

Torrio, O'Banion, Alterie, Nick Juffra who was among the earliest bootleggers to be prosecuted and already had a record as a bootlegger, and thirty-four others, including four policemen, were indicted. Torrio, himself, was a second offender, and would be subject to a sentence of five years on a conspiracy charge alone.

10. THE GOLD COAST BREWER AND THE UNDERWORLD CHIEF

It was the general understanding of city and government officials that Torrio and O'Banion were the real operators of the Sieben plant, with a politician and a "fixer" back of them sharing in the profits and distributing the graft, but that in this case, as in the Puro Products case, a pre-Volstead brewer was involved in the ownership. It seems that pre-Volstead brewers, who remained in the business, had called these gangsters in to do their convoying and to "front" [2] for them in case of a "fall." [3]

---

[2] Take the brunt of the law if discovered.
[3] Charles Gregston analyzes this alliance between pre-Volstead brewers and their new gangster partners as follows:

"John Torrio and a Chicago brewer are the twin kings of commercialized crime in Cook County today. They are the men back of the O'Banions and

Torrio brought O'Banion, the most daring and brilliant of the Combine's gunmen, from safe-blowing to liquor leadership. O'Banion soon earned a sizable "split" for himself. He had eyes "on better things" when he was killed, November 10, 1924.

Walter Stevens, Dan McFall, Dan McCarthy, Louis Alterie, Earl Weiss, Scarface Al Capone—all are, or were, subordinates in the crime syndicate,

---

Druggans, the guns and the gangs. They are the organizers, the directors, the 'fixers' and the profit-takers. Torrio is absolute in the field of vice and gambling; the brewer is king of the 'beer-racket.' They work together and the others, with a few exceptions, work for them.

"A strange pair: Torrio is a native of Italy, a Tammany graduate, a postgraduate pupil of the late 'Big Jim' Colosimo. His colleague is the youngest of four brothers who were rich brewers before prohibition. While Torrio was learning the tricks of ward politics in New York and the rewards of sin in the old Twenty-second Street district, and later in Burnham, his twin king of crime was living pleasantly on what is called the 'Gold Coast,' the son of a wealthy and established family. A common genius for organization brought them together soon after prohibition had ushered in the new era of crime through which Chicago is passing.

"They have made organized crime pay tremendous dividends. The brewer's earnings, from the syndicated beer 'racket' he works under political protection, have been reckoned at $12,000,000 a year since 1920. Nobody has ever risked a guess at the clearings of the many-sided Torrio.

"They are joint rulers of the underworld today. No one can run beer in Chicago without first seeing and paying the beer king. No one can cut in on the gambling 'racket' without Torrio's sanction. Immune from prosecution themselves, the two kings of crime can count on the law as well as their own gunmen when they want an intruder driven out. And they have the power to protect their henchmen from prosecution when murder becomes necessary, as it sometimes does. And the brewer is so completely above the law, so thoroughly protected from prosecution, that it is unsafe to mention his name, though the police and the prosecutors of crime know quite well who he is.

"Beer running offered Torrio a splendid opportunity. He had developed a machinery for 'fixing' the law and he had gangsters at his service; stepping up from vice and gambling to beer was easy and natural. Simultaneously the brewer was dabbling in violation of the Eighteenth Amendment. His brothers are said to have been frowning on his ventures, but their warnings weren't heeded.

"Natural attraction brought the pair together and their dovetailing abilities put crime on its new basis. Gunmen were lured away from the risks of highway robbery and safe-blowing to get into the far more lucrative business of peddling beer and driving out competitors. Breweries were leased from their despairing owners and reopened. Cheating saloon-keepers, thousands of them, found it easy to sell beer profitably after paying the syndicate $50 a barrel or more, and $35 easily covered the cost of production and the expense of 'fixing' the public officials, policemen and prohibition agents.

"The brewer knew the methods of modern business and applied them to syndicated beer runing. Torrio knew gangsters and recruited them. Thus Druggan and Lake were drawn away from the hoodlum activities of the Valley Gang into a 'racket' that made both of them rich beyond all their dreams. Working breweries for the combine, they soon were riding in expensive cars, dressing like millionaires and living in fashionable neighborhoods."—*Daily News*, November 17, 1924.

some of them important enough to be profit sharers, some mere hired men. They all danced when Torrio and his colleagues moved the strings—gangsters, gangleaders, and politicians.

Somehow, Torrio had found a way to keep the forces of the state's attorney's office away from his gunmen, and the raiding squads of Sheriff Hoffman out of his dives. Under public pressure sporadic raids were made, resulting in temporary and often momentary stoppage of operations.

11. THE OUTCOME OF THE SIEBEN CASE

A retrospect of the Sieben Brewery case three years after the indictment shows that thirty-eight men were indicted, including pre-Volstead owners, brew-masters, and brewery workers, laborers, and truck drivers, and policemen as well as gangsters. Four months after the raid, pleas of guilty were entered for eleven of the defendants, and the O'Banion case was dismissed on account of his death by murder. John Torrio was sentenced to nine months in the Du Page County Jail and five thousand dollar fine; Ed O'Donnell, eight months in the Kane County Jail and two thousand dollar fine; Nick Juffra, six months in the De Kalb County Jail and two thousand dollar fine; Joseph Warszynski, three months in the De Kalb County Jail; Joseph Lanenfeld, three months in the Kane County Jail; Richard Wilson, two hundred dollar fine; George J. Murphy, two hundred dollar fine; Arthur Barrett, two hundred dollar fine, and Jack Heinan, two hundred dollar fine. Warszynski and Lanenfeld were two of three negligent policemen assigned to the Sieben Brewery. District Attorney Edward A. Olson on the same day dismissed the cases of twenty-one other defendants. Among these were minor gangsters, two policemen, one politician, and the pre-Volstead owners.

On January 31, 1925, the judgment against Nick Juffra was vacated. Juffra was the most persistent offender of all the early beer runners. He had been arrested twenty-four times between the advent of prohibition and the Sieben Brewery case. The case of George Frank, the brew-master, was not heard until March 20, 1925. He then entered a plea of guilty and received a sentence of three months in the Lake County Jail and a three thousand dollar fine. The case of Louie Alterie still stands undismissed and unprosecuted, three years after.

12. IMMUNITY AND POLITICAL CONNECTIONS

Dion O'Banion enjoyed an amazing immunity from prosecution, although Police Chief Collins had accused him of responsibility for twenty-five murders. He was a Torrio man.

Terry Druggan and Frankie Lake were immune until they later became entangled in the toils of the Federal Government.

Frankie McErlane, the most brutal gunman who ever pulled a trigger in Chicago, went scot free when, in the interests of Torrio he and Dapper Dan McCarthy had exercised their talents for murder.

13. QUALITIES OF LEADERSHIP

The story of a midnight "hi-jacking" not only illustrates the level headedness which made it possible for Torrio to command the allied gun chiefs of Chicago, but also throws some light on the elements of the continuous warfare which resulted when Torrio's prestige was destroyed through the unwillingness of Mayor Dever and Chief of Police Collins to deal with him. It is a contrast of the expediency of the seasoned leader against the childish irresponsibility of his young lieutenant.

Two policemen held up a Torrio beer squad on a west side street one night and demanded money. By telephone, over a wire which had been tapped by the police, the convoy gangsters reported this to Dion O'Banion. O'Banion replied, "Three hundred dollars? To them bums? Why say, I can get 'em knocked off for half that much." Scenting trouble, police headquarters sent rifle squads to prevent murder if O'Banion should send killers after the "hi-jacking" policemen, but in the meantime the beer runner went over O'Banion's head and put the problem up to Torrio, "The Big Boss." He was back on the wire in a little while with a new message for O'Banion: "Say Dionie, I just been talking to Johnny and he said to let them cops have the three hundred. He says he don't want no trouble."

Such was the difference in temper that made Torrio all-powerful and O'Banion just a superior sort of "plug-ugly." Torrio was shrewd enough to keep out of needless trouble. When murder must be done it was done deftly and thoroughly, as in the case of O'Banion himself, who was shot in his florist shop on November 10, 1924, supposedly by the Gennas, Torrio followers; and of Big Jim Colosimo, Meegan, and Bucher. O'Banion, on the other hand, learned his methods from such practitioners as Gene Geary, convicted slayer, who was sent to Chester as insane, and Louis Alterie and Nails Morton, his "pal."

O'Banion first became friendly with them when he was Gimpy O'Banion, a singing waiter in the old McGovern place at North Clark and West Erie Streets. O'Banion had been a choir boy at the Holy Name Cathedral. The singing of songs, especially Irish sentimental songs, always won over the brutal Geary.

O'Banion, Alterie, Yankee Schwartz, Earl (Hymie) Weiss, and others of the Torrio following, had techniques unlike Torrio's quieter, "brainier" methods which made him boss.

14. THE WANING OF TORRIO'S PRESTIGE

To bear out the statement that the armed forces of Torrio were composed of the alliance of gun chiefs of Chicago, we list below some of the names:

Dion O'Banion	Dan McFall
Terry Druggan	Louie Alterie
Frankie Lake	Hymie Weiss
Frank McErlane	Scarface Al Capone
Dapper Dan McCarthy	The Genna Brothers
Walter Stevens	The West Side O'Donnells

In the Sieben Brewery case the prestige of Torrio was injured, because it was conclusive evidence that Mayor Dever and Chief of Police Collins were not under his control. Likewise, there was a concurrent weakening of his power over his gangs when the Genna and O'Banion feud began with the murder of O'Banion. Then Torrio himself was wounded by gunfire; when he recovered he actually welcomed the jail sentence, and safety. The Dever onslaughts upset the underworld regime and destroyed the equilibrium. The beer wars followed.

15. CONCLUSION

The career of John Torrio epitomizes an important stage in the development of organized crime in Chicago. Trained as a lieutenant of Colosimo, he was thoroughly versed in the technique of dealing with gangsters and politicians. As a manager of resorts under Colosimo he had survived all the crusades against vice and had learned how to utilize to full advantage the control of suburban villages like Burnham as open and unmolested centers for outlawed enterprises.

The four years following Colosimo's death (1920–1924) witnessed the steady rise of Torrio to a position of dominant leadership in the underworld of organized crime, a leadership which came to a sudden end with his arrest and conviction in the Sieben Brewery case. In this short period, which coincided with the introduction of constitutional prohibition, Torrio applied all that he had learned in his years of apprenticeship, to the organization on a city and country-wide basis of the new business of bootlegging. The general plan of conducting criminal business enterprises as outlined by Torrio, and which with modifications made by Capone still persists, may be summarized as follows:

1. The operation of pre-prohibition breweries was engineered by

Torrio with the connivance of officials and sometimes with the participation of brewery owners. With the improvement of prohibition enforcement the old-time brewery now plays a minor role in the illegal manufacture of alcohol.

2. Criminal business enterprises, like vice, gambling, and bootlegging,
were carried on under adequate political protection. Torrio's power
rested, in large part, on his ability to insure protection to his fellow
gangsters. Immunity from punishment appears to be an almost indispensable element in maintaining the prestige and control of a gangster chief,
as indicated by Torrio's retirement after serving his prison sentence.

3. Torrio was unusually successful in securing agreements among gangsters by the method of an orderly assignment of territory for bootlegging
operations. Yet certain gangsters, like the South Side O'Donnells, were
not included in these arrangements, and some gangster chiefs, like
O'Banion, chafed under Torrio's generalship. Torrio's victory over open
enemies like the O'Donnells was in part due to ruthless warfare and in
part to police activity against his rivals to which his own gangsters were
largely immune.

4. The scheme of orderly cooperation between gangsters engaged in
bootlegging which came into existence during the Torrio regime, was
disrupted before his retirement by the incoming of the Dever administration which destroyed the previous arrangements for political protection.

5. Bootlegging, because of its enormous profits, naturally became the
main illegal business enterprise promoted by Torrio and his fellow
gangsters. But with political protection they continued to carry on and to
extend the field of operation of vice and gambling enterprises.

6. Torrio was quick to perceive the importance of taking advantage of
the fact that the metropolitan region of Chicago falls under many different municipal governments. He not only utilized the suburban villages
which he already controlled in the metropolitan region of Chicago as
centers for bootlegging, gambling, and vice, but he extended his control
over other outlying communities. Cicero, as well as Burnham, River
Forest, and Stickney, became notorious as completely controlled for the
purposes of organized crime.

With the retirement of Torrio, Al Capone, his chief lieutenant, became
the principal contender for the position of leadership of the forces of
organized crime. While Capone has not as yet succeeded in securing the
position of uncontended supremacy held by Torrio, he has profited by
the experience of the latter. He has, for example, endeavored to detach
himself from first-hand participation both in criminal activities and in

gangster feuds. He has taken extraordinary precautions to protect himself by an armed force of body-guards against attacks by enemy gangsters. Capone has entered new fields of organized crime like business "racketeering" and has even attempted something like an inter-city federation of the activities of organized crime. And finally, he has adjusted the operations of his criminal enterprises more carefully than did Torrio to meet the exigencies of changes in the political situation.

19. Town and Country

The decline of small town moral supremacy in the aftermath of war helped give city life a stronger appeal to the American imagination in the Twenties than it had ever held, or has held since. Cities were the place to be, not to get away from. They were centers for business opportunity, for personal freedom, for cultural enjoyment, and they grew rapidly during the decade, putting up ever taller buildings in downtown areas and filling up outlying vacant land with new homes and stores. Skyscrapers created new skylines for the financial district in New York and along Michigan Avenue in Chicago. As city centers became less congenial places to live in, immigrant families could prove their successful assimilation into American life by moving to new single-family homes in nearby city neighborhoods, leaving their tenement apartments to Negroes newly arrived from the South.

Small towns, meanwhile, grew increasingly aware of their need for self-improvement, if they were to compete with the lure of the big cities. Planning and zoning experts began to apply their skills to small towns, and the more advanced towns of the Twenties laid down sidewalks, paved streets, put parks in vacant areas, and, most urgently of all, built imposing new high schools to provide their children with the academic opportunities they needed for advancement in the complex modern world.

Even the rapidly spreading use of the automobile contributed at first to the centralizing trend; people in the Twenties used their cars to get into city and town centers, rather than to escape them. But the automobile was also shaping the growth of new, low-built, and sprawling cities like Detroit and Los Angeles, and creating the problems of traffic and parking that already plagued most cities and good-sized towns. No leader of the automobile industry gave more publicized interest to the technological and cultural forces that were transforming American life in the Twenties than Henry Ford. During the Twenties he published a controversial anti-Semitic newspaper, the Dearborn *Independent,* and began collecting the remarkable array of American artifacts, machines, and buildings that form the holdings of the Henry Ford Museum and Greenfield Village, Ford's monuments to an American past his methods and products were so greatly altering. Into the Ford Motor Company in the Twenties came also many photographs of contemporary American town and country scenes. The following photographs from the Ford Archives, Henry Ford Museum, Dearborn, Michigan, reflect both the changes and the continuities in the American environment of the Twenties.

1. *New York City during a bus strike, ca. 1920.*

2. *Detroit from the air, 1927.*

3. *Detroit street scene, 1923.*

4. *Commercial Garage, Ridgewood, N.J., ca. 1920.*

5. *Johnston's Garage, Inc., New Paltz, N.Y., ca. 1920.*

6. *Interior, F. J. Hedges' Garage, East Hampton, N.Y., ca. 1920.*

7. *Interior, Drexler Motor Co., Thibodaux, La., late Twenties.*

8. *South Main Street, Henderson, Tex., ca. 1928.*

9. *4-H Club Event, Wayside Inn, Sudbury, Mass., mid-Twenties.*

10. *Railroad Street, Ironton, Ohio, 1923.*

11. *A railroad crossing, Carleton, Mich., 1925.*

20. Teamwork Pays Off

When news broke of the "Black Sox" scandal—that eight baseball players on the Chicago White Sox had taken bribes from gamblers to throw the 1919 World Series—the world of sports seemed to share in the general collapse of cultural order and moral certainty that prevailed in the minds of Americans after the war. Major league baseball recovered from that stigma, however, and went on with other sports to new heights of popularity and cultural prominence in the Twenties. Sports benefited from the economic prosperity of the decade, as well as from less tangible cultural needs—the longing for heroes, the desire for direct forms of competition in an increasingly complex society, the lure of sharing vicariously in the money and fame that sports brought to boys who were poor, like Babe Ruth, or members of minority ethnic and nationality groups. Sports did not play any one overriding role in the culture of the Twenties, for the sports world was ample, and accommodated many.

A great sports success story in the Twenties was the University of Notre Dame football team. Under the leadership of Coach Knute Rockne, Notre Dame teams from 1918 to 1930 went through five undefeated seasons and won 105 games, losing only twelve, and tying five. The Fighting Irish gained the loyalty of thousands of followers known as "subway alumni," big city dwellers who had not attended a college but who took pleasure in rooting for a team dominated by boys with immigrant backgrounds.

Rockne was killed in a plane crash in March, 1931. A year later, McCready Huston (1891–   ), a free-lance writer and novelist, published *Salesman from the Sidelines: Being the Business Career of Knute K. Rockne* (New York, 1932). The book gave an account of Rockne's business connection with the Studebaker Corporation, manufacturer of motor cars, from 1928 until his death. Huston's theme was that Studebaker hired Rockne to instill in their car dealers and salesmen a new set of values—instead of prizing individual methods and personal success, they should be convinced of the superior power of team play, practice, and planning, techniques that had brought success to Notre Dame football. To demonstrate Rockne's message, Huston printed the following text of a "typical Rockne sales address."

A Sales Promotion Address
KNUTE ROCKNE

That introduction by Mr. Hoffman was a lot shorter than he generally makes. He introduced Senator Johnson one evening and after the affair was over a friend said to him, "Paul, weren't you kind of nervous introducing the 'big shots' like the Senator?" Mr. Hoffman said, "Yes, but for just the first forty-five minutes or so." I want to thank him for his kind words, but they are the words of a friend; the only chaps who really know the football coach are the alumni.

I remember last September I received from one of these men a letter which went somewhat as follows: "I am delighted to hear that you recovered your health, but my personal opinion is that if that blood clot had been in your head instead of your leg you never would have been laid up."

Now, Mr. Hoffman made some jesting remarks regarding my work in business, and interviewing reporters on business, and when I was out in Los Angeles last summer I looked up his record and I found that before he became a star salesman and distributor and finally a vice president of Studebaker, he used to pick up some odd money officiating at basketball games and I tried to find out why he quit so suddenly. I found that he began blowing his whistle too often. The crowd objected; and the last game he worked he blew the whistle so often that the people thought he was a traffic policeman. That night he went back to the hotel and he awoke in the morning with four dogs in bed with him. I found out he hasn't whistled since.

Before I joined Mr. Hoffman on this tour I was up at Rochester, Minnesota, resting a bit and enjoying myself. Mr. Hoffman called me long distance one day and said he would give me twenty-five dollars a week and my expenses if I would go along with him on a speaking tour of Studebaker meetings. He even said he would pay me a little more than that, but I finally told him I wasn't interested and hung up. As I said, I was enjoying myself except for a few annoying incidents. Every once

Knute Rockne, a sales promotion speech, from McCready Huston, *Salesman from the Sidelines: Being the Business Career of Knute K. Rockne* (New York, 1932), pp. 93–115.

in a while a bellboy would come down the hall dribbling one of my checks back to me marked "no funds." That wasn't so bad until one of the boys brought one back marked "no bank." I immediately called up Mr. Hoffman and asked, "When do we leave?"

I don't know just what I am going to talk about. Mr. Hoffman asked me what I thought about Free Wheeling, for you know I have a new Free Wheeling automobile. Studebaker gives me one every year—very embarrassing. I told him I thought Free Wheeling was great. I said, "It seems to me Free Wheeling is going to be to the automobile business what the forward pass was to football. It has opened up the game, made it more pleasurable for both the spectators and the players." Free Wheeling opens up new areas and vistas of delight for the motorist.

But that is not what I am going to talk about. I don't know just what I can contribute to this meeting; perhaps my contribution will be along the lines of the assistance we got from one of our alumni last fall at one of the games.

This chap was up in the grandstand with some friends and he had a little bottle on his hip from which every now and then he took a nip. At this particular moment we had the ball on our forty-yard line—sixty yards to go for a touchdown. The alumnus turned to his cronies and said, "Watch this kid Carideo; he's a smart quarterback. I'll tell you what he'll do. He will cross them up and throw a forward pass on the first down." But what did Carideo do? He sent Savoldi right through the center of the line for twelve yards. Nonplussed by this, our tippling alumnus turned to his friends and said, "Well, Carideo was just feeling them out to find the weak spot. Now that he has found it he will send Savoldi through there again; you see if he don't." Instead Carideo sent Schwartz around end for fifteen yards. That did not bother our friend. He again turned to his friends as the teams lined up, saying, "Watch him now; whenever he begins using Schwartz that's the tip-off that means he is heading for a touchdown. He is going to continue using Schwartz, Schwartz, Schwartz." But instead of doing that Carideo dropped back and threw a forward pass to Conley at end which was completed on the two-yard line. One of the cronies by this time was quite irritated and asked the alumnus, "Well, Mr. Wisecracker, what is he going to do now?" To which the alumnus replied, "I got them down that far; they can go the rest of the way themselves."

I don't know anything about selling automobiles; I never sold one in my life; but perhaps a few remarks here on the psychology that is necessary for success in a football organization might not be out of place because it seems to me that the same psychology that makes for success in a football organization will make for success in any organization, and particularly in a selling organization.

Now in the fall when we make our first call for the team, about three hundred and fifty lads assemble in a large room in the library; and it is my idea to talk to them on the correct psychology before I take them out on the field. I talk to them on ambition and I tell them that most of what I read about ambition is bunk. There is not plenty of room at the top. There is very little room at the top. There is room at the top only for the few who have the ability and the imagination and the daring and the personality and the energy that make them stand out from among their fellow men. But there is success for any man in his own job if he does it as well as it can be done. As far as I am able to observe the greatest satisfaction I can get on this earth is to do the particular job I am doing as well as it can be done; and I think that holds good for every one. There may be other things that are easier, but they generally leave a headache or a heartache the day after.

I tell the lads there are five types I do not want. And I say the first type I have in mind is the swelled head. The man who was a success a year ago and who is content to rest on his laurels, who wants to play on his reputation. Dry rot sets in and he ceases to make an effort. To that kind of boy there will come quite a shock because the chances are there will be someone playing in his place.

The second type is the chronic complainer. They crab at everyone but themselves. And I say no organization can afford to have that type of man among them because complaining is infectious. And I say the complainer is in for quite a shock, too, because as soon as I can find out who the complainers are, why some evening when they come out for practice there will be no suits in their lockers.

And third is the quitter. The quitter is the fellow who wishes he could play but who is not willing to pay the price; and I tell the boys if one of that type is here he might just as well quit now and not wear out the equipment.

I don't want boys to dissipate physically or emotionally. I tell them that I have no brief against playing pool long hours in the afternoon, dancing half the night, or learning to drive an automobile with one hand; but I tell them we have no time for it. If we are going to compete with organizations who do not do that sort of thing and who are saving all their energy for the contest, I say do not dissipate any energy emotionally. By that I mean they should not give way to emotions such as jealousy, hatred or anything of that sort. I say that this sort of thing destroys any organization; and then I tell them that we should look upon one another in a friendly way. Look for the good in one another and be inspired by the fine qualities in those around us and forget about their faults. I tell them that the chances are that I will notice their faults and won't stutter when I mention them to the particular individual who has them.

There is a sixth type of man who suffers from an inferiority complex. He generally comes from a small community and he says to himself, "What chances have I got to get on the first string of thirty-three men when there are 350 boys trying for it? I don't believe I've got a chance and I don't believe I can make it." If there are any among you who feel that way, forget about it and get a superiority complex. I say to them, "You are just as good as any man here. And by getting a superiority complex you can show the coach you belong at the top of the thirty-three men where you think you would like to be."

I remember one year about four years ago I divided the men on the field in groups,—the ends, tackles, guards, centers, quarterbacks, etc. I walked up to the group of guards. Now guard is a position demanding a certain amount of physical ruggedness. There were fifteen good-sized boys in the group and one little chap whose name was Metzger. I said to him, "Aren't you a little slight and small to be playing guard?" "Yes," he answered, "but I am a little rough." The same confidence enabled him, in spite of the fact that he weighed only 149 pounds, to hold his own against any opponent whether he weighed two hundred pounds or more.

In two weeks I call them together again and tell them that there are certain among them who have great potentialities but that they haven't shown any improvement. There are certain among them that I do not want unless they change.

The first is the chap who alibis, one who justifies his own failure, and I tell them that a boy who does this had better watch out or he will get into a second class, that of feeling sorry for himself, in which case the bony part of his spine turns into a soft substance known as soap and he is absolutely worthless.

The second class of lad—I generally have very few of them—is the slicker, the mucker, who tries to get by by playing unfair football. I tell that type of boy that we cannot afford to have him on the team for he will bring discredit on the school and on our organization. I also impress on him that slugging and unfairness do not pay either in a game or in life after leaving school.

Then, third, there is the boy who lacks courage, who is afraid. What is courage? Courage means to be afraid to do something and still going ahead and doing it. If a man has character, the right kind of energy, mental ability, he will learn that fear is something to overcome and not to run away from.

And before the first game of the year I talk to them along the same lines on ambition. I say ambition, the right kind of ambition, means that you must have the ability to co-operate with the men around you, men working with you; and it is my observation that ability to co-operate is more essential than individual technique. In this day and age no individual stands alone; he must be able to co-operate in every sense of the word; and that is not a very easy thing to do in football because I know in our college we often get boys who have been spoiled by the home press in their high school days. They kick the ball well, and pass pretty well, and once in a while they run with it. They are all pretty good—if you don't believe it they have clippings along with them to prove it. Teaching co-operation is not always the easiest thing in the world to do, especially to a group of boys. I remember one lad who looked good in practice, a sophomore, and we decided to start him the first game of the year.

Three times they called this chap's number and three times he made long runs for touchdowns, sixty, seventy, eighty yards in length; and, of course, on each of these runs he had excellent co-operation from his team mates. The next morning I picked up the paper to see if the local sport writer would give credit where credit was due. Did he say that the outstanding feature of the game was the wonderful blocking and tackling, unusual for so early in the season? No; this sport writer knew his public and he wrote what he thought the public would like. They had five columns telling all about the halfback and full-length pictures of him—front view, side view, and rear view.

Well, this young man never had anything like that happen to him before in his life, so the first thing we knew he was suffering from that disease which we call in athletics "elephantiasis of the occipital lobe." It is not a very dangerous malady but it renders the victim useless for the time being. We gave him the usual serum treatment—ridicule from his team mates, the student body, and his best girl. That usually reduces the fever and swelling.

A few weeks later we went East to play the Army, up there on the plains above the Hudson River. This, of course, was long before the Army games were moved to New York City. By that time we thought the young man had recovered from the malady so we decided to play him. We had a beautiful setting; clouds of variegated colors were floating in the sky;

the boy's relatives were there to see him play. Anyhow, after a few minutes during which time this young man posed around evidently wondering how he looked from the grandstand, I put in the game a third string halfback who was anxious to go out and do his bit for the team and we were lucky enough to nose out the Army.

Monday, back in South Bend, we had our first practice after the game. The flash was sulking in a corner of the field. I did not pay any attention to him. Tuesday he was still sulking. I still ignored him. Wednesday he came to me and said, "Coach, I think I will turn in my suit." I replied, "I was just thinking of asking you for it." He said, "This is the most unfair treatment I ever received in my life. You disgraced and humiliated me in front of my folks." I said, "Don't you know why I took you out?" He did not seem to know. "I will refresh your memory," I said. "On two occasions when the Army kicked to us and after we failed three times to make any gain, George Gipp dropped back in punt formation and sent one of those long spirals soaring down the field. Every one of your team mates ran down the field just as fast as he could in order that the Army quarterback might not bring that ball back an inch. All but you. You were gamboling leisurely down the field. You were saving yourself for later on when they were to call your number. With the aid of your team mates you were going to get headlines in the New York papers.

"However, the Army fumbled on their own twenty-yard line and we recovered the ball. We lined up just twenty yards from the Army's goal line and little Joe Brandy, quarterback, turned to the team and said, 'This is our chance; now is the time to drive it over.' And he barked out the signals, clear, crisp and staccato, calling for a play where the ball comes to you and you take it around right end. Running just in front of you was your team mate, the other halfback, George Gipp; and his particular responsibility on that play was to take the end out and keep him out; and he did. You wriggled and squirmed for eleven yards before you were finally tackled on the Army's nine-yard line. I remembered the cheering of the crowd, mentioning just your name, as the teams lined up. Again Joe Brandy called signals, calling for the same play, except this time around the other end. The same play, except this time George Gipp carried the ball. You were expected to do for him and for the team what he did for you—take the Army end out and keep him out. And what did you do? You did not even annoy him, and George Gipp was tackled for a four-yard loss. The teams lined up and the same play was called again. You were given a second chance to see if you could fulfill your obligation to your team. And what did you do? The second time you went out there and leaned against the end, who tackled Gipp a second time for a loss. So I took you out, not because we failed to score at that particular moment, but because you did not have the sense of responsibility to co-operate and the sense of obligation, not so much to me as to your pals on the team."

Well, that lad had character. He was well bred. He learned his lesson and came out and did his bit for the team. The next year he developed into an All-American halfback, if that means anything.

In any organization no one man can enjoy the spotlight all the time while the rest of the boys are doing the chores. Each one has to take a turn doing the chores.

After that I began the practice of putting up signs in the locker room where the players had to read them. I put up a half dozen signs. One sign which applied in this particular case read, "Success is based on what the team does; not how you look." The result is I have not had much trouble along that line since, although of course, now and then I may have to hang that sign in an individual locker. When I do the boy will bring that sign back to me and say, "You got me all wrong, Coach." And I say, "Was that hanging in your locker? Oh, I beg your pardon." But it has its effect just the same.

Now I want to impress the necessity of co-operation on the minds of you distributors, dealers, and sellers of automobiles and trucks. Unless you understand the problems of production, enginering, bookkeeping, service, advertising and all departments that go to make up your organization, your organization cannot succeed. The failure of any one of them may cause you to fail.

Later on after a game or two, and particularly after a game where I have seen the lads give up, I talk to them further some noon on ambition. I tell them that there can be no ambition without perseverance. By perseverance I mean the ability to stick in there and keep giving the best of one's self. The ability to keep in there and keep trying when the going is tough and you are behind and everything seems hopeless. There can be no success, no reward, unless every man has the ability to stay in there until the last whistle blows.

I was down in New York not long ago, and in the company of Lawrence Perry I visited the Players' club. He was showing me through the club and was telling me about its being founded by Booth, the famous Shakespearian actor, and how Booth was the first president and under his guidance the club had always maintained a very high standard of membership. As we were going through we came to a room where there was a table and chair, and Perry told me that Booth was wont to come here to read and study. One afternoon while sitting and reading, he died. The table and chair were left in the same place in memory of Booth, and the book has been left open at the very place where he was reading at the time he passed away. Out of curiosity I stepped up to find out what he had been reading. It was Pope's "Essay on Man." "Hope springs eternal in the human breast." "If hope eludes you, all is lost."

Going back to Notre Dame I carried this message to the boys. I talked to them about it until I felt that every one of them was thoroughly imbued with that psychology. That year we had played our schedule of eight games, and the ninth and last game was with Southern California in Los Angeles. With but seven or eight minutes to play we were ahead seven to six. I, of course, thought the game was pretty well over and felt that the one-point lead we had was sufficient to win; but just then the Southern California boys began to collect themselves and started an irresistible drive down the field. I changed my guards and tackles and still on they came, three and four yards at a time, over our goal line for a touchdown, and although they missed the goal kick, or point after touchdown, that made the score 12 to 7 in favor of Southern California with about three minutes to play. "Well," I said, "I guess it's all over but the shouting."

We elected to receive the kickoff and brought the ball back to the twenty-yard line. Here we tried three plays without making an inch, so finally on the fourth down we kicked down the field to Southern California, who, much to my pleasant surprise, punted the ball right back as if to say, "There it is; what are you going to do with it?"

We had seventy yards to go. In those three plays on the twenty-yard line I had seen something I had hoped I wouldn't see. I saw ten men still doggedly trying for all they were worth, but the eleventh lad, a little third-string quarterback, was through. As far as he was concerned, the game was over. Hope had eluded him. I don't blame him, for he was just a normal lad only nineteen years old.

I turned around to a little chap sitting behind me on the bench who had been injured earlier in the season and had not played much—little Art Parisien. I said, "Art, how do you feel? Do you think if I put you in there you can pull old 83 and 84, those left-handed passes of yours, and maybe still pull the game out of the fire?" Before I had finished talking he had his headgear on and was on the field. As he was leaving he turned around and shouted back to me, "Coach, it's a cinch."

That may sound like egotism, but it wasn't. A man once defined egotism to me as "the anesthetic that deadens the pain of one's stupidity." You can be assured that that was not the case with this lad. He felt that he could do it for he had done it just a short time previously against Northwestern in Chicago, and he felt that he could do it because he was filled with hope.

On the first play he pulled a play of nine yards straight through the line, after which he called time out. Then he called those ten lads around him—for he could not talk to them until after the first play—and you could see him imbuing them with his optimism. He lifted those ten team mates of his; and to my pleased surprise, they did pull old 83, that left-handed pass, and it was good for twenty-three yards. I thought that was fine but I still didn't see how we had a chance. I thought it would at least sound good to the alumni over the radio.

There was now left only two and a quarter minutes to play. Next he pulled an end run to the right side of the field for position and there was less than a minute to play. Then he pulled old 84, that left-handed pass, to a lad name Niemic, who went over for the winning touchdown.

Winning the game is not important, although interesting. The interesting thing to me was the fact that this team wouldn't be beaten. It proved to me that the team or individual that wouldn't be beaten couldn't be beaten.

That applies to you automobile men out there on the firing line. You men are facing keen competition this year, perhaps facing more opposition than you ever faced in your lives, but I say that is the sort of thing you should thrill to—any kind of challenge. Any kind of organization ought to thrill to it. I think your organization, the Studebaker organization, has demonstrated that you can go better when the going is tough, so I say to you that this year you should thrill to this challenge.

Now I remember last Fall when we went out to Los Angeles to play Southern California, Earl Carpenter, Paul Hoffman's partner in Los Angeles, wrote a letter to Mr. Hoffman shortly before the game and told him to advise me not to go out to the coast because I would surely suffer a relapse because of the beating we would get from Southern California. He said they have the strongest team they ever had on the Pacific Coast, which means, of course, the strongest in the country. I read that letter to the players at Tucson, Arizona, on the way out to Los Angeles, and they thrilled to the challenge.

I remember very well just before the game in the dressing room everything was quiet. I could hear the band playing in the distance, and gradually the music died away as the band marched off the field. Pretty soon the referee rapped on the door and said we had three minutes to get out on the field. I turned to the team and said, "Boys, today you are going up against a great football team, how great we don't know, but I don't think they are a bit better than you are. I think you're just as good as they are." I went on:

"I think I know just about what shape you are in physically. I think I know what shape you are in mentally, and how much football you know; but there is one thing I don't know and that is—what is in your hearts. That is going to tell the story on the field this afternoon and it is up to you to go out there and show ninety thousand people just what is in your hearts.

"Now if we win the toss we are going to receive the ball, but if they receive we are going out there and tackle hard and play a good defense. I want you full of pep. Hit them hard and take the heart out of them in the first few minutes; and you men in the backfield play heads-up football all the time and watch for forward passes; and when that ball is in the air, go and get it. When we get that ball that is when we go to work. I want every man to block with everything he has in him and I want every man on the team to dig in his toes, lift those knees high, and when we start driving down the field for the goal line, that is when I want you to go, go, go, go, go, go!"

PART FOUR

FOUNDATIONS OF THE REPUBLIC

21. The Spiritual Power of Commerce

The Republican presidents from 1921 to 1929, Warren G. Harding and Calvin Coolidge, held a place in the affections of the American electorate out of all proportion to their later reputations in the perspective of history. Much of their power lay in their ability to connect their era with the past, an accomplishment of considerable importance to their constituents, though it may seem insignificant, or even incomprehensible, to later generations.

Cultural and social continuity was of great concern to the middle class native Americans who principally comprised the Republican Party in the Twenties. Their sense of cultural control and cultural order had been undermined in the aftermath of war. Moreover, they themselves were in transition, moving to a new cultural orientation constructed around the themes of business enterprise and commercial progress. They wanted to be reassured they were not breaking away from traditional standards, that their lives were still governed by the old genteel values of thrift, industry, individuality, and decorum. And they wished to be reminded, in a fatherly way, not to deviate from the old middle-class norms. During his nearly six years in office Coolidge (1872–1933) especially displayed great rhetorical ability in uniting old values comfortably with new business practices.

Coolidge's person, in itself, was enough to demonstrate the steadfast survival of past values into the present. His origins lay in the plain life of rural Vermont. Moving to a small town in Massachusetts, he climbed slowly up the ladder of political success. In 1918 he won the governorship of Massachusetts, and there he gained national fame by firmly handling the Boston police strike of 1919. Nominated for vice president by the Republicans in 1920, he succeeded to the presidency in August, 1923, when Harding died, and won the office in his own right in 1924. Even as he upheld old standards Coolidge vigorously advocated new departures in the areas of American policy of greatest interest to his business-oriented constituents, as in the following address delivered before the Chamber of Commerce of the State of New York on November 19, 1925.

Government and Business
CALVIN COOLIDGE

This time and place naturally suggest some consideration of commerce in its relation to Government and society. We are finishing a year which can justly be said to surpass all others in the overwhelming success of general business. We are met not only in the greatest American metropolis, but in the greatest center of population and business that the world has ever known. If any one wishes to gauge the power which is represented by the genius of the American spirit, let him contemplate the wonders which have been wrought in this region in the short space of 200 years. Not only does it stand unequaled by any other place on earth, but it is impossible to conceive of any other place where it could be equaled.

The foundation of this enormous development rests upon commerce. New York is an imperial city, but it is not a seat of government. The empire over which it rules is not political, but commercial. The great cities of the ancient world were the seats of both government and industrial power. The Middle Ages furnished a few exceptions. The great capitals of former times were not only seats of government but they actually governed. In the modern world government is inclined to be merely a tenant of the city. Political life and industrial life flow on side by side, but practically separated from each other. When we contemplate the enormous power, autocratic and uncontrolled, which would have been created by joining the authority of government with the influence of business, we can better appreciate the wisdom of the fathers in their wise dispensation which made Washington the political center of the country and left New York to develop into its business center. They wrought mightily for freedom.

The great advantages of this arrangement seem to me to be obvious. The only disadvantages which appear lie in the possibility that otherwise business and government might have had a better understanding of each other and been less likely to develop mutual misapprehensions and sus-

Calvin Coolidge, "Government and Business," *Foundations of the Republic: Speeches and Addresses* (New York, 1926), pp. 317–332. An address before the Chamber of Commerce of the State of New York, New York City, November 19, 1925.

picions. If a contest could be held to determine how much those who are really prominent in our government life know about business, and how much those who are really prominent in our business life know about government, it is my firm conviction that the prize would be awarded to those who are in government life. This is as it ought to be, for those who have the greater authority ought to have the greater knowledge. But it is my even firmer conviction that the general welfare of our country could be very much advanced through a better knowledge by both of those parties of the multifold problems with which each has to deal. While our system gives an opportunity for great benefit by encouraging detachment and breadth of vision which ought not to be sacrificed, it does not have the advantages which could be secured if each had a better conception of their mutual requirements.

While I have spoken of what I believed would be the advantages of a more sympathetic understanding, I should put an even stronger emphasis on the desirability of the largest possible independence between government and business. Each ought to be sovereign in its own sphere. When government comes unduly under the influence of business, the tendency is to develop an administration which closes the door of opportunity; becomes narrow and selfish in its outlook, and results in an oligarchy. When government enters the field of business with its great resources, it has a tendency to extravagance and inefficiency, but, having the power to crush all competitors, likewise closes the door of opportunity and results in monopoly. It is always a problem in a republic to maintain on the one side that efficiency which comes only from trained and skillful management without running into fossilization and autocracy, and to maintain on the other that equality of opportunity which is the result of political and economic liberty without running into dissolution and anarchy. The general results in our country, our freedom and prosperity, warrant the assertion that our system of institutions has been advancing in the right direction in the attempt to solve these problems. We have order, opportunity, wealth, and progress.

While there has been in the past and will be in the future a considerable effort in this country of different business interests to attempt to run the Government in such a way as to set up a system of privilege, and while there have been and will be those who are constantly seeking to commit the Government to a policy of infringing upon the domain of private business, both of these efforts have been very largely discredited, and with reasonable vigilance on the part of the people to preserve their freedom do not now appear to be dangerous.

When I have been referring to business, I have used the word in its all-inclusive sense to denote alike the employer and employee, the production of agriculture and industry, the distribution of transportation and commerce, and the service of finance and banking. It is the work of the world. In modern life, with all its intricacies, business has come to hold a very dominant position in the thoughts of all enlightened peoples. Rightly understood, this is not a criticism, but a compliment. In its great economic organization it does not represent, as some have hastily concluded, a mere desire to minister to selfishness. The New York Chamber of Commerce is not made up of men merely animated with a purpose to get the better of each other. It is something far more important than a sordid desire for gain. It could not successively succeed on that basis. It is dominated by a more worthy impulse; its rests on a higher law. True business represents the mutual organized effort of society to minister to the economic requirements of civilization. It is an effort by which men provide for the material needs of each other. While it is not an end in itself, it is the important means for the attainment of a supreme end. It rests squarely on the law of service. It has for its main reliance truth and faith and justice. In its larger sense it is one of the greatest contributing forces to the moral and spiritual advancement of the race.

It is the important and righteous position that business holds in relation to life which gives warrant to the great interest which the National Government constantly exercises for the promotion of its success. This is not exercised as has been the autocratic practice abroad of directly supporting and financing different business projects, except in case of great emergency; but we have rather held to a democratic policy of cherishing the general structure of business while holding its avenues open to the widest competition, in order that its opportunities and its benefits might be given the broadest possible participation. While it is true that the Government ought not to be and is not committed to certain methods of acquisition which, while partaking of the nature of unfair practices, try to masquerade under the guise of business, the Government is and ought to be thoroughly committed to every endeavor of production and distribution which is entitled to be designated as true business. Those who are so engaged, instead of regarding the Government as their opponent and enemy, ought to regard it as their vigilant supporter and friend.

It is only in exceptional instances that this means a change on the part of the national administration so much as it means a change on the part of trade. Except for the requirements of safety, health and taxation, the law enters very little into the work of production. It is mostly when we come to the problems of distribution that we meet the more rigid exactions of legislation. The main reason why certain practices in this direction have been denounced is because they are a species of unfair competition on the one hand or tend to monopoly and restraint of trade on the other. The whole policy of the Government in its system of opposition to monopoly, and its public regulation of transportation and trade, has been animated by a desire to have business remain business. We are politically free people and must be an economically free people.

It is my belief that the whole material development of our country has been enormously stimulated by reason of the general insistence on the part of the public authorities that economic effort ought not to partake of privilege, and that business should be unhampered and free. This could never have been done under a system of freight-rate discriminations or monopolistic trade associations. These might have enriched a few for a limited period, but they never would have enriched the country, while on the firmer foundation of justice we have achieved even more ample individual fortunes and a perfectly unprecedented era of general prosperity. This has resulted in no small part from the general acceptance on the part of those who own and control the wealth of the Nation, that it is to be used not to oppress but to serve. It is that policy, sometimes perhaps imperfectly expressed and clumsily administered, that has animated the National Government. In its observance there is unlimited opportunity for progress and prosperity.

It would be difficult, if not impossible, to estimate the contribution which government makes to business. It is notorious that where the government is bad, business is bad. The mere fundamental precepts of the administration of justice, the providing of order and security, are priceless. The prime element in the value of all property is the knowledge that its peaceful enjoyment will be publicly defended. If disorder should break out in your city, if there should be a conviction extending over any length of time that the rights of persons and property could no longer be protected by law, the value of your tall buildings would shrink to about the price of what are now water fronts of old Carthage or what are now corner lots in ancient Babylon. It is really the extension of these fundamental rights that the Government is constantly attempting to apply to modern business. It wants its rightful possessors to rest in security, it wants any wrongs that they may suffer to have a legal remedy, and it is all the time striving through administrative machinery to prevent in advance the infliction of injustice.

These undoubtedly represent policies which are wise and sound and necessary. That they have often been misapplied and many times run into excesses, nobody can deny. Regulation has often become restriction, and inspection has too frequently been little less than obstruction. This was the natural result of those times in the past when there were practices in business which warranted severe disapprobation. It was only natural that when these abuses were reformed by an aroused public opinion a great deal of prejudice which ought to have been discriminating and directed only at certain evil practices came to include almost the whole domain of business, especially where it had been gathered into large units. After the abuses had been discontinued the prejudice remained to produce a large amount of legislation, which, however well meant in its application to trade, undoubtedly hampered but did not improve. It is this misconception and misapplication, disturbing and wasteful in their results, which the National Government is attempting to avoid. Proper regulation and control are disagreeable and expensive. They represent the suffering that the just must endure because of the unjust. They are a part of the price which must be paid to promote the cause of economic justice.

Undoubtedly if public vigilance were relaxed, the generation to come might suffer a relapse. But the present generation of business almost universally throughout its responsible organization and management has shown every disposition to correct its own abuses with as little intervention of the Government as possible. This position is recognized by the public, and due to the appreciation of the needs which the country has for great units of production in time of war, and to the better understanding of the service which they perform in time of peace, resulting very largely from the discussion of our tax problems, a new attitude of the public mind is distinctly discernible toward great aggregations of capital. Their prosperity goes very far to insure the prosperity of all the country. The contending elements have each learned a most profitable lesson.

This development has left the Government free to advance from the problems of reform and repression to those of economy and construction. A very large progress is being made in these directions. Our country is in a state of unexampled and apparently sound and well distributed prosperity. It did not gain wealth, as some might hastily conclude, as a result of the war. Here and there individuals may have profited greatly, but the country as a whole was a heavy loser. Forty billions of the wealth of the Nation was directly exhausted, while the indirect expenditure and depreciation can not be estimated. The Government appreciated that the only method of regeneration lay in economy and production. It has followed a policy of economy in national expenditures. By an enormous reduction in taxation it has released great amounts of capital for use in productive effort. It has sought to stimulate domestic production by a moderate application of the system of protective tariff duties. The results of these efforts are known to all the world.

Another phase of this progress is not so well understood, but upon its continuance depends our future ability to meet the competition of the lower standards of living in foreign countries. During the past five years the Department of Commerce has unceasingly directed attention to the necessity for the elimination of waste. This effort has been directed toward better cooperation to improve efficiency in the use of labor and materials in all branches of business. This has been sought by the necessary cooperative action among individual concerns within industrial groups, and between producers and consumers. This does not imply any diminution of fair competition or any violation of the laws against restraint of trade. In fact, these proposals have been a protection to the smaller units of business and a most valuable asset alike to the producer, wage earner and consumer.

The result of the realization of these wastes and the large cooperative effort that has been instituted in the community to cure them, whether with the assistance of the Government departments or by independent action of the groups, has been the most profound factor in this recovery made in the past five years. There can be no question that great wastes have been eliminated by these activities in the business community through such actions as the abolition of car shortages; by improved equipment and methods of management of our railways; the cooperation with shippers to save delays; the remarkable advance in electrification of the country with all of its economies in labor and coal; the provision of better economic and statistical information as to production, stocks, and consumption of all commodities in order that producers and consumers may better adjust supply to demand, thereby eliminating speculation and loss; the great progress made in the technology of standardizing quality and dimensions in heavy manufactured products like building materials and commodities generally which do not involve problems of style or individuality; the reduction of seasonal employment in the construction and other industries and of losses through fire and through traffic accidents; advancement of commercial arbitration; development of farmers' cooperatives for the more economical and stable marketing of farm produce; and in general the elimination of waste due to lost motion and material throughout our whole economic fabric.

All this represents a movement as important as that of twenty years ago for the regulation of corporations and conservation of our natural resources. This effort for conservation of use of materials and conservation of energy in which our whole country has engaged during these five years has been in no small part responsible for the rich reward in the increasing comfort and living standards of the people. But in addition to bringing about a condition in which the Government debt is being rapidly liquidated while at the same time taxes are greatly reduced, capital has become abundant and prosperity reigns. The most remarkable results of economy and the elimination of waste are shown in the wage and commodity indexes. In 1920 wages were about 100 per cent above the pre-war rates and the average wholesale price of commodities was about 120 per cent above the pre-war rates. A steady increase in the wage index took place, so that during the last year it was 120 per cent above the pre-war rate. As the cost of our production is so largely a matter of wages, and as tax returns show that for the last year profits were ample, it would naturally have been expected that the prices of commodities would have increased. Yet during this period the average wholesale price level of commodities declined from 120 per cent above the pre-war level that it was in 1920, to only 57 per cent above the pre-war level in 1925. Thus, as a result of greater economy and efficiency, and the elimination of waste in the conduct of the National Government and of the business of the country, prices went down while wages went up. The wage earner receives more, while the dollar of the consumer will purchase more. The significance and importance of this result can not be overestimated.

This is real and solid progress. No one can deny that it represents an increase in national efficiency. It must be maintained. Great as the accomplishments have been, they are yet but partly completed. We need further improvement in transportation facilities by development of inland waterways; we need railroad consolidations; we need further improvement of our railway terminals for more economical distribution of commodities in the great congested centers; we need reorganization of Government departments; we need still larger extension of electrification; in general, we need still further effort against all the various categories of waste which the Department of Commerce has enumerated and so actively attacked, for in this direction lies not only increased economic progress but the maintenance of that progress against foreign competition. There is still plenty of work for business to do.

By these wise policies, pursued with tremendous economic effort, our country has reached its present prosperous condition. The people have been willing to work because they have had something to work for. The per capita production has greatly increased. Out of our surplus savings we have been able to advance great sums for refinancing the Old World and developing the New. While Europe has attracted more public attention, Latin America, Japan, and even Australia, have been very large participators in these loans. If rightly directed, they ought to be of benefit to both lender and borrower. If used to establish industry and support commerce abroad, through adding to the wealth and productive capacity of those countries, they create their own security and increase consuming power to the probable advantage of our trade. But when used in ways that are not productive, like the maintenance of great military establishments or to meet municipal expenditures which should either be eliminated by government economy or supplied by taxation, they do not appear to serve a useful purpose and ought to be discouraged. Our bankers have a great deal of responsibility in relation to the soundness of these loans when they undertake to invest the savings of our country abroad. I should regret very much to see our possession of resources which are available to meet needs in other countries be the cause of any sentiment of envy or unfriendliness toward us. It ought everywhere to be welcomed with rejoicing and considered as a part of the good fortune of the entire world that such an economic reservoir exists here which can be made available in case of need.

Everyone knows that it was our resources that saved Europe from a complete collapse immediately following the armistice. Without the benefit of our credit an appalling famine would have prevailed over great areas. In accordance with the light of all past history, disorder and revolution, with the utter breaking down of all legal restraints and the loosing of all the passions which had been aroused by four years of conflict, would have rapidly followed. Others did what they could, and no doubt made larger proportionate sacrifices, but it was the credits and food which we supplied that saved the situation.

When the work of restoring the fiscal condition of Europe began, it was accomplished again with our assistance. When Austria determined to put her financial house in order, we furnished a part of the capital. When Germany sought to establish a sound fiscal condition, we again contributed a large portion of the necessary gold loan. Without this, the reparations plan would have utterly failed. Germany could not otherwise have paid. The armies of occupation would have gone on increasing international irritation and ill will. It was our large guarantee of credit that assisted Great Britain to return to a gold basis. What we have done for France, Italy, Belgium, Czechoslovakia, Poland, and other countries, is all a piece of the same endeavor. These efforts and accomplishments, whether they be appreciated at home or received with gratitude abroad, which have been brought about by the business interests of our country, constitute an enormous world service. Others have made plans and adopted agreements for future action which hold a rank of great importance. But when we come to the consideration of what has been done, when we turn aside from what has been promised, to examine what has been performed, no positive and constructive accomplishment of the past five years compares with the support which America has contributed to the financial stability of the world. It clearly marks a new epoch.

This holds a distinctly higher rank than a mere barter and sale. It reaches above the ordinary business transaction into a broader realm. America has disbanded her huge armies and reduced her powerful fleet, but in attempting to deal justly through the sharing of our financial resources we have done more for peace than we could have done with all our military power. Peace, we know, rests to a great extent upon justice, but it is very difficult for the public mind to divorce justice from economic opportunity. The problem for which we have been attempting a solution is in the first instance to place the people of the earth back into avenues of profitable employment. It was necessary to restore hope, to renew courage. A great contribution to this end has been made with American money. The work is not all done yet. No doubt it will develop that this has not been accomplished without some mistakes, but the important fact remains that when the world needed to be revived we did respond. As nations see their way to a safer economic existence, they will see their way to a more peaceful existence. Possessed of the means to meet personal and public obligations, people are reestablishing their self-respect. The financial strength of America has contributed to the spiritual restoration of the world. It has risen into the domain of true business.

Accompanying these efforts to assist in rehabilitation have lately come the negotiations for the settlement of our foreign debts. Ten nations have already made settlements for $6,383,411,669 of these debts, exclusive of accrued interest. The principal sums and interest which have been funded and are to be paid to the United States aggregate $15,056,486,000. There remain nine nations, with debts in the principal amount of $3,673,-342,362, which have not yet been settled. Of the nine nations, France represents $3,340,000,000, Greece $15,000,000, and Yugoslavia $51,000,000. Of the remaining six, Rumania is now negotiating a settlement, Nicaragua is paying currently, and a moratorium for twenty years has been granted Austria by act of Congress. Armenia has ceased to exist as a nation, the Government of Russia has not been recognized, and Liberia owes but $26,000.

It has been the belief of the Government that no permanent stabilization of European finances and European currency can be accomplished without a definite adjustment of these obligations. While we realize that it is for our advantage to have these debts paid, it is also realized that it is greatly for the advantage of our debtors to have them finally liquidated. We created these values and sent them abroad in a period of about two years. We are extending the time for their return over a term of sixty-two years. While settlements already made and ratified by Congress, and those which will be presented for ratification, are very generous, I believe they will be alike beneficial to ourselves and the countries concerned. They maintain the principle of the integrity of international obligations. They help foreign governments to reestablish their fiscal operations and will contribute to the economic recovery of their people. They will assist both in the continuance of friendly relations, which are always jeopardized by unsettled differences, and the mutual improvement of trade opportunities by increasing the prosperity of the countries involved.

The working out of these problems of regulation, Government economy, the elimination of waste in the use of human effort and of materials, conservation and the proper investment of our savings both at home and abroad, is all a part of the mighty task which was imposed upon mankind of subduing the earth. America must either perform her full share in the accomplishment of this great world destiny or fail. For almost three centuries we were intent upon our domestic development. We sought the help of the people and the wealth of other lands by which to increase our numerical strength and augment our national fortune. We have grown exceedingly great in population and in riches. This power and this prosperity we can continue for ourselves if we will but proceed with moderation. If our people will but use those resources which have been intrusted to them, whether of command over large numbers of men or of command over large investments of capital, not selfishly but generously, not to exploit others but to serve others, there will be no doubt of an increasing production and distribution of wealth.

All of these efforts represent the processes of reducing our domestic and foreign relations to a system of law. They consist of a determination of clear and definite rules of action. It is a civilizing and humanizing method adopted by means of conference, discussion, deliberation, and determination. If it is to have any continuing success, or any permanent value, it will be because it has not been brought about by one will compelling another by force, but has resulted from men reasoning together. It has sought to remove compulsion from the business life of the country and from our relationship with other nations. It has sought to bestow a greater freedom upon our own people and upon the people of the world. We have worshiped the ideals of force long enough. We have turned to worship at the true shrine of understanding and reason.

In our domestic affairs we have adopted practical methods for the accomplishment of our ideals. We have translated our aspirations into appropriate actions. We have followed the declaration that we believe in justice, by establishing tribunals that would insure the administration of justice. What we have been able to do in this respect in relation to the different States of our Union, we ought to encourage and support in its proper application in relation to the different nations of the world. With our already enormous and constantly increasing interests abroad, there are constantly accumulating reasons why we should signify our adherence to the Permanent Court of International Justice. Mindful of our determination to avoid all interference in the political affairs, which do not concern us, of other nations, I can think of no more reassuring action than the declaration of America that it will whole-heartedly join with others in the support of the tribunal for the administration of international justice which they have created. I can conceive of nothing that we could do, which involves assuming so few obligations on our part, that would be likely to prove of so much value to the world. Beyond its practical effect, which might be somewhat small, it would have a sentimental effect which would be tremendous. It would be public notice that the enormous influences of our country were to be cast upon the side of the enlightening processes of civilization. It would be the beginning of a new world spirit.

This is the land of George Washington. We can do no less than work toward the realization of his hope. It ought to be our ambition to see the institutions which he founded grow in the blessings which they bestow upon our own citizens and increase in the good which their influence casts upon all the world. He did not hesistate to meet peril or encounter danger or make sacrifices. There is no cause which can be supported by any other methods. We can not listen to the counsels of perfection; we can not pursue a timorous policy; we can not avoid the obligations of a common humanity. We must meet our perils; we must encounter our dangers; we must make our sacrifices; or history will recount that the works of Washington have failed. I do not believe the future is to be dismayed by that record. The truth and faith and justice of the ancient days have not departed from us.

22. Working Women, Unoccupied Wives

Women as well as blacks benefited from the wartime manpower shortage, but work opportunities alone could not have produced the fundamental transformation that reshaped the social role and self-image of women in the Twenties. During the Second World War millions of women worked, over a longer period of years, but after that war women contentedly resumed a lifestyle celebrating female dependence and family togetherness. What provided women with the cultural foundation for their new independence and career ambitions in the Twenties was the breakup of genteel cultural controls after the war.

When the old modes of persuasion failed, genteel culture did not try to coerce women into observing prewar restrictions on behavior, as it resorted to coercion against drinkers, radicals, and immigrants. One compelling reason may have been that the energy transforming woman's place in American society—as in the triumphant woman's suffrage movement, in literary and intellectual circles, in scholarship and the social sciences—came predominantly from women with genteel middle-class backgrounds. The respectable rebels with serious ambitions to utilize their skills and intelligence, to extend their education, to enter professional and scholarly careers, created a cultural movement which supported the more publicized and widely experienced aspects of women's liberation from a passive domestic role—the working girls living independently, the new candor about sex, smoking in public, drinking in speakeasies and nightclubs.

But the Great Depression undermined the social and cultural conditions supporting the new role of women in the Twenties. In the following generation the trends of the Twenties were in fact reversed, and it was not until a new generation emerged at the end of the Nineteen-Fifties that women began again to think about their economic, intellectual, and sexual lives in a style resembling that of the Twenties. "The New Status of Women in America," an essay by Mary Ross, a Vassar graduate and an editor on *The Survey,* has the considerable value of seeking, at the end of the Twenties, to separate lasting and long-range trends from the fashions and habits of the moment.

The New Status of Women in America

MARY ROSS

Rather contrary to the views circulated by feminists and their foes, I believe that a clue to the new element in the status of American women is to be found in economic *dependence*. Slowly, almost unconsciously, there was evolved through the last century in this country a middle-class philosophy that the man's work should support the family. This is something new in the history of humankind. The work of the world never has been done by one sex unaided.

There have been whole classes—both men and women—endowed with sufficient hereditary wealth so that they did not need to engage in productive work. There have been women with such charm and beauty that they were "supported" for these exceptional qualities, much as the artist at times has been freed from the need to work for bread and butter by the interest and pride of a patron. But only in very recent times has it been possible for a people to live without the work of most of the children; and still more recently has arisen the idea that most middle-class Americans accept as a matter of course that the women as well should be exempt from the need to share in the economic support of the family. Europeans still look with surprise at the unoccupied wives of hardworking American business men. And it is with this phenomenon, I believe, that there have arisen during the past two or three generations many of the puzzling questions involved in the present position of women in America.

Preliminary figures from the Census of 1930 estimate that of some 37,000,000 American women between the ages of sixteen and sixty-four, about 10,000,000 are employed in "gainful occupations." Approximately 23,000,000 others are listed as "housewives" and all but a small proportion of these are doing all the work involved in "keeping" the home. Yet in an economic sense it is the first group—those who are working for money— who are closer to the traditional position of woman's lot. They are working

Mary Ross, "The New Status of Women in America," *Woman's Coming of Age: A Symposium*, Samuel D. Schmalhausen and V. F. Calverton, eds. (New York, 1931), pp. 536–549.

for the reasons for which women always have worked—to support themselves and their children. A series of detailed studies made by the federal Women's Bureau dispel any allusion that the work of wage-earning women is a gesture of mere "self-assertion" or "freedom." From the earlier government researches made of representative groups of working women, it is likely that 40 per cent of these women are or have been married. The march of American women towards the pay envelope was an effort to meet an old need in a new way.

Between 1890 and 1920 the proportion of single women (and the Census includes as single the widowed and divorced) increased 21 per cent; the proportion of working wives with living and present husbands just doubled. In 1920 (later figures are not yet available) one working woman in four had a husband from whom she was neither divorced nor separated. In a group of 40,000 working women in four different communities studied by the Women's Bureau, more than half of the wives had children. In one of the places, Passaic, N. J., three-fifths of the wives had one or more children under the age of five. Another study considered the comparative contribution of men and women workers in Manchester, N. H., to family support. Both wives and spinsters were working to keep themselves and their families. "Comparing single men and single women, the women contributed more extensively, both actually and relatively. Comparing married men and women, relatively to their earnings, the two sexes contributed the same proportion—practically all." ("The Share of Wage-earning Women in Family Support," a Bulletin of The Women's Bureau, No. 30, p. 65.) Especially at a time like the present when jobs are at a premium, it is likely to be assumed that wage-earning women indulge in work to get fur coats, permanent waves or other personal luxuries. For the vast majority, what facts there are paint a very different picture.

The new element in the status of these 10,000,000 American women is not that they must work but that the work which will bring an economic return generally must be done away from their homes and their children. In addition to a day spent in factory or office, most of them are still carrying many of the old tasks associated with women's work—cooking, washing, sweeping, mending, for themselves and often for husbands and children as well. What this means in strain and worry is hard to overestimate. The Industrial Revolution transferred the work of men from the farm or the home workshop to the factory, and by and large it limited rather than increased the responsibility and planning demanded of the individual worker. As its wheels have become increasingly powerful and all-embracing, in this country most children and some women have been exempted from the need to produce wealth—but for the remainder of the women, the anonymous millions who appear as mere units in these Census figures, the old lot of work has become increasingly complicated.

For most of these women the question of status is the question of how to get on at all, how to keep food in the children's mouths and shoes on their feet, to meet the rent bill, and with good luck to put by enough to let a promising child go through high school, to tide over the weeks when some one is out of work or sick, to mitigate the wage-less interval of old age. When the question of "status" crosses their minds, it is probably in the form of a hope some day to attain the luxury of the class next higher up, where the women—or at least the wives—do not have to go "out" to work.

It is in just this—the so-called middle class—that I believe some of the most interesting, and for the future most important, questions of status are now beginning to emerge. Probably it is permissible to look to the position of married women for the changes that are likely to prove significant. The spinster has and is blazing new trails; but except insofar as these have an influence upon her married sister, they are not likely to have an immediate influence upon the upcoming generation. Possibly this middle class is most reliable as a barometer in tribal ways, for it is not so protected by wealth and social position as to ignore changes in social pressures, yet it has sufficient leeway beyond the requirements of mere existence to admit of change and occasional experimentation. In the so-called typical American home, probably boasting a Ford and a bathtub, admitting a child or two, will be found the great majority of those 23,000,000 housewives, and with them questions of status important not only to themselves and their children but also to the army of women who work for wages.

And changes there are—at the present time—in the direction of economic dependence. In many of these families, perhaps in most, one would not have to go back further than the grandparents of the present adult generation to find something pretty close to the pioneer condition. We have heard repeatedly of our soap-and-candle-making grandmothers, of their chests of wools and linen spun and woven by their own hands, their cupboards of home-made jelly, home-raised, killed and cured hams, and the like. The corollary to this fact of history is usually stated only in terms of women: that the well-known industrial era has "robbed" women of their former jobs. Most of the talking about this change has been done, quite naturally, by women, for it is the women on whom the brunt of novelty has borne. And quite naturally these women, already perplexed by their own problems, have usually ignored the male side of the picture.

If the inarticulate husband and father of the past couple of generations had been aware of what was happening to him, he might well have murmured that after countless generations in which women had borne a substantial share of the economic (but not necessarily pecuniary) support of the family, now it seemed as though all the bills came home to him.

In *The Independent* of February 17, 1910, Simon Patten, the economist, made a prophetic analysis of a process that was already under way and since has gone much further. "Forty years ago," he wrote, "a man could live comfortably on $1,000 a year. Under the magic of his wife's hand this $1,000 became $1,500 or $2,000. The wife created more value by industry in the home than her husband did out of it. . . . Now all things are done outside the home and must be purchased with the $1,000 income. The wife no longer contributes to the family income by creating values, and with the increased standards of elaborate dressing, she is often its chief burden."

The parents now struggling with shoe bills and rent checks were children in the 1890's. Servants were still plentiful, cheap and willing, for the factories did not yet offer opportunities more alluring in money and independence, and immigration was at flood tide. Dressmaking was still done at home, a college education was the exception and still a privilege chiefly reserved for promising sons; wives, though they had lost much of their status as skilled producers, still retained considerable value as *entrepreneurs*. But as the general houseworker has been moving towards extinction and the machine has developed increasingly cheap and subtle skills, much of that value has left her. There is little use to complain of the change; steel *is*, for most purposes, more durable, more economical, than fingers. It has become money that makes the mare go—money to pay for canned tomatoes and a can-opener, to meet the bill of the commercial laundry, to buy clothing that large-scale industry can turn out at very little more than the materials alone will cost the housewife. We are used to the truism that machines have come to do far more cheaply and efficiently than fingers can most of the things that were women's work in the household. What has not been as clearly emphasised in middle-class circles is that as machines have taken over these tasks women have given up a good share of the economic contributions to the family that was theirs only a generation or two ago. What must be paid for in money usually has come to be the responsibility of the man alone.

Strangely enough, in view of the general alarm at a falling birthrate among the so-called upper classes and an increasing rate of divorce, little mention has been made in an analogous decline in the economic value of the unique feminine activity—the bearing of children. A recent dispatch from Jerusalem reports the concern of a British deputy over the amounts that Arabs pay for their wives. The price of a wife among these tribes, he reported, ranges from $100 to as much as $2,500; a man may go badly into debt, sell his land, put a lien on his future to buy one. When primitive tribes buy wives, they give wealth for wealth in return for the services of a woman who not only will scratch up the soil and plant grain and dress and cook the game, but who also will become the mother of sons to serve in battle and of daughters to bring wealth back into the family when they in turn are given in marriage.

In the pioneer home children were a necessity; even in the farm home to-day they are likely to be an economic asset. In the earlier industrial decades—and still unfortunately in the parts of these United States—the work of young children brought income into the family which probably more than counter-balanced what little had to be spent on their food, clothing, and shelter. When feudal lands, or even American farm lands, were to be consolidated the marriage of a son or daughter could be made a stroke of family fortune; when family businesses were being built up through the nineteenth century it was important economically, as well as sentimentally, to have a son and heir to take over the concern and further it. But now, as an economic activity, the bearing of children has become valuable only to princesses and peasants. For the greater part of our American people children are coming to represent an economic liability. Less and less is it socially permissible—or individually desirable—even to assume that they will aid in supporting the parents in old age. A farmhouse may be big enough to give a grandparent privacy; its activities may afford a sense of some usefulness. But the outlook is very different in all ways in a city apartment, where space costs per room, where food must be bought, where there is no front porch for a rocking chair.

In one of his invaluable statistical studies, Dr. Louis I. Dublin has assembled data to show that in an American family with an annual income of $2,500 it costs the parents approximately $7,200 in money, aside from the value of their personal service, to bring a child into the world and raise it to the age of eighteen. (Statistical Bulletin, Metropolitan Life Insurance Company, Vol. VII, No. 5, page 5). Against this, in our predominately urban civilization, can be set little economic return by the child himself. If these calculations be correct, such a family must spend from two to three years of all of a very moderate income for each child supported through, say, a high school course.

Nor does it seem likely that children will become less expensive. Education has moved out of the luxury class for the preferred and become, at the middle-class level, almost a necessity. Maybe a college degree is not a logical prerequisite for entrance to a large business house, but it is likely to prove at least a social asset and an increasing number of firms require it. Nor is it only the sons who must be educated. In another compilation, published in the *Atlantic Monthly* for September, 1926, Dr. Louis I. Dublin pointed out that in 1890 there were 163,000 girls in secondary schools in this country; in 1924, 1,963,000. In 1890 there were 84,000 women in the colleges and normal schools; in 1924, just short of 450,000.

Aside from the increasing costs of school and college bills—and even if the tuition comes free the pupil usually must be helped with at least part of the living cost—the sciences of preventive medicine bring many demands on conscientious parents not known before this generation. Tonsil removals, teeth-straightening, anti-diphtheria inoculations, periodic health examinations, summer camps—these are largely phenomena of the twentieth century. Moreover, the city parent must pay at every turn for things for his children that come without cost in the country—for space to play and sunshine in the apartment, for trips to the country, for swimming lessons in a pool instead of a plunge in the pond.

On the economic side, it is just here that becomes apparent one of the pressing question marks as to the present status of American women. When children are a financial liability instead of an asset, when the capacity of a couple to support them is measured by the money income of the husband alone, will the wealth of the country increase rapidly enough so that men's incomes can stand the brunt? Or will women in general turn work into current economic channels, if not for mere bread and butter, then in order to make possible the emotional satisfactions that can accrue to both partners only through parenthood?

I believe that to an extent usually not recognised by casual observers the comparatively small group of American "breadwinning women" in the professions and business represent earning for the sake of the family— for children present or future—for an investment in the joint future of husbands and hence themselves. They may not be obliged to work, in the sense that the money is necessary to pay the rent and the butcher and grocer; but it will provide the extra things—the better education, the occasional trip abroad, the week-end shack in the country—that are desirable family investments. Their work may be necessary to make possible the luxury of a child. I know of married women working in Wall Street, for example, who say that when the bank account reaches $2,000 they will take a year off to have a baby. And just this seems to me the important element in the present status of women in America—the effort to adapt their work to the existing order so that it will give them the satisfactions they crave as women. It is not "new" in motivation or purpose, but merely in method.

Whether such a change in method will work for good or evil is rather beside the point. There was vast indignation when maiden aunts became bachelor girls who preferred to work for pay in offices rather than wash dishes in a relative's home for their keep and an occasional dole of money. No one, I think, supposes they will go back; probably not many people feel now that the change has been disastrous. No longer is it generally a point of pride for a man to support able-bodied female relatives as he did when their work about the house had a tangible value; he might well feel indignant if it were required of him. Similarly for many women so educated that they have an economic value apart from child-bearing and housekeeping, it seems a strange choice to give up the possibility of children, or the best chances that they might give their children and also their husbands, in order to maintain the tradition of not working for money. They act not on "principle," but for simple reasons of practicability.

The increase of education has brought an increasing number of women to whom such a choice is open; and, in the ranks of the middle class, it is bringing increasing need for a choice. For an education for a profession, for example, is no longer so rare as to command a premium; and there is some evidence, at least, that the ranks of the so-called cultured have been slipping in economic status. Three years ago a committee made a careful study of incomes and living costs of the faculty of Yale University, where incomes probably compare favourably with those in all but a few similar institutions of the country. ("Incomes and Living Costs of a University Faculty." Edited by Yandell Henderson and Maurice R. Davie, Yale University Press, 1928). They found that "there is reason to believe that the economic conditions of this profession are now such as effectively to discourage many young men of high quality of intellect and force of character from adopting this profession." They found, moreover, that the real value of salaries at Yale, measured in their purchasing power in essentials and not taking account of the entirely new items such as telephones, cars, or appendectomies that have become almost essential to family budgets during that period, fell greatly between 1900 and 1914 and still further from 1923 to 1927. Their figures show that "the faculty as a whole, in spite of considerable increases, is unable by 12 per cent to live upon its salaries as well to-day as it could in 1913, remembering always that the 1913 salary scale was already far below what would have enabled the faculty to live then as well as it did in 1900" (page 29).

Somewhat of this same pressure has been brought, I believe, upon ministers, doctors, lawyers—and still the numbers of new recruits to these professions swell the professional schools. This is the pressure that may well reabsorb that leisure which the wives of professional men gained quite suddenly in the closing decades of the past century, assuming, as it seems reasonable to assume, that people still will want to be and to have doctors, lawyers, college professors and the like, and that women still will want to marry particular representatives of these professions. After an extensive study of living costs at the University of California, Dr. Jessica Peixotto concluded that in that community "not less than $7,000 is requisite to maintain a reasonable comfort basis for professional life. With any sum less than $7,000 much energy is deflected from constructive tasks . . . to go toward efforts to force a lesser total upward." (Jessica B. Peixotto, "Getting and Spending at the Professional Standard of Living." New York: The Macmillan Company, 1927). Yet a recent compilation of income by the National Bureau of Economic Research showed that a little less than 2 per cent of our 45,000,000 income receivers—about one in fifty —had as much as $5,000 a year.

For the wage-earning groups prosperity, even at the advertising point, meant that in December, 1927, President Coolidge and Mr. Hoover pointed proudly to the fact that our average industrial wage was $4 a day. If work was steady, that meant $1,200 a year; and at the time this boast was made, another branch of the government estimated that it cost well over $2,000 a year to maintain a family of five merely in health and decency. Supposing the family to be four instead of five, that still leaves a gap to be filled by the contribution of wife or children. Herein one succinct explanation of the 10,000,000 American women gainfully employed.

As the rise of the American middle class through the past century raised a considerable number of women above the need for economic activity, it gave scope for new developments not primarily economic in their nature. When one speaks of the unoccupied wives of American business men, that adjective must be construed carefully, for these women could arise to protest that they are far from idle. They raise their children—one, two, occasionally three or four of them—with a care probably unknown to any past generation. It is they who founded the great culture-club movement which was floated on the easy money of the nineties; they who spend the great American income, sustain its movie industry, buy or borrow the novels, support the fashion and the beauty-culture businesses, keep bridge and travel and religious and medical cults at high levels of activity, and help along the two-car-family standard.

Out of this sudden burst of female leisure have come many good things, much of the foundation of American philanthropy, for example. But the investment of that leisure is reaching, I believe, the point of diminishing returns. Many of the activities it founded have developed a point of specialisation which demands the professional: philanthropy, for example, has become professionalised social work. And the culture which rests on one-sex participation is sterile.

When women began to emerge from isolated unoccupation in their individual homes, there was a kick to be gotten, undoubtedly, out of mere sociability—Browning clubs, euchre parties, pink teas. The enormous force of the women's club movement and the drive for woman suffrage have borne evidence of women's capacity for joint action. But, as George Meredith points out that the art of comedy, the play of the mind, can flourish only in a society where the wits of men and women touch each other, so, it would seem to me, our exclusively female activities are growing stale even to those who have been most deeply concerned with them. The cocktail party, held at an hour when men (and women!) can come straight from the office, is likely to be more alluring than the pinkest of pink teas. The country club where both skirts and plus-fours appear on greens, presses hard on the city club created for male or female.

In the past leisure has been the possession of the rich and powerful, and in general, the joint possession of both men and women of those classes. It is this shared leisure of both sexes that is both interesting and productive—at its best, creative of art in living. A very different thing from a day which includes a shopping expedition, bridge-party, an hour with the children, and dinner with a husband too tired to talk of much but the stock market. For a time it has been a prop to female egos to believe that one was sustaining the charity or art of the world in preference to making jelly or re-cutting the children's old clothes, when a woman with intelligence and a chance for choice knew that she could save by doing the work herself only if her time was considered worth little or nothing. It has been a prop to male egos that have withstood the battle to a competence to be able to exhibit an unoccupied wife as proof of their own financial strength. But over a period of time most people cannot live by ego alone, and for some this process of fattening wives on husbands' work is getting dull. Or such at any rate would seem to me the implication of daughters from well-to-do homes who hunt up jobs and work hard at them; of the penchant for activity that has drawn a number of wealthy women into businesses of their own as their children grew up; of the avid questions which well-to-do wives and mothers ask of one who has managed to have both children and a profession; and the research by women, such as that at Smith College, to study how a life can be integrated to include both without sacrifice of either.

We have passed in America, I believe, the days of self-assertive and antagonistic feminism. The very word feminist has come to seem a trifle archaic. It came into full cry in the first decades of this century from women quite remote in purpose from the millions of Census breadwinners —women who were bound to "be" something, do something, to show the world. Because most of the non-domestic activities that they could choose were ordinarily associated with the work of men, their striving for assertion was likely to take the form of showing that they were as good or better than men. Naturally it made the men mad. Hence the talk that it was "unwomanly" for a woman to be a doctor or a lawyer or what she would. And that deepest of taunts—the denial of one's sex—embittered still further a sterile battle whose ammunition now is nearly spent.

By and large American women seemed to have proved to their own satisfaction and to that of the schools and universities that a woman can be a competent doctor or lawyer or financial specialist. Many of the women who did the demonstrating were brave and really interested in what they were doing on behalf of themselves and others; others were chiefly self-assertive. They worked against heavy odds, and usually had to buy success at the price of marriage and children, sometimes of charm and personal appearance, of being considered queer—as some of them undoubtedly were. The reaction came, perhaps most clearly about the time of the World War, in the swing from feminist to flapper. It was obvious by that time that women could get money or professional status for themselves according to their individual opportunities and advantages; but why get it, a young generation asked, at the probable price of so many other things? Wasn't it more sensible for an attractive girl to try to marry wealth and status, if she wanted them, than to try to get them for herself when the rewards in profession and business typically were for women less than for men and when she ran a risk of missing marriage altogether if she were too much concerned with work?

It seems to me that now in the big cities, where the stress is greatest, there is the small start of a reaction away from the flapper. Money is the symbol of this reaction but its essence involves more than money. It is the joint acceptance by women and men of sharing responsibility for the circumstances which delimit the possibilities of both and of children—present or hoped for. Many of these must be attained through the hard medium of cash. For our generation, more than that of any earlier time, money or its absence may determine leisure, health, education, self-direction as well as the kinds of satisfaction expressed in terms of golf and motor-cars. Such a partnership precludes the assumption on which much current middle-class practice—that one must earn while the other spends. And at its best it gives a chance for shared enjoyment and mutual understanding that is difficult when husband and wife move in worlds that hardly touch. Such an arrangement, if one could hazard a look at the future, might make an adjustment of "status" that would be brilliant not only for women but also for men.

But lest one seems to be overstepping the present into Utopia, it is well to point to some of the peculiarly trying difficulties in the current status of American women. Up and down the economic ladder, for all who must consider it, runs the one problem that is peculiarly modern: the one-time unity of a home that combined the work and leisure of a man and wife and their children has been split up. How evolve some equivalent that will give room for the common needs of food and sex and parenthood and fun? Unless American prosperity can be reborn and evolved with sufficient sturdiness to make it unnecessary for women to be economic producers, this situation will continue to place a special strain on women both physically and psychically.

Most women, I believe, desire both marriage and children, and especially since the conventional dictates of the church and the social order have lost most of their force, it is the women who want children who will carry on the race. Until the present century, it has been possible for the mother to aid in their support as well as their care while working under the same roof which housed the children. If she must go out to find work that brings an economic return which the family needs or wants, she must face a division of interest and responsibility, generally working as long a day as would a man, then coming home to take up again an emotional responsibility which usually she cannot and does not want to delegate.

It is difficult to shove professional interests aside for a few years and resume them as the children get older without finding one's self out of step. For many women who have been educated to be aware of other interests, it seems hard to regard the rearing of a child or two as the emotional outlet of a "life work." One's grandmother is likely to have had six or eight and to have run a number of infant home industries besides.

Moreover the average length of life in this country has been so greatly extended during the past half century, while the birth rate has fallen, that childbearing and rearing takes in points of time a far smaller proportion of the lives of women than was formerly the case.

Under the conditions prevailing in England from 1836–46 (analogous figures for this country are not available) only three-quarters of the girl babies born lived to be five years old, only half to the age of forty-six. Under the conditions of health and disease which existed in that country in 1910–12, three-quarters will live to the age of 40 and half till they are 64. It seems fair to suppose that in many a family the grandmother of the present young adult generation spent eight or nine out of her twenty adult years bearing and nursing her children, while the granddaughter is spending perhaps three or four out of forty. There is no longer the same need for a reserve supply of maiden aunts and other useful relatives to bring up other people's motherless children. Indirectly as well as directly the job that has been uniquely that of womankind seems to have dwindled in its proportion to an adult life. There has come, too, to the modern American mother a whole array of resources to take over some of the responsibility that once was hers alone: the baby health station, the kindergarten or nursery school, the public school and its health clinics, the public health nurse, the gamut of specialists in the growth, behaviour and needs of children.

A part of the dilemma of the present generation is a psychological hazard that may wane with time and other custom. The young middle-class husbands and wives of to-day were reared in homes of the brown plush era where the woman typically had little economic responsibility—and what she had was along the traditionally womanly lines. There is likely to be hurt pride on the male side and a sense of grievance on the female when circumstances dictate a change in that pattern. Such secondary reactions may well be bred out in a couple of generations in children who grow up under other arrangements and without the old expectations. At the present time it seems hard even for a husband who is appreciative of the advantages of his wife's wage-earning not to expect, unconsciously, in addition to this help the undivided interest and tranquillity that a stay-at-home mother may have had at the end of a day. With the best will in the world it is hard to forget the old divisions between "men's work" and "women's work" in an apartment kitchenette even though the well-being of every one will be aided by a pooling of all the energies left over from the outside jobs to do what still must be done at home. It is difficult—perhaps it is impossible—for a man to appreciate the emotional demands that young children make upon their mother and to take account of these, if they are to be added to a day comparable to his, in totting up the family's budget of vitality. While women still are newcomers in industrial and professional pursuits outside their homes, it is extremely difficult for them to find work except under the standards of men's work—and to these, if they add children, they must add these emotional expenditures that are one price of maternity. This new adaptation of the old status of women—looked at closely—has little of the glamour of "emancipation." It bristles with a thousand questions.

For some reason whose explanation I shall have to leave to the psychologists and anthropologists, money seems to have become a symbol of masculinity. Even a modern husband—if one may venture a brash generalization—probably could accept without a twinge of injured pride a pile of shirts that his wife had made laboriously and wastefully, if he considered her time and effort of any value; he might easily be hurt if she went out and earned the money to buy him those shirts, even though that process were much easier and pleasanter for her. He doesn't like to think that a woman's earning is necessary or desirable, though he quite readily would assume that loyalty to him presupposed her work for him at home. A modern young man out of a job will eat the food which his girl-friend cooks for him in her kitchenette—she, it may be assumed, earning the cost of the food and the kitchenette and supplying the elbow grease as well—when he would be hurt if she suggested paying for his dinner at a resturant where it would cost her nothing in work and probably no more in money.

In the little wave of self-conscious feminism that rose through a quarter-century preceding the War, many women were intent on earning money as a symbol not only of freedom but also of supremacy and self-sufficiency. They challenged the men—there wasn't much else for them to do if they wanted to do the things that were habitually those of men. It is this attitude of challenge, of a demand for equality, that still lingers as the connotation of the phrase "the new status of women in America." But the challenge at its peak affected only a negligible number of American women. The change which is moulding the lives of millions is a later chapter in the history of that industrial revolution which began to shift the workplace of men so radically a century ago.

For women as for men, the shift has brought "freedom" in a negative way: no longer is it necessary to work as a member of a family group in order to hold an economic footing. A man found it hard to run a farm without his wife and the unpaid labour of his children. Now he can run, say, a taxicab, all the more easily for not having what we call encumbrances. Similarly a woman had to marry to get a home to work in, unless she worked, unpaid, in that of a relative. Now she can get a job and a furnished room. If there are no children to support, she can usually resign from an unsuccessful marriage and look for some means of livelihood other than being a wife.

On the positive side, however, the picture is less clear. For men, typically, marriage requires a far heavier measure of family support than before. For a very considerable number of the women who marry it means two jobs—wage-earning and the remaining work of the housewife, for the doing of which by another, her wage is usually insufficient. At the other end of the scale it means that much of the economic capacity of women is used predominantly in consumption—in contriving to make the husband's salary go as far as it can, and that the economically productive work still left in the home brings a return far less than the woman's capacities might earn in outside occupation. The new thing is the leisure that has come to one sex. The old thing—and the thing which is the crux of the questions that beset women who have freedom to examine their status—is how to gather together the elements that make a life satisfying.

23. The Great God Fashion

Women's fashions were radically transformed in the Twenties. Hemlines went up from the ankles to the knees, and in offices, on buses, at parties, women showed their knees in public for the first time. Flesh-tinted silk stockings were worn, also for the first time, and the development of the brassiere during the Twenties encouraged many women to discard the Victorian corset. Moreover, two major developments in the economics of women's fashions that had begun before the war became socially significant only after it. One was the internationalization of style, with Paris taking the lead in setting fashion trends; the other was the mass production of ready-made clothing, making fashionable-looking clothes available at moderate prices.

Surveys taken during the Twenties disclosed that most men did not notice what a woman was wearing. Why then did fashion assume such great importance in the Twenties? Critics of the emphasis on fashion asserted that women were dressing not for men, but in competition with other women. Since working girls wanted to wear and could afford attractive and fashionable clothes, well-to-do women were threatened with losing a major symbol of status. Timeliness thus became a critical point for fashion-conscious women. They defined themselves as those who wore the latest original creations before the dresses were copied and mass-produced for shop girls. As soon as a style became common, fashionable women discarded it. These attitudes created the syndrome of style changes which the critics deplored as wasteful, especially on the budget of a married woman who wished to keep herself more attractively dressed than her husband's office girls.

The fashion pages of the *Ladies Home Journal* did not feature the shortest skirts or the most radical "flapper" styles, but they did speak authoritatively on clothing for millions of respectable middle-class women. Owned, like *The Saturday Evening Post,* by the Curtis Publishing Co., the *Journal* had been enormously successful as a touchstone of genteel culture and taste during the thirty-year editorship of Edward W. Bok, from 1899 to 1919. During the Twenties, under Bok's successors, the *Journal* changed to keep pace with the times. It gave considerably more space to fashions and especially to Paris fashions, a subject that Bok had resisted, implying that it was of interest chiefly to courtesans. The following illustrations show changing fashions of the Twenties, as depicted in the pages of the *Journal* from 1919 to 1930.

160   The Ladies' Home Journal for June, 1919

"These are So Pretty for Girls,"

They Will Help to Make

AS MISS FERGUSON'S impeccable taste in dressing is one of her many justly famed talents, you will be interested in these two pages of summer clothes for girls, which she has stamped with her approval.

IT IS to just such simple girlish frocks as these above that many women owe their youthful appearance and slender silhouettes. Lustrous melon-shaded sport satin makes No. 2216 a charming frock for summer afternoon wear. When a blouse dress (No. 2209) in a new crinkly crêpe silk requires a collar and gilet of contrasting texture nothing could be daintier for this purpose than crisp white organdie. White satin cording outlines the circle clusters.

WHEN one chooses such a picturesque dress as No. 2211, with a quaint little bodice of turquoise taffeta and a skirt of crêpe Georgette, gay with rosewreaths and dainty with flutings of plaited net, a black chiffon-plumed poke is an assured acquisition. Have you noticed how distinctive a dark-blue tailored suit appears against a background of gay-colored dresses? Its success would be certain if made of silk tricolette like No. 2210-1931 and worn over a filmy blouse of net and lace. Correct in every line is the good-looking blouse dress (No. 2176) made of cool white linen strikingly embroidered in black.

THE end of the school middy is the beginning of such pretty dresses as these two on the left, which are so becoming to slender young girls. Practical textures such as cotton crepe and plaid sponge made the first dress, with long tassels hanging from bound buttonholes, delightfully girlish. In glistening white madras is the other one (No. 2206) with a dainty cool organdie chemisette tied with a black ribbon. Pockets are still essential, as you can see by the pretty band edging the blouse. Net is a sheer favorite for blouses, and when made over a lace-frilled guimpe like No. 2215 with a rose-color ribbon they are ravishing.

1. Ladies Home Journal, *June, 1919.*

DESIGNS BY HARRY COLLINS

2667-2668

2657-2658

2660

2665

2657-2658

GORGEOUS AFTERNOON GOWN of white rough pongee (No. 2660). Effectively trimmed in bands of brick-color rough pongee, put on with a loop stitch of white mercerized cotton. This gown may be worn with guimpe.
Patterns may be had in sizes 36 to 42 inches.

AFTERNOON SUIT of attractive simplicity (No. 2667-2668); made of navy poiret twill with ruffles and narrow belt. The skirt is plain, but adds line to the suit.
Patterns for the coat (No. 2667) may be had in sizes 16 years, and 36 to 42 inches.
Patterns for the skirt (No. 2668) may be had in sizes 16 years, and 26 to 32 inches.

AFTERNOON GOWN of taupe serge (No. 2665), with straight and simple lines that are more eloquent than any amount of description.
Patterns may be had in sizes 36 to 46 inches.

SPORT SUIT of green and tan rough silk (Nos. 2657-2658). The box plaits form trimming on coat and skirt. Breezy and elegant. The front of the coat is shown on the seated figure on the left.
Patterns for the coat (No. 2657) may be had in sizes 16 years, and 36 to 42 inches.
Patterns for the skirt (No. 2658) may be had in sizes 16 years, and 26 to 32 inches.

2. Ladies Home Journal, *June, 1920.*

3. Ladies Home Journal, *June, 1921.*

302

All sketches above from Molyneux

4. Ladies Home Journal, *November, 1924.*

5. Ladies Home Journal, *November, 1926.*

6. Ladies Home Journal, *November, 1927.*

7. Ladies Home Journal, *November, 1929.*

306

8.　Ladies Home Journal, *February, 1930.*

24. Dangers of Mother Love

When genteel culture lost its persuasive force after the war, among the first to seek new sources of direction and guidance were parents and teachers, who required some form of cultural perspective in the raising and training of children. In retrospect nearly everyone could see flaws in traditional family life and education. Certain aspects of growing up had been treated repressively and furtively, others were distorted by excessive emotion and sentiment. Nevertheless, genteel culture at least had claimed to know the techniques for mastering the world, and provided young people a coherent vision of their future. Middle-class parents and teachers had not lost confidence in the future during the Twenties, but they doubted the efficacy of many old methods, and around them old values were openly challenged or ignored on many fronts. They needed a new principle to give order to their world, one that could help them fit their children for the life to come.

Their search was answered by professional social science. The social sciences had been expanding as academic disciplines for several decades, and in the Twenties for the first time they found widespread public willingness to follow their research conclusions as precepts for everyday living. Social science stepped in to fill the role genteel culture had vacated, as arbiter of values and instructor in preferred attitudes toward life. The most forceful claims to prescriptive power were made in the name of behaviorism. The pioneer behaviorist was the psychologist John B. Watson (1878–1958), professor at Johns Hopkins from 1908 to 1920. Beginning in 1913 Watson published a series of books and articles proclaiming that psychology could be made a "purely objective experimental branch of natural science." Human behavior, he said, consisted of body-motor responses to environmental stimuli, and he claimed that behavioral research would someday explain every aspect of human life in terms of stimulus and response.

Behaviorism's assault on the psychological idealism of genteel culture was congenial to the mood of the Twenties, and Watson's influence soared. In 1924 he became a vice-president of the J. Walter Thompson Company, an advertising agency. Four years later he addressed himself to the needs of parents and teachers in his *Psychological Care of Infant and Child* (New

York, 1928), two chapters of which are reprinted here. Watson's views of child rearing quickly found their way into many college textbooks and teacher training manuals.

Psychological Care of Infant and Child
JOHN B. WATSON

Once at the close of a lecture before parents, a dear old lady got up and said, "Thank God, my children are grown—and that I had a chance to enjoy them before I met you."

Doesn't she express here the weakness in our modern way of bringing up children? We have children to enjoy them. We need to express our love in some way. The honeymoon period doesn't last forever with all husbands and wives, and we eke it out in a way we think is harmless by loving our children to death. Isn't this especially true of the mother today? No matter how much she may love her husband, he is away all day; her heart is full of love which she must express in some way. She expresses it by showering love and kisses upon her children—and thinks the world should laud her for it. *And it does.*

Not long ago, I went motoring with two boys, aged four and two, their mother, grandmother and nurse. In the course of the two-hour ride, one of the children was kissed thirty-two times—four by his mother, eight by the nurse and twenty times by the grandmother. The other child was almost equally smothered in love.

But there are not many mothers like that, you say—mothers are getting modern, they do not kiss and fondle their children nearly so much as they used to. Unfortunately this is not true. I once let slip in a lecture some of my ideas on the dangers lurking in the mother's kiss. Immediately, thousands of newspapers wrote scathing editorials on "Don't kiss the baby." Hundreds of letters poured in. Judging from them, kissing the baby to

John B. Watson, *Psychological Care of Infant and Child* · (New York, 1928), pp. 69–87, 184–187.

death is just about as popular a sport as it ever was, except for a very small part of our population.

Is it just the hard heartedness of the behaviorist—his lack of sentiment —that makes him object to kissing? Not at all. There are serious rocks ahead for the over-kissed child. Before I name them I want to explain how love grows up.

Our laboratory studies show that we can bring out a love response in a newborn child by just one stimulus—*by stroking its skin.* The more sensitive the skin area, the more marked the response. These sensitive areas are the lips, ears, back of the neck, nipples and the sex organs. If the child is crying, stroking these areas will often cause the child to become quiet or even to smile. Nurses and mothers have learned this method of quieting an infant by the trial and error process. They pick the child up, pat it, soothe it, kiss it, rock it, walk with it, dandle it on the knee, and the like. All of this kind of petting has the result of gently stimulating the skin. Unscrupulous nurses have learned the very direct result which comes from stroking the sex organs. When the child gets older, the fondling, petting, patting, rocking of the body will bring out a gurgle or a coo, open laughter, extension of the arms for the embrace.

The love life of the child is *at birth* very simple as is all of its other emotional behavior. Touching and stroking of the skin of the young infant brings out a love response. No other stimulus will.

This means that there is no "instinctive" love of the child for the parents, nor for any other person or object. It means that all affection, be it parental, child for parent or love between the sexes, is built up with such bricks and mortar. A great many parents who have much too much sentiment in their make-up, feel that when the behaviorist announces this he is robbing them of all the sacredness and sweetness in the child-parent relationship. Parents feel that it is just natural that they should love their children in this tangible way and that they should be similarly loved by the child in return. Some of the most tortured moments come when the parents have had to be away from their nine-months old baby for a stretch of three weeks. When they part from it, the child gurgles, coos, holds out its arms and shows every evidence of deepest parental love. Three weeks later when they return the child turns to the attendant who has in the interim fondled and petted it and put the bottle to the sensitive lips. The infant child loves anyone who strokes and feeds it.

It is true that parents have got away from rocking their children to sleep. You find the cradle with rockers on it now only in exhibits of early

American furniture. You will say that we have made progress in this respect at any rate. This is true. Dr. Holt's book on the care of the infant can take credit for this education. But it is doubtful if mothers would have given it up if home economics had not demanded it. Mothers found that if they started training the infant at birth, it would learn to go to sleep without rocking. This gave the mother more time for household duties, gossiping, bridge and shopping. Dr. Holt suggested it; the economic value of the system was easy to recognize.

But it doesn't take much time to pet and kiss the baby. You can do it when you pick him up from the crib after a nap, when you put him to bed, and especially after his bath. What more delectable to the mother than to kiss her chubby baby from head to foot after the bath! And it takes so little time!

To come back to the mechanics of love and affection. Loves grow up in children just like fears. *Loves* are home made, built in. In other words loves are *conditioned*. You have everything at hand all day long for setting up conditioned love responses. The touch of the skin takes the place of the steel bar, the sight of the mother's face takes the place of the rabbit in the experiments with fear. The child *sees* the mother's face when she pets it. Soon, *the mere sight of the mother's face* calls out the love response. The touch of the skin is no longer necessary to call it out. A conditioned love reaction has been formed. Even if she pats the child in the dark, the *sound* of her voice as she croons soon comes to call out a love response. This is the psychological explanation of the child's joyous reactions to the sound of the mother's voice. So with her footsteps, the sight of the mother's clothes, of her photograph. All too soon the child gets shot through with too many of these love reactions. In addition the child gets honeycombed with love responses for the nurse, for the father and for any other constant attendant who fondles it. Love reactions soon dominate the child. It requires no instinct, no "intelligence," no "reasoning" on the child's part for such responses to grow up.

THE ADULT EFFECTS OF TOO MUCH CODDLING IN INFANCY

To understand the end results of too much coddling, let us examine some of our own adult behavior. Nearly all of us have suffered from over-coddling in our infancy. How does it show? It shows as *invalidism*. As adults we have too many aches and pains. I rarely ask anybody with whom I am constantly thrown how he feels or how he slept last night. Almost invariably, if I am a person he doesn't have to keep up a front around, I get the answer, "Not very well." If I give him the chance, he expatiates along one of the following lines—"my digestion is poor; I have a constant headache; my muscles ache like fire; I am all tired out; I don't feel young any more; my liver is bad; I have a bad taste in my mouth"— and so on through the whole gamut of ills. Now these people have nothing wrong with them that the doctors can locate—and with the wonderful technique physicians have developed, the doctor can usually find out if anything is wrong. The individual who was not taught in his youth by his mother to be dependent, is one who comes to adult life too busy with his work to note the tiny mishaps that occur in his bodily makeup. When we are deeply engaged in our work, we never note them. Can you imagine an aviator flying in a fog or making a landing in a difficult field wondering whether his luncheon is going to digest?

We note these ills when our routine of work no longer thrills us. We have been taught from infancy to report every little ill, to talk about our stomach, our elimination processes, and the like. We have been allowed to avoid the doing of boresome duties by reporting them, such as staying away from school and getting relieved from sharing in the household chores. And above all, we have, by reporting them, got the tender solicitude of our parents and the kisses and coddling of our mothers. Mother fights our battles for us and stands between us and the things we try to avoid doing.

But society doesn't do this. We have to stick to our jobs in commercial and professional life regardless of headaches, toothaches, indigestion and other tiny ailments. There is no one there to baby us. If we cannot stand this treatment we have to go back home where love and affection can again be commandeered. If at home we cannot get enough coddling by ordinary means, we take to our armchairs or even to our beds. Thereafter we are in a secure position to demand constant coddling.

You can see invalidism in the making in the majority of American homes. Here is a picture of a child over-conditioned in love. The child is alone putting his blocks together, doing something with his hands, learning how to control his environment. The mother comes in. Constructive play ceases. The child crawls its way or runs to the mother, takes hold of her, climbs into her lap, puts its arms around her neck. The mother, nothing loath, fondles her child, kisses it, hugs it. I have seen this go on for a two-hour period. If the mother who has so conditioned her child attempts to put it down, a heartbroken wail ensues. Blocks and the rest of the world have lost their pulling power. If the mother attempts to leave the room or the house, a still more heartbroken cry ensues. Many mothers often sneak away from their homes the back way in order to avoid a tearful, wailing parting.

Now over-conditioning in love is the rule. Prove it yourself by counting the number of times your child whines and wails "Mother." All over the house, all day long, the two-year-old, the three-year-old and the four-year-old whine "Mamma, Mamma," "Mother." Now these love responses which the mother or father is building in by over conditioning, in spite of what the poet and the novelist may have to say, are not constructive. They do not fight many battles for the child. They do not help it to conquer the difficulties it must meet in its environment. Hence just to the extent to which you devote time to petting and coddling—and I have seen almost all of the child's waking hours devoted to it—just to that extent do you rob the child of the time which he should be devoting to the manipulation of his universe, acquiring a technique with fingers, hands and arms. He must have time to pull his universe apart and put it together again. Even from this standpoint alone—that of robbing the child of its opportunity for conquering the world, coddling is a dangerous experiment.

The mother coddles the child for two reasons. One, she admits; the other, she doesn't admit because she doesn't know that it is true. The one she admits is that she wants the child to be happy, she wants it to be surrounded by love in order that it may grow up to be a kindly, good-natured child. The other is that her own whole being cries out for the expression of love. Her mother before her has trained her to give and receive love. She is starved for love—affection, as she prefers to call it. It is at bottom a sex-seeking response in her, else she would never kiss the child on the lips. Certainly, to satisfy her professed reason for coddling, kissing the youngster on the forehead, on the back of the hand, patting it on the head once in a while, would be all the petting needed for a baby to learn that it is growing up in a kindly home.

But even granting that the mother thinks she kisses the child for the perfectly logical reason of implanting the proper amount of affection and kindliness in it, does she succeed? The fact I brought out before, that we rarely see a happy child, is proof to the contrary. The fact that our children are always crying and always whining shows the unhappy, unwholesome state they are in. Their digestion is interfered with and probably their whole glandular system is deranged.

SHOULD THE MOTHER NEVER KISS THE BABY?

There is a sensible way of treating children. Treat them as though they were young adults. Dress them, bathe them with care and circumspection. Let your behavior always be objective and kindly firm. Never hug and kiss them, never let them sit in your lap. If you must, kiss them once on the forehead when they say good night. Shake hands with them in the morning. Give them a pat on the head if they have made an extraordinarily good job of a difficult task. Try it out. In a week's time you will find how easy it is to be perfectly objective with your child and at the same time kindly. You will be utterly ashamed of the mawkish, sentimental way you have been handling it.

If you expected a dog to grow up and be useful as a watch dog, a bird dog, a fox hound, useful for anything except a lap dog, you wouldn't dare treat it the way you treat your child. When I hear a mother say "Bless its little heart" when it falls down, or stubs its toe, or suffers some other ill, I usually have to walk a block or two to let off steam. Can't the mother train herself when something happens to the child to look at its hurt without saying anything, and if there is a wound to dress it in a matter of fact way? And then as the child grows older, can she not train it to go and find the boracic acid and the bandages and treat its own wounds? Can't she train herself to substitute a kindly word, a smile, in all of her dealings with the child, for the kiss and the hug, the pickup and coddling? Above all, can't she learn to keep away from the child a large part of the day since love conditioning must grow up anyway, even when scrupulously guarded against, through feeding and bathing? I sometimes wish that we could live in a community of homes where each home is supplied with a well-trained nurse so that we could have the babies fed and bathed each week by a different nurse. Not long ago I had opportunity to observe a child who had had an over sympathetic and tender nurse for a year and a half. This nurse had to leave. When a new nurse came, the infant cried for three hours, letting up now and then only long enough to get its breath. This nurse had to leave at the end of a month and a new nurse came. This time the infant cried only half an hour when the new nurse took charge of it. Again, as often happens in well regulated homes, the second nurse stayed only two weeks. When the third nurse came, the child went to her without a murmur. Somehow I can't help wishing that it were possible to rotate the mothers occasionally too! Unless they are very sensible indeed.

Certainly a mother, when necessary, ought to leave her child for a long enough period for over-conditioning to die down. If you haven't a nurse and cannot leave the child, put it out in the backyard a large part of the day. Build a fence around the yard so that you are sure no harm can come to it. Do this from the time it is born. When the child can crawl, give it a sandpile and be sure to dig some small holes in the yard so it has to crawl in and out of them. Let it learn to overcome difficulties almost from the moment of birth. The child should learn to conquer difficulties away from your watchful eye. No child should get commendation and notice and petting every time it does something it ought to be doing anyway. If your heart is too tender and you must watch the child, make yourself a peephole so that you can see it without being seen, or use a periscope. But above all when anything does happen don't let your child see your own trepidation, handle the situation as a trained nurse or a doctor would and, finally, learn not to talk in endearing coddling terms.

Nest habits, which come from coddling, are really pernicious evils. The boys or girls who have nest habits deeply imbedded suffer torture when they have to leave home to go into business, to enter school, to get married—in general, whenever they have to break away from parents to start life on their own. Inability to break nest habits is probably our most prolific source of divorce and marital disagreements. "Mother's boy" has to talk his married life over with his mother and father, has constantly to bring them into the picture. The bride coddled in her infancy runs home to mother or father taking her trunk every time a disagreement occurs. We have hundreds of pathological cases on record where the mother or father attachment has become so strong that a marital adjustment even after marriage has taken place becomes impossible. To escape the intolerable marriage tie the individual becomes insane or else suicides. In the milder cases, though, the struggle between young married people coddled in infancy shows itself in whines and complaints and the endless recounting of ills. Not enjoying the activities that come with marriage they escape them by tiredness and headaches. If his wife does not give mother's boy the coddling, the commendation and the petting the mother gave him, she doesn't understand him, she is cold, unwifely, unsympathetic. If the young wife does not constantly receive the gentle coddling and admiration her father gave her then the husband is a brute, unsympathetic, un-understanding. Young married couples who do not swear a solemn oath to fight out their own battles between themselves without lugging in the parents soon come upon rocks.

In conclusion won't you then remember when you are tempted to pet your child that mother love is a dangerous instrument? An instrument which may inflict a never healing wound, a wound which may make infancy unhappy, adolescence a nightmare, an instrument which may wreck your adult son or daughter's vocational future and their chances for marital happiness.

❋   ❋   ❋

After this brief survey of the psychological care of infant and child the behaviorist hastens to admit that he has no "ideals" for bringing up children. He does not know how the ideal child should be brought up. The standards imposed by present society are not his standards. He is often criticized for not rushing in with plans for instructing children how to grow up in accordance with the specifications of his Utopia.

As a matter of fact there are as many ways of bringing up the child as there are civilizations. The behaviorist might advocate a very different manual of psychological care for the Chinese infant from the one he would prescribe for native Australian or African offspring. There is no ideal system of civilization—there are only actual civilizations, hence the child must be brought up along practical lines to fit a given civilization. Had the child we picture here grown up in the days of Cotton Mather, he would probably have spent most of his time in the stocks for insubordination. Had he been brought up at the time of the French Revolution, he would have been looked upon as a gentleman who did not understand the virtues of fire and rape, and if in the times of the Crusaders, as a worker fit only to be farrier or artisan. Finally, had he reached adulthood in the balmy military days of Huguenot versus Catholic, he would have been called by both parties a wicked heretic only fit to be burned at the stake.

We must face the fact that standards of training are changing as our civilization changes—and civilization is changing under our very eyes at a far more rapid rate than it has ever changed in the past. I do not except here the changes that went on at the time of the French Revolution or those that are going on in the Soviet Republic. In both these instances the changes affected mainly the nobility. I believe that the internal structure of our American civilization is changing from top to bottom more rapidly and more fundamentally than most of us dream of. Consequently today less than ever before, is it expedient to bring up a child in accordance with the fixed molds that our parents imposed upon us.

We have tried to sketch in the foregoing chapters a child as free as possible of sensitivities to people and one who, almost from birth, is relatively independent of the family situation. Naturally we have had to give the child customary manners and to build up conventions in him, and to give him a daily personal routine since he must have such habits if his guts (emotional equipment) are to give him time to do anything else.

Above all, we have tried to create a problem-solving child. We believe that a problem-solving technique (which can be trained) plus boundless absorption in activity (which can also be trained) are behavioristic factors which have worked in many civilizations of the past and which, so far as we can judge, will work equally well in most types of civilizations that are likely to confront us in the future.

25. The Gospel and the World

Religious life during the Twenties was marked by great public confrontations and spectacles—Aimee Semple McPherson in her flowing robes, preaching at the Angelus Temple in Los Angeles; Clarence Darrow challenging William Jennings Bryan on the literal truth of the Bible, at the trial of John T. Scopes at Dayton, Tennessee, in 1925, for breaking state law by teaching the doctrine of evolution. But beyond the deep and serious conflict between fundamentalism and liberalism in the American Protestant churches, there lay an even more significant issue: whether religion could relate at all to the modern urban-industrial culture that, for the first time in the Twenties, began clearly and openly to dominate American life.

It was probably a matter of chance that placed the young minister Reinhold Niebuhr (1892–   ), at a major center of the new industrial culture in the Twenties. The son of a clergyman of Wright City, Missouri, Niebuhr was educated at Elmhurst College and Eden Theological Seminary, then went on for two more years of study at Yale Divinity School, where he received a B.D. degree in 1914 and an M.A. in 1915. He was ordained a minister in the Evangelical Synod of North America in 1915 and accepted a pastorate at Bethel Evangelical Church in Detroit.

Detroit in 1915 was on the threshold of becoming the automobile manufacturing center of the world. In the thirteen years Niebuhr spent there, from 1915 to 1928, Detroit's population jumped from 500,000 to one and one-half million. Racial clashes broke out, particularly over housing, and the auto industry fought to prevent unions from organizing their workers. "During these years," Niebuhr later wrote, "I became interested in problems of industrial justice and became painfully aware of the fact that the 'liberal' church preached the good life in terms of as complete irrelevance to the problems of industrial society as the orthodox church." Niebuhr left Detroit in 1928 to join the faculty of Union Theological Seminary in New York. The following year he published his first book, *Leaves from the Notebook of a Tamed Cynic* (Chicago & New York, 1929), a diary of his pastorate in Detroit; selections are reprinted here. Three years later, in 1932, Niebuhr brought out *Moral Man and Immoral Society,* his famous attack on the liberal doctrines in religion, politics, and social thought.

Leaves from the Notebook of a Tamed Cynic
REINHOLD NIEBUHR

1920

I am really beginning to like the ministry. I think since I have stopped worrying so much about the intellectual problems of religion and have begun to explore some of its ethical problems there is more of a thrill in preaching. The real meaning of the gospel is in conflict with most of the customs and attitudes of our day at so many places that there is adventure in the Christian message, even if you only play around with its ideas in a conventional world. I can't say that I have done anything in my life to dramatize the conflict between the gospel and the world. But I find it increasingly interesting to set the two in juxtaposition at least in my mind and in the minds of others. And of course ideas may finally lead to action.

A young woman came to me the other day in——and told me that my talk on forgiveness in the C—— Church of that town several months ago has brought about a reconciliation between her mother and sister after the two had been in a feud for five years. I accepted the news with more outward than inward composure. There is redemptive power in the message! I could go on the new courage that came out of that little victory for many a month.

I think I am beginning to like the ministry also because it gives you a splendid opportunity to have all kinds of contacts with people in relationships in which they are at their best. You do get tired of human pettiness at times. But there is nevertheless something quite glorious about folks. That is particularly true when you find them bearing sorrow with real patience. Think of Mrs. —— putting up with that drunkard of a husband for the sake of her children—and having such nice children. One can learn more from her quiet courage than from many a book.

Reinhold Niebuhr, *Leaves from the Notebook of a Tamed Cynic* (Chicago and New York, 1929), pp. 27–28, 49, 78–79, 82–84, 111–113, 116–117, 141–144, 147–150, 154–155, 163–165, 195–198.

1923

This has been a wonderful Christmas season. The people have been splendid. It is fun to go into the homes and see the laughter and joy of the children. It is rewarding to see how the people respond to our call for Christmas giving among the poor. The church was piled high yesterday with groceries and toys of every description. There is so much that is good in human nature.

Of course the cynics will say that it is easier to be charitable than to be just, and the astute social observers will note that what we give for the needy is but a small fraction of what we spend on ourselves. After all, the spirit of love is still pretty well isolated in the family life. If I had a family maybe that thought would never occur to me. The old Methodist preacher who told me some time ago that I was so cantankerous in my spirit of criticism about modern society because I am not married may be right. If I had about four children to love I might not care so much about insisting that the spirit of love shall dominate all human affairs. And there might be more value in loving the four children than in paying lip service to the spirit of love as I do.

1925

We went through one of the big automobile factories today. So artificial is life that these factories are like a strange world to me though I have lived close to them for many years. The foundry interested me particularly. The heat was terrific. The men seemed weary. Here manual labor is a drudgery and toil is slavery. The men cannot possibly find any satisfaction in their work. They simply work to make a living. Their sweat and their dull pain are part of the price paid for the fine cars we all run. And most of us run the cars without knowing what price is being paid for them.

Looking at these men the words of Markham's "The Man with the Hoe" came to me. A man with a hoe is a happy creature besides these suffering souls.

"The emptiness of ages in his face"

.   .   .   .

"Who made him dead to rapture and despair,
A thing that grieves not and that never hopes,
Stolid and stunned, a brother to the ox?"

We are all responsible. We all want the things which the factory produces and none of us is sensitive enough to care how much in human values the efficiency of the modern factory costs. Beside the brutal facts of modern industrial life, how futile are all our homiletical spoutings! The church is undoubtedly cultivating graces and preserving spiritual amenities in the more protected areas of society. But it isn't changing the essential facts of modern industrial civilization by a hair's breadth. It isn't even thinking about them.

The morality of the church is anachronistic. Will it ever develop a moral insight and courage sufficient to cope with the real problems of modern society? If it does it will require generations of effort and not a few martyrdoms. We ministers maintain our pride and self-respect and our sense of importance only through a vast and inclusive ignorance. If we knew the world in which we live a little better we would perish in shame or be overcome by a sense of futility.

1925

On a Western Trip

Out here on the Pacific coast, particularly in Los Angeles, one is forcibly impressed with the influence of environment upon religion. Every kind of cult seems to flourish in Los Angeles, and most of them are pantheistic. Every sorry oriental religious nostrum is borrowed in the vain effort to give meaning to pointless lives and to impart a thrill to vacuous existences. The pantheism is partly due, no doubt, to the salubrious nature of the southern California climate. Wherever nature is unusually benignant, men tend to identify God and the natural world and to lose all moral vigor in the process.

But that is hardly the whole explanation. There are too many retired people in Los Angeles. They left the communities where their personalities had some social significance in order to vegetate on these pleasant shores. In this sorry and monotonous existence they try to save their self-respect by grasping for some religious faith which will not disturb their ease by any too rigorous ethical demands. Of course Aimee Semple McPherson is more successful than the pantheistic cults. She fights the devil and gives the people a good show. She storms against the vices which flourish in this paradise without touching their roots. Furthermore she has the art of casting the glow of religious imagination over sensuality without changing its essential nature. In that art she seems to be typical rather than unique for this whole civilization. If she is unique it is only in her success.

They are always telling me that Detroit is the most typically American of our cities. Perhaps Detroit is typical of the America which works feverishly to get what it wants, while Los Angeles is typical of the America which has secured what it wants. On the whole I prefer the former to the latter. An honest enthusiasm even for inadequate ends is better than a vacuous existence from which even the charm of an imperfect ambition has departed. Of course the paganism of power is more dangerous than the paganism of pleasure, but from the perspective of a mere observer it is more interesting. Who would not prefer Napoleon to his imbecile brothers who merely luxuriated in the prosperity created by his ambition?

Only in the case of complete innocency, as that of a child's, is life more beautiful in repose than in activity. Character is created by a balance of tensions, and is more lovely even when the balance is imperfect than in a state of complete relaxation.

Of course Los Angeles has more culture than our midwestern cities. Culture flourishes in leisure and sometimes redeems it. But it will be a long time before this kind of leisure will produce more than dilettantism.

1926

The excitement about the Federation of Labor convention in Detroit subsided, but there are echoes of the event in various magazines. Several ministers have been commended for "courage" because they permitted labor leaders to speak in their churches who represented pretty much their own convictions and said pretty much what they had been saying for years.

It does seem pretty bad to have the churches lined up so solidly against labor and for the open shop policy of the town. The ministers are hardly to blame, except if they are to be condemned for not bringing out the meaning of Christianity for industrial relations more clearly in their ministry previous to the moment of crisis. As it was, few of the churches were sufficiently liberal to be able to risk an heretical voice in their pulpits. The idea that these A. F. of L. leaders are dangerous heretics is itself a rather illuminating clue to the mind of Detroit. I attended several sessions of the convention and the men impressed me as having about the same amount of daring and imagination as a group of village bankers.

The ministers of the country are by various methods dissociating themselves from the Detroit churches and are implying that they would have acted more generously in a like situation. Perhaps so. There are few cities in which wealth, suddenly acquired and proud of the mechanical efficiency which produced it, is so little mellowed by social intelligence. Detroit produces automobiles and is not yet willing to admit that the poor automata who are geared in on the production lines have any human problems.

Yet we differ only in degree from the rest of the country. The churches of America are on the whole thoroughly committed to the interests and prejudices of the middle classes. I think it is a bit of unwarranted optimism to expect them to make any serious contribution to the reorganization of society. I still have hopes that they will become sufficiently intelligent and heroic to develop some qualifying considerations in the great industrial struggle, but I can no longer envisage them as really determining factors in the struggle. Neither am I able for this reason to regard them as totally useless, as some of the critics do.

The ethical reconstruction of modern industrial society is, to be sure, a very important problem, but it is not the only concern of mankind. The spiritual amenities and moral decencies which the churches help to develop and preserve in the private lives of individuals are worth something for their own sake. Yet it must be obvious that if anyone is chosen by talent and destiny to put his life into the industrial struggle, the church is hardly his best vehicle.

The church is like the Red Cross service in war time. It keeps life from degenerating into a consistent inhumanity, but it does not materially alter the fact of the struggle itself. The Red Cross neither wins the war nor abolishes it. Since the struggle between those who have and those who have not is a never-ending one, society will always be, in a sense, a battleground. It is therefore of some importance that human loveliness be preserved outside of the battle lines. But those who are engaged in this task ought to realize that the brutalities of the conflict may easily negate the most painstaking humanizing efforts behind the lines, and that these efforts may become a method for evading the dangers and risks of the battlefield.

If religion is to contribute anything to the solution of the industrial problem, a more heroic type of religion than flourishes in the average church must be set to the task. I don't believe that the men who are driven by that kind of religion need to dissociate themselves from the churches, but they must bind themselves together in more effective association than they now possess.

1926

That resolution we passed in our pastors' meeting, calling upon the police to be more rigorous in the enforcement of law, is a nice admission of defeat upon the part of the church. Every one of our cities has a crime problem, not so much because the police are not vigilant as because great masses of men in an urban community are undisciplined and chaotic souls, emancipated from the traditions which guided their fathers and incapable of forming new and equally potent cultural and moral restraints. The children of the puritans are in this respect no better than the children of the immigrants. Both have reacted against traditions which do not fit their new cricumstances and both are unable to escape license by new and better standards.

Perhaps the real reason that we live such chaotic lives in urban communities is because a city is not a society at all, and moral standards are formed only in societies and through the sense of mutual obligation which neighbors feel for one another. A big city is not a society held together by human bonds. It is a mass of individuals, held together by a productive process. Its people are spiritually isolated even though they are mechanically dependent upon one another. In such a situation it is difficult to create and preserve the moral and cultural traditions which each individual needs to save his life from anarchy.

All of us do not live in moral chaos. But in so far as we escape it, it is due to our loyalty to religious, moral and cultural traditions which have come out of other ages and other circumstances. That is why churches, Protestant, Catholic and Jewish, however irrelevant their ethical idealism may be to the main facts of an industrial civilization, are nevertheless indispensable. It is enough that our society should be morally chaotic without also losing the kind of moral restraint which still determines the life of many individuals.

There is something very pathetic about the efforts of almost every one of our large cities to restore by police coercion what has been lost by the decay of moral and cultural traditions. But of course we do have to save ourselves from anarchy, even if it must be done by force. Only I think the church would do well to leave the police problem alone. If violence must be used temporarily, let the state do so without undue encouragement from the church. The church must work in another field and if it has failed in that field, it cannot recoup its failures by giving advice to the police department. The priest as a sublimated policeman is a sorry spectacle.

1927

Talked today at the open forum which meets every Sunday afternoon in the high school. The "lunatic fringe" of the city congregates there, in addition to many sensible people. The question period in such meetings is unfortunately monopolized to a great extent by the foolish ones, though not always. Today one old gentleman wanted to know when I thought the Lord would come again, while a young fellow spoke volubly on communism and ended by challenging me to admit that all religion is fantasy. Between those two you have the story of the tragic state of religion in modern life. One half of the world seems to believe that every poetic symbol with which religion must deal is an exact definition of a concrete or an historical fact; the other half, having learned that this is not the case, can come to no other conclusion but that all religion is based upon fantasy.

Fundamentalists have at least one characteristic in common with most scientists. Neither can understand that poetic and religious imagination has a way of arriving at truth by giving a clue to the total meaning of things without being in any sense an analytic description of detailed facts. The fundamentalists insist that religion is science, and thus they prompt those who know that this is not true to declare that all religious truth is contrary to scientific fact.

How can an age which is so devoid of poetic imagination as ours be truly religious?

1927

Our city race commission has finally made its report after months of investigation and further months of deliberation on our findings. It has been a rare experience to meet with these white and colored leaders and talk over our race problems. The situation which the colored people of the city face is really a desperate one, and no one who does not spend real time in gathering the facts can have any idea of the misery and pain which exists among these people, recently migrated from the south and unadjusted to our industrial civilization. Hampered both by their own inadequacies and the hostility of a white world they have a desperate fight to keep body and soul together, to say nothing of developing those amenities which raise life above the brute level.

I wish that some of our romanticists and sentimentalists could sit through a series of meetings where the real social problems of a city are discussed. They would be cured of their optimism. A city which is built around a productive process and which gives only casual thought and incidental attention to its human problems is really a kind of hell. Thousands in this town are really living in torment while the rest of us eat, drink and make merry. What a civilization!

Incidentally I wish the good church people who hate our mayor so much because he doesn't conform to their rules and standards could appreciate how superior his attitudes and viewpoints on race relations are to those held by most church people. It seems to me rather unfortunate that we must depend upon the "publicans" for our social conscience to so great a degree while the "saints" develop their private virtues and let the city as such fry in its iniquities.

1927

I wonder if it is really possible to have an honest Thanksgiving celebration in an industrial civilization. Harvest festivals were natural enough in peasant communities. The agrarian feels himself dependent upon nature's beneficence and anxious about nature's caprices. When the autumnal harvest is finally safe in the barns there arise, with the sigh of relief, natural emotions of gratitude that must express themselves religiously, since the bounty is actually created by the mysterious forces of nature which man may guide but never quite control.

All that is different in an industrial civilization in which so much wealth is piled up by the ingenuity of the machine, and, at least seemingly, by the diligence of man. Thanksgiving becomes increasingly the business of congratulating the Almighty upon his most excellent co-workers, ourselves. I have had that feeling about the Thanksgiving proclamations of our Presidents for some years. An individual, living in an industrial community might still celebrate a Thanksgiving day uncorrupted by pride, because he does benefit from processes and forces which he does not create or even guide. But a national Thanksgiving, particularly if it is meant to express gratitude for material bounty, becomes increasingly a pharisaic rite.

The union Thanksgiving service we attended this morning was full of the kind of self-righteous bunk which made it quite impossible for me to worship. There was indeed a faint odor of contrition in one of the prayers and in an aside of the sermon, but it did not spring from the heart. The Lord who was worshiped was not the Lord of Hosts, but the spirit of Uncle Sam, given a cosmic eminence for the moment which the dear old gentleman does not deserve.

It is a bad thing when religion is used as a vehicle of pride. It would be better to strut unashamedly down the boardwalk of nations than to go through the business of bowing humbly before God while we say, "We thank thee Lord that we are not as other men."

1927

Mother and I visited at the home of —— today where the husband is sick and was out of employment before he became sick. The folks have few connections in the city. They belong to no church. What a miserable existence it is to be friendless in a large city. And to be dependent upon a heartless industry. The man is about 55 or 57 I should judge, and he is going to have a desperate time securing employment after he gets well. These modern factories are not meant for old men. They want young men and they use them up pretty quickly. Your modern worker, with no skill but what is in the machine, is a sorry individual. After he loses the stamina of youth, he has nothing to sell.

I promised —— I would try to find him a job. I did it to relieve the despair of that family, but I will have a hard time making good on my promise. According to the ethics of our modern industrialism men over fifty, without special training, are so much junk. It is a pleasure to see how such an ethic is qualified as soon as the industrial unit is smaller and the owner has a personal interest in his men. I could mention quite a few such instances. But unfortunately the units are getting larger and larger and more inhuman.

I think I had better get in contact with more of these victims of our modern industrialism and not leave that end of our work to mother alone. A little such personal experience will help much to save you from sentimentality.

1927

The new Ford car is out. The town is full of talk about it. Newspaper reports reveal that it is the topic of the day in all world centers. Crowds storm every exhibit to get the first glimpse of this new creation. Mr. Ford has given out an interview saying that the car has cost him about a hundred million dollars and that after finishing it he still has about a quarter of a billion dollars in the bank.

I have been doing a little arithmetic and have come to the conclusion that the car cost Ford workers at least fifty million in lost wages during the past year. No one knows how many hundreds lost their homes in the period of unemployment, and how many children were taken out of school to help fill the depleted family exchequer, and how many more children lived on short rations during this period. Mr. Ford refuses to concede that he made a mistake in bringing the car out so late. He has a way of impressing the public even with his mistakes. We are now asked to believe that the whole idea of waiting a year after the old car stopped selling before bringing out a new one was a great advertising scheme which reveals the perspicacity of this industrial genius. But no one asks about the toll in human lives.

What a civilization this is! Naïve gentlemen with a genius for mechanics suddenly become the arbiters over the lives and fortunes of hundreds of thousands. Their moral pretentions are credulously accepted at full value. No one bothers to ask whether an industry which can maintain a cash reserve of a quarter of a billion ought not make some provision for its unemployed. It is enough that the new car is a good one. Here is a work of art in the only realm of art which we can understand. We will therefore refrain from making undue ethical demands upon the artist. Artists of all the ages have been notoriously unamenable to moral discipline. The cry of the hungry is drowned in the song, "Henry has made a lady out of Lizzy."

1928

This Federal Council meeting is an interesting study in the geography of morals. The race commission presented a report today in which it tried to place the council on record as favoring the enforcement of the fifteenth amendment as well as the eighteenth. It was obviously an effort to exploit the strong prohibition sentiment of the churches for the sake of committing them to the espousal of the interests of the disfranchised Negroes in the south. That is not a bad political strategy. But it did not quite work.

A good brother from the southern Presbyterian church warned that to interfere with this "political issue" would "soil the garments of the bride of Christ." To him the eighteenth amendment represented a "moral" issue but the fifteenth was a "political" one. I have a sneaking suspicion that the fifteenth amendment expresses more of the genius of the gospel than the eighteenth, but that is neither here nor there. What was interesting was the way in which various church leaders tried to rescue us from the embarrassment into which the council was brought by this proposal.

A good brother who was raised in the south and now lives in the north tried to act as mediator. He introduced his remarks with the usual nice story about how much he loved his Negro mammy. Some day he ought to have a lesson in ethics and learn how much easier it is to love those who acknowledge their inferiority than those who challenge our superiority. It is indeed a virtuous woman who can love her social competitor as sincerely as she loves her faithful maid.

Another mediator was a southern bishop who has many northern connections. He made much of the fact that the south disregards only the spirit and not the letter of the enfranchising amendments to the constitution. The bishop is really a man of some courage who has spoken out bravely on the industrial conditions in the south. But he was evidently afraid in this instance either to accept or to reject a Christian view of race relations. So he stuck to casuistry about the letter of the law. He has probably preached many a sermon on the text about the letter killing and the spirit making alive. At any rate everyone who spoke revealed how geographic and historical circumstance had qualified Christian conviction.

That was as true of those of us who took an uncompromising position as the southern equivocators and the semi-southern mediators. To the southerners we are not Christian idealists but merely "Yankee" meddlers. And perhaps we are. At any rate it was easy to see from the debate that the north cannot help the south much in solving its race problem. If it is solved the solution must come out of the conscience and heart of the south.

After all, the problem, as every moral problem, is not merely conditioned by geography but by mathematics. Contact between races when the one race is almost as numerous as the other is quite a different story from a relationship in which the subject race is numerically very much weaker than the dominant group. Therefore let us not judge, lest we be judged. It is so easy to repent of other people's sins.

Nevertheless it does not make one feel very comfortable to have a great church body seek some politic solution for a problem in which the ideal of Christian brotherhood leaves little room for equivocation.

1928

I always thought I was a fairly brutal realist, but I am beginning to suspect that the whole thing is a pose to hide the sentimental preacher. At any rate now that the time has come to sever my connections with the church I find it almost impossible to take the step. There is nothing quite like the pastoral relationship. I would almost be willing to sacrifice the future for the sake of staying here and watching the lovely little kiddies grow up, and see the young boys and girls that I have confirmed blossoming into manhood and womanhood. There must be something bogus about me. Here I have been preaching the gospel for thirteen years and crying, "Woe unto you if all men speak well of you," and yet I leave without a serious controversy in the whole thirteen years.

It is almost impossible to be sane and Christian at the same time, and on the whole I have been more sane than Christian. I have said what I believe, but in my creed the divine madness of a gospel of love is qualified by considerations of moderation which I have called Aristotelian, but which an unfriendly critic might call opportunistic. I have made these qualifications because it seems to me that without them the Christian ethic degenerates into asceticism and becomes useless for any direction of the affairs of a larger society.

I do not say that some one ought not to undertake an ascetic revolt against civilization. Certainly there would be a peace in it which no one can find who tries to adapt the principles of love to a civilization built upon the drive of power and greed. Those of us who make adjustments between the absolute ideal of our devotion and the necessities of the immediate situation lack peace, because we can never be sure that we have our adjustment at the right place.

Every moral position which has left the absolute basis is in danger of becoming a rationalization of some selfish purpose. I am not unconscious of the fact that my tendency to criticise others so severely for their alleged rationalizations and hypocrisies springs from my own sense of insecurity.

I persevere in the effort to combine the ethic of Jesus with what might be called Greek caution because I see no great gain in ascetic experiments. I might claim for such a strategy the full authority of the gospel except that it seems to me more likely to avoid dishonesty if one admits that the principle of love is not qualified in the gospel and that it must be qualified in other than the most intimate human associations. When one deals with the affairs of a civilization, one is trying to make the principle of love effective as far as possible, but one cannot escape the conclusion that society as such is brutal, and that the Christian principle may never be more than a leaven in it.

There has never been a time when I have not been really happy in the relationships of the parish ministry. The church can really be a community of love and can give one new confidence in the efficacy of the principles of brotherhood outside of the family relation. The questions and qualms of conscience arise when one measures the church in its relationships to society, particularly to the facts of modern industry. It is at this point where it seems to me that we had better admit failure than to claim any victory. The admission of failure may yet lead to some kind of triumph, while any premature confidence in the victory of a Christian ethic will merely obfuscate the conscience.

Modern industry, particularly American industry, is not Christian. The economic forces which move it are hardly qualified at a single point by really ethical considerations. If, while it is in the flush of its early triumphs, it may seem impossible to bring it under the restraint of moral law, it may strengthen faith to know that life without law destroys itself. If the church can do nothing else, it can bear witness to the truth until such a day as bitter experience will force a recalcitrant civilization to a humility which it does not now possess.

26. Good Temper in Bad Times

The decade of prosperity came crashing to an end in the Wall Street panic of autumn, 1929, and America entered the Great Depression. Many of the social and cultural transformations of the Twenties were halted, and some were reversed. As unemployment increased, women and blacks lost their new standing in the labor market. With factories laying off workers, the movement of people into the cities slowed, and in some cases urban population declined as workers returned to their small-town homes and farms.

At the same time other new trends of the Twenties were advanced by the Depression. The economic collapse dealt an even more severe blow to middle class status and values than the breakup of genteel cultural control after the First World War. With the middle class foundering as never before, the institutions and values of mass culture gained dominance over American cultural life. People had less money to spend, but more time on their hands; radio and movies, which in 1929 were just beginning to talk, gave them diversion, entertainment, a sense of shared experience in their mass plight.

The most interesting aspect of the Crash and the Depression, in the long-range view, was the calmness and good humor with which Americans in general responded to their adversity. Left-wing groups agitated, some farmers protested, and among intellectuals there was a prevailing belief that the nation would take either the Communist or the Fascist road. But the people at large were passive and confused, devoid of the social and political perspectives on which they could act. They viewed the halt in the advance of modern civilization almost with a sense of relief. It gave them a chance to pause, to look around, and contemplate, even to enjoy, what they had accomplished. In a time of trouble many hoped to recover the cohesive ties of family and community that the Twenties had undone. One of the best accounts of everyday life in the depth of the Depression described New York City in the last months of 1931. "New York in the Third Winter," which appeared in *Fortune* magazine in January, 1932, was not signed, but it was later made known that the author was James Thurber (1894–1961), then a journalist, thereafter to become a major humorist and artist of his time.

New York in the Third Winter
JAMES THURBER

A Frenchman, let us say, or a resident of Iowa, reading in his paper that there are, in round numbers, about 750,000 persons out of work in New York (160,000 of them at the end of their tether), might excusably get the idea that the depression has become, in our greatest city, nothing short of a spectacle. If, then, the Frenchman or the Iowan comes to New York to see the spectacle, he must be grievously disappointed. There is no big parade of the unemployed, stalking through the streets, muttering ominously; there are no hungry mobs besieging bread shops; there is not even a pall of gloom hanging heavy over the town. The visitor must be surprised to discover that, at first and even at second glance, New York City is outwardly much the same as it was in pre-depression days. He will, of course, encounter talk about bad times wherever he goes, but it is more likely to be faintly facetious than downright dejected. The depression has, as a matter of fact, brought forth almost as many jokes as did the old Model T Ford. Even little shopkeepers, forced out of business, announce their plight with a touch of ironic humor. In the window of a small store in Fourteenth Street is a sign reading "Busted and Disgusted." On Third Avenue there is another one reading "This Is No Place for Me. Selling Out." That, of course, is not the kind of spirit that stalks through the streets muttering or throwing bricks through bakery windows. It is not the spirit that leads to riot. Hence to the visiting Frenchman or to the guest from Iowa, New York has no spectacle to offer—nor is there the immediate promise of one. Even the restless Communists of Union Square are well-fed enough to get mad about Gandhi instead of Hoover, to worry about politics instead of economics.

Wandering about the city looking for Disaster, the visitor from out of town will very likely find no more than he would have found in New York in any other winter—the kind of Disaster, that is, which impinges on the eye. He will see throngs jamming into the subways during the

[James Thurber], "New York in the Third Winter," *Fortune*, vol. 5, January 1932, pp. 41, 43, 46, 48, 109, 121.

rush hours—despite the fact that these averaged 144,110 fewer patrons per day in the last fiscal year; he will see well-dressed people crowding the lobbies of theatres during the *entr'acte*—although only three-fourths as many shows are available; he will see business and pleasure going along ostensibly, if not actually, the same as before. New York is a proud city. It does not put up placards saying "I Feel Bad." It puts up placards saying "I Will Share." The official byword of the depression is thus one of Service and Coöperation, not of Despair.

The person who lives in New York sees, naturally, signs of the times which would escape the attention of an outsider. Take, for a colorful example, the taxicab drivers, a unique set of gentlemen as typical of New York in their way as the cowboys were of the old West. They used to be gay, talkative, wisecracking. Now they are silent and a touch grim.

Just before the depression, there were 20,000 licensed cabs on the streets of New York. About 1,500 of these have disappeared in the last year, but the field is still enormously overcrowded. People no longer jump into a cab to ride a few blocks. They walk. Taximen make less than one-half, sometimes less than one-third, once in a while only a slight fraction of their normal earnings—which used to run about $7 a day. Of the 1,500 cabs which dropped out, about 600 were so-called "gyp cabs"—that is, they charged twenty cents for the first quarter-mile and ten cents for each additional quarter-mile. The usual rate is fifteen-and-five. With these gyp cabs vanished also most of the old and decrepit vehicles. "You gotta have a smart lookin' hack," the drivers will tell you. "Smartness" in taxis has, indeed, reached an almost ludicrous point. Bright robin's-egg-blue cabs, cabs trimmed in glaring colors, cabs with dazzling diagonal lines make the streets look like a carnival. Anything to attract attention. There is something typical of the times in the sight of a solemn-faced chauffeur sitting idle at the wheel of a cab which looks like a Mardi gras float.

In the diversions and entertainments of the day—and the night—there must be some key to the temper of the people. New York is, of course, first and foremost a city of theatregoers. It has eighty-six legitimate theatres. On the first of December—a midseason day picked at random—there were twenty-eight shows running (many were just creeping along). On the same day last year, there were thirty-nine. Of course, the show business is volatile and subject to change with. slight notice. A comparison of any day this season with the same day last year is an imprecise affair, but the theatre generally has a harder time getting people into its seats now than ever before. Seven or eight years ago a just-average comedy or drama often had a fairly good run—two to three months, let us say, anyway; the same kind of play nowadays is likely to close in a week. Audiences shop carefully in Broadway. One comedy which opened on a Monday night amid the high hopes of its author and producer—because it was similar in tempo and writing to another comedy by the same author which had a run of three months four years ago—closed the same week. The most money that was taken in any night was $270. This meant that only about a hundred people paid to get in. The house was, of course, "papered." Free tickets were sent out wholesale to friends of the author and producer, and to special lists of organizations, societies, etc., which all box offices keep handy in order to fill the theatre and make a flop happy in its last hours, to rouge the cheeks of the dying play. The night this play closed, almost every seat was occupied—and the visitor from France or Iowa probably wrote home that the theatre is flourishing. Nevertheless, $30,000 was lost on the production, of which $7,000 had been spent on scenery—brand-new scenery that was hauled away by a theatrical warehouse company which didn't pay a nickel for it. At the theatre next door to this one, another play was doing even less business the same week—as low as $60, or about twenty paid admissions to a performance. Nor will producers spend money nursing a drooping play.

Prices for seats have been cut—slightly, not radically. The old $5 and $6 charges for musical shows have come down to around $4 in most cases, but dramas and comedies keep pretty consistently to a $3 top. Actors who are in demand are still as highly paid as before, but the run of mimes are glad to sign a contract for 25 per cent less than they have been accustomed to. A big hit today will take in as much money and enjoy as long a run as it would have in more normal days. One of the solid successes of the town, Eugene O'Neill's *Mourning Becomes Electra*—the three-plays-in-one show—charges $6 for all orchestra seats and some balcony seats. On the first of December, it was impossible to get good seats until after the eleventh of December. *Strange Interlude,* O'Neill's equally long and equally successful play of 1928–29, charged $4.40 for its best seats.

An unusual feature of the 1931 theatrical season began to be apparent soon after it got under way: serious, even tragic plays did as well as plays of lighter theme, sometimes much better. Comedies have to be very good indeed to draw crowds. Perhaps misery's desire for company brings people to plays which depict the trials and tribulations of life. There is one outstanding exception, however, to this phenomenon: the popularity of burlesque shows. Almost a dozen of them are going great guns at one time. The featured act of each of them involves a young woman who, to the plaudits of the crowd, takes off her things, one at a time, until she is as nearly undressed as the law allows—and it allows more than formerly. The best of these specialized *artistes* get big salaries—one named Hinda Wassau, for instance, $475 a week. The houses are crowded. The desire of this type of pleasure-seeker for madder music (if not stronger wine) is also borne out by the appeal of the large, cheap dance halls. There the cavortings are characterized by an abandom so remarkable that these resorts are no place for the New Yorker to take his out-of-town visitor unless the latter is made of stern and imperturbable stuff. All of this does not come under the head of gayety. There is in it something of the note of hysteria common to the carryings-on in towns behind the battle lines in time of war. "Let joy be unconfined, for tomorrow we starve."

This same spirit of madness shows up sometimes in the so-called "whoopee cruises," those little jaunts in big ships out beyond the twelve-mile limit and back, in the course of which everybody stays up all night, or nearly so, and raises a type of ned which, while not so unrestrained as the ned raised in the dance halls, still partakes of the same flavor. It is not true, of course, that the whole town has gone wild. The instances cited are special ones. Drinking conditions, for example, are in general probably not much different from last year or the year before last or the year before that. There are probably more people than ever who seek Escape in parties at home, but the riotousness has gone out of highball drinking. It has settled into a kind of ritual, almost a routine. The edge of abandon in drinking—even in the much-maligned Greenwich Village—has worn blunt. Backgammon, bridge, word games are more popular than ever. They are cheaper than the theatre or any other form of entertainment which you have to get dressed up and go out to.

The fact that there are many more dark theatres now than there were might somehow or other be worked into a plausible reason for a corresponding increase in the sale of novels and other books, which after all are a similar diversion. Book sales, however, are not good. A book that sells 40,000 copies now—and not many do—would have sold 60,000 or 75,000 before the Gloom. There has been a certain tendency to cut prices, but that hasn't helped much. The strange boom that started up a couple of years ago in contemporary first editions, boosting prices to an artificial level, has collapsed. A fine copy of Galsworthy's *The Man of Property* brought as much as $1,150 in New York in 1929. Now it would fetch less than one-quarter of that amount. Shaw and Barrie and Kipling have suffered almost as much. An excellent copy of Barrie's *A Window in Thrums,* which sold for $260 two years ago, brought only $30 at an auction in November. The same is true of the works of certain American authors who were unduly exploited: Edith Wharton, Owen Wister, Thornton Wilder, and others.

It is interesting to turn from the general run of books to the works of a man who even in these times has sold 400,000 copies in a year—Mr. Ely Culbertson, the bridge expert. His is probably one of the biggest of the depression fortunes and bridge one of the few big depression businesses. Culbertson sells daily more than 1,500 of his booklets on bridge and 750 of his big books on the subject. His income is more than $200,000 a year. He is proud of the fact that he made bridge a big business. Each of his teachers—and he has 1,600—must take a five-day course from him, at $60. He writes in *Life* and in 140 newspapers, talks on the radio, and lectures (he had more than 400 invitations to lecture in 1931). Mr. Culbertson says that Americans spent $10,000,000 this year on bridge lessons and that, counting card sales and all, nearly $100,000,000 was spent directly and indirectly on bridge.

And how are the hotels getting along? Bravely, one finds. The manager, the *maitre d'hôtel,* meet you with the same poise, the same suave smile, but behind all the fortitude is a definite and grave concern. One authority on hotels in New York says he doesn't know of one that isn't losing money. Rates are being cut, 25 per cent and more. Customers, in fact, are sought at any price, despite the existence of an optimistic document, signed by most hotel men during the summer, setting forth an agreement to do nothing of the kind. The Pennsylvania and the New Yorker are among the exceptions to this corner-cutting. The New York Central Railroad, concerned in the welfare of the Hotel Commodore, drums up business for it in their hinterland offices. The Ritz has sent out letters to hundreds of its old customers, asking them why they don't patronize it any longer; most of them answer that they are staying in the country. The Savoy-Plaza lost $1,018,905 in the first nine months of 1931. The Bowman group lost $594,774 in the first nine months. Virtually all of the big hotels have had to cut down their minimum room rates.

The Ritz's minimum is now $6; it was $8. Pierre's (now in the hands of its bondholders) was planned to average more than $10 a room, has rented some for as low as $6.

The new Waldorf Hotel, opening, hesitated to announce prices in advance, fearful of further slashing among its neighbors. Finally, it set a minimum figure of $6 a room. Not long after its opening, it was a shining exception in point of occupancy: for a while in November it was 100 per cent filled. But its average has been nearer 60 per cent—which, indeed, is better than the city's average of 50 per cent. The Waldorf's competitors say novelty and exceptionally low rates are the reasons—*de luxe* tower apartments with fireplaces and grand pianos, they claim, have yielded only 65 per cent of the revenue which the owners anticipated.

Hotel restaurant trade has gone to pieces. Some of the dining rooms are virtually empty at meal time. A number of them have eliminated music. The speakeasies are responsible for this in large part. People feel the need of a bracing cocktail, or maybe two, at lunch time and dinner. Not all of the speakeasies are making money, of course, but very few of them, considering that there are thousands and thousands, close down. They ease along, making small profits at worst, big profits at best. The big elaborate ones, especially, are thriving—the ones that embellish their bars until they take on something of the look of a *de luxe* taxicab. Every now and again a new one opens, with a more ornate and impressive bar than the last one. One boasts a bar of colored tile, another a great horseshoe counter; customers of a third group about a hexagon. The bars have to be impressive, and the food has to be excellent. Buyers for speakeasy kitchens are up at dawn, selecting the best.

After the visitor has had a cocktail and eaten the chef's specialty, he will probably want to see the Empire State Building.* It is not only one of the phenomena of our day, but it might be said to be the royal palace of the kingdom of real estate, and as such it deserves a visit. The kingdom of real estate in New York is in a bad way, as it is everywhere—only in New York it is bad on a magnificent scale. During the boom, the sound of the riveter was loud in the city. Now it is so quiet you can hear a girder fall for miles away. Great monuments to the boom-time building

---

* *To visit the tower of which—a curious depression statistic—over 550,000 persons have paid $1 apiece.*

loom up, half filled or less, all over the city. Landlords of office buildings as well as apartment buildings are willing to enter into all sorts of curious compromises with their tenants—such tenants as they have. Evictions are no longer common, many landlords being willing to take what they can get when they can get it. A fourteen-room apartment in Park Avenue in the Seventies, which rented normally for $16,000 a year, rented this year for $12,000. Another, whose price was $15,000, dropped to $10,000. Cooperative apartments have taken, as the saying is, a terrible beating, of which this example is fairly typical: one apartment bought for $60,000 ($10,000 maintenance) was sublet for $10,000, with no allowance for interest on the $60,000. Many an important-looking apartment building, flaunting its elegant doorman to the world, echoes hollowly to the tread of its handful of tenants. People have moved into the suburbs, or they have moved into more modest apartments, some of which, such as the Tudor City group, are profiting probably as much now as they would if times were better.

But to return to the Empire State Building, the tallest and most impressive office building—unless the Chrysler spire fetches you more than the Empire's mooring mast—in the town. The situation varies from week to week, but on a certain day last month, less than one-third of the outside shops on the ground floor were rented. Elevators had stopped running from the forty-second to the sixty-seventh floor. Many floors were not finished at all—merely big plastery spaces.

There were 457 listings on the directory board in the marbled and vasty lobby. But they didn't represent 457 different firms. Some Japanese in Room 727 had seventeen separate listings—from Shohei Ikegami to Reisuke Ishida. The Starrett Corp. on the twenty-sixth floor had twenty-seven listings. The du Pont company, which occupies all of the tenth floor, had achieved thirty-five separate and scattered mentions. The highest office in the building (not counting the lonely and remote studios of the National Broadcasting Co. on the eighty-fifth floor and the office of John J. Raskob on the eightieth) was that of the Model Brassiere Co. —on the forty-first floor. Five women collecting funds for the unemployed in the lobby had taken in, by 11:30 one morning, only $8.50. Of course, the Empire State is young—not yet a year old—and it has all of life before it. It is brave. It says stoutly that it is "just under half full . . ."

What now of the city's famous stores? If one expects to find Macy's or Saks or even the smaller shops so empty that one can hear a price drop, one is terribly disappointed. They are just as crowded and bustling as ever. Of course, prices have come down. They have, in fact, been thrown down. The advertising pages of every paper he picks up scream price cuts at the reader. Even places like Cartier and F. A. O. Schwarz and Brooks Brothers (a widely disparate trio), concerns which once on a time mentioned only Quality, in a dignified tone, are playing up the cheapness of their wares. Saks-Fifth Avenue went so far as to take a full page in the tabloid *Daily Mirror* to advertise its sale of $1,000,000 worth of fine diamond jewelry. (Every place you turn, some store offers you a bargain in jewelry. Marcus & Co. has a $50,000 emerald ring which it will be pleased to part with for $37,500. Fifty per cent off on jewelry is common. It is all very glittering and enticing and tantalizing.)

The famous shops for women, such as Bergdorf Goodman, Jay Thorpe, Kurzman, places into whose windows the average woman during the normalcy could merely wistfully stare, are now offering apparel at prices within that woman's reach. Exclusive little shops on side streets have a clientele now they never had before—for they now listen to reason, will consider any offer. Of course, there isn't a jam at the doors before opening time, for the average woman hasn't as much money as she had, but the chance to buy, say, a pair of Bergdorf Goodman shoes for $16 will prompt many a wife to unbalance the family budget. Bergdorf Goodman's, it is only fair to say, is one of several who have not exactly joined the rush of screamers into the advertising columns, but offers its reductions more or less quietly to its regular clientele: sables at 40 per cent under what they were two winters ago; $16,000 mink coats marked down to $12,000 (this last bargain was snapped up). Some of the smart shops, Tappé, for example, send telegrams to their long-absent patrons, wanting to know, rather plaintively, what is the matter—as if everybody didn't know!

What, you might ask at this point, hasn't been hard hit? Are there businesses which make more during a depression than during a normalcy? Well, shoe-repair shops, for one thing, and necktie-cleaning shops. Things like that. One shop that does nothing but clean ties has more work, almost, than it can do. Its small trucks race busily about town. Men no longer throw away a necktie after they have worn it a few times. But these are petty examples. Here is one on a larger scale: Childs restaurants sold two million $1 dinners this year as against half a million in 1930. One of the few figures comparable to this which springs to mind—or, rather, emerges after a careful research into such profitable enterprises as stick up their lonely heads here and there—is in quite another field than the restaurant business. It is the 1,750,000 copies (maybe more by the time this is read) sold every month by the remarkable magazine, *Ballyhoo,* dedicated to making flagrant fun of advertising and advertisers and the press in general. The sales of most magazines have dropped, but *Ballyhoo* was wildfire from the start. It is a phenomenon difficult to account for. Some analyzers think it is because people like to see ballyhoo attacked; others claim that, in buying the magazine, the people are "falling for" just another ballyhoo. Anyway, there it is.

Credit bureaus (to name another successful business and one whose success is understandable) have never had better times. All the credit bureaus in New York found themselves understaffed this fall and unprepared to cope with the rush of work. In October, their business increased 35 per cent. In spite of this, stores assert that people are taking only 4 per cent longer to pay than they did two years ago, and that they lose only about ½ per cent more on their credit business than they used to. The stores are very nice to delinquent but well-meaning debtors. If a person explains that he cannot pay his bill, he is courteously referred to the credit bureau. The person estimates the amount of money over and above his living expenses which he can prorate among his creditors once a month. No loss of credit results from this system.

Professional men, who always have a hard time collecting their money, have a worse time now. In happy days, their losses ran from 15 to 33 per cent. In depression times they are incalculable. This is particularly true, of course, of the physicians. People not only don't pay for the curing, or treatment, of old aches and maladies, but they let new ones go untreated. They stay away from doctors. They also stay out of hospitals. The deficit of the fifty-five hospitals affiliated with the United Hospital Fund will be $12,000,000 this year. One trouble is people reneging on their pledges—a few regular donors have gone even further and written plaintive notes asking the return of last year's gifts. Those who are forced to take to hospital beds choose them in wards or in semi-private rooms, and dispense with the attentions of a special nurse. The Presbyterian's famous Harkness Pavilion is only about 40 per cent full. In one hospital, where the top price for a room is $42 a day, most of such rooms were occupied (if occupied at all) by persons who were paying only $12 or $14 for them. Maternity floors were not nearly so well filled up as a year ago. By the last of September it had been figured that the total number of births in the five boroughs of Greater New York would show a decrease of 5,000 since last year. Deaths, down about 3,000 in 1930, will be up over 4,000 in 1931.

The little odds and ends of New York life in the third winter of the depression are myriad. Let us just set down a few as they spring to mind, without reason or order. Stenographers who were making $40 to $50 two years ago are glad to make $20 and $25 now, if they can get it. Architects, once well paid, have been known to go to work for as little as $20 a week. The Racquet & Tennis is said to be one of the few clubs in town with a sizable waiting list, and even that has been dwindling rapidly. In 1931, there were 3,000 apple sellers on the streets, as against twice that many a year ago. The city has prohibited apple selling on certain streets; the novelty of the thing has worn off; people are sick of apples. Open accounts in savings banks in New York increased 445,000 in 1931. Borden's and Sheffield's no longer ask for a deposit on milk bottles. A lady with a small baby, living in a hotel near Gramercy Park, took one quart of Grade A milk each morning, for five days, from Borden's and then, for some reason or other, shifted to another firm. An agent of Borden's called on her in person to demand the reason why. She gave him her reason, whatever it was—a whim, probably. But, as Oliver Herford's expression is, "a whim of iron." Three days later the representative was back. "I wonder," he said, when the lady answered his ring, "if we couldn't go into that matter again?" And all for one quart of milk a day!

Silk stockings that sold for $1.95 have been reduced to eighty-seven cents. The Pullman company is offering 20 per cent off on upper berths. Steamship business has fallen way off. In the first nine months of 1931, 50,000 fewer American citizens left New York Harbor outward bound in ships than for the same period in 1930. The high-priced suites on liners have come down 30 per cent, other first-class fares 10 per cent. There were 37,883 fewer telephones in New York in 1931 than the year before— but the rate is still higher than it was in boom times. On the other hand, the George Washington Bridge has done better than it expected! Eight million cars will have crossed it by its first birthday, with $4,400,000 taken in. Nor has it hurt the Holland Tunnel traffic. New York failures from January to November this year totaled 23,332—about 1,500 more than for the same period last year. A Stock Exchange seat sold in 1929 for $495,000 (ex-rights); this October it sold for $156,000. A Curb seat was worth $254,000 in 1929, the latest quotation is $40,000.

The Union Club cut its $2.50 dinner to $2, announcing the fact by a discreet card to its members. College football continued to draw its huge crowds, offering, as it did, two hours of practical obliviousness to one's troubles. But price, for the first time in the game's history, became a factor. Wherever $4 and $5 were asked for tickets, attendance tended to fall off; reductions, on the other hand, were followed by broken attendance records. Football fans further insisted upon a run for their money; teams with off years were woefully neglected. Nedick's orange-drink stands sold the beverage which made them famous for five cents instead of ten, beginning this fall. Walgreen's have reduced sodas from twenty to fifteen cents. Drug stores and sandwich shops no longer charge five cents extra if you want your sandwich bread toasted. The sale of expensive candies has fallen off, while that of nickel candy bars (some people eat one and call it a lunch) has increased. Two years ago, Schrafft's did not sell any candy for less than $1 a pound; now you can get chocolates there for sixty cents. Lofts sells 100,000 pounds of candy a day, largely the thirty-nine, forty-nine, and fifty-nine cents a pound boxes. Broadway night clubs are melancholy. The Harlem clubs are always the same, depression in and depression out. Thompson's lunch rooms have the cheapest prices since 1916. Vaudeville theatres have forbidden their performers to make unworthy jokes about the depression (or about Herbert Hoover). When unemployment fund workers called at two nice shops in Madison Avenue near Sixty-first Street, they were presented with a nickel from each. The vice president of a downtown firm brings a bunch of white carnations to his office every morning and makes each department head wear one, so that they will at least *look* gay. Almost nobody buys orchids, or antique andirons, or thoroughbred wire-haired terriers right now. Life goes on.

Selected Bibliography

Aaron, Daniel. *Writers on the Left: Episodes in American Literary Communism.* New York, Harcourt, Brace & World, Inc., 1961.

Allen, Frederick Lewis. *Only Yesterday: An Informal History of the Nineteen-Twenties.* New York, Harper & Bros., 1931.

Bernstein, Irving. *The Lean Years: A History of the American Worker 1920–1933.* Boston, Houghton Mifflin Co., 1960.

Blackmur, R. P. "Anni Mirabiles, 1921–1925: Reason in the Madness of Letters," in *A Primer of Ignorance,* edited by Joseph Frank. New York, Harcourt, Brace & World, Inc., 1967, pp. 3–80.

Chambers, Clarke A. *Seedtime of Reform: American Social Service and Social Action 1918–1933.* Minneapolis, University of Minnesota Press, 1963.

Cowley, Malcolm. *Exile's Return: A Literary Odyssey of the 1920's.* Revised Edition. New York, The Viking Press, 1951.

Cruse, Harold. *The Crisis of the Negro Intellectual.* New York, William Morrow, 1967.

Fitzgerald, F. Scott. "Echoes of the Jazz Age," in *The Crack-Up,* edited by Edmund Wilson. New York, New Directions, 1945, pp. 13–22.

Galbraith, John Kenneth. *The Great Crash, 1929.* Boston, Houghton Mifflin Co., 1955.

Giedion, Siegfried. *Mechanization Takes Command: A Contribution to Anonymous History.* New York, Oxford University Press, 1948.

Grazia, Sebastian de. *Of Time, Work, and Leisure.* New York, The Twentieth Century Fund, Inc., 1962.

Hicks, John D. *Republican Ascendancy, 1921–1933.* New York, Harper & Bros., 1960.

Higham, John. *Strangers in the Land: Patterns of American Nativism, 1860–1925.* New Brunswick, N. J., Rutgers University Press, 1955.

Hoffman, Frederick J. *The Twenties: American Writing in the Postwar Decade*. New York, The Viking Press, 1955.

Joughin, Louis, and Edmund M. Morgan. *The Legacy of Sacco and Vanzetti*. New York, Harcourt, Brace and Co., 1948.

Kazin, Alfred. *On Native Grounds: An Interpretation of Modern American Prose Literature*. New York, Harcourt, Brace & Co., 1942.

Kouwenhoven, John A. *Made in America: The Arts in Modern Civilization*. Garden City, N.Y., Doubleday and Co., 1948.

Leuchtenburg, William E. *The Perils of Prosperity, 1914–1932*. Chicago, The University of Chicago Press, 1958.

Lynd, Robert S. and Helen Merrell Lynd. *Middletown: A Study in Modern American Culture*. New York, Harcourt, Brace and Co., 1929.

May, Henry F. *The End of American Innocence: A Study of the First Years of Our Own Time, 1912–1917*. New York, Alfred A. Knopf, 1959.

———. "Shifting Perspectives on the 1920's," *Mississippi Valley Historical Review*, vol. 43, December, 1956, pp. 405–427.

Meyer, Donald. *The Positive Thinkers: A Study of the American Quest for Health, Wealth and Personal Power from Mary Baker Eddy to Norman Vincent Peale*. New York, Doubleday & Co., 1965.

Mills, C. Wright, *White Collar: The American Middle Classes*. New York, Oxford University Press, 1951.

Mowry, George E. *The Urban Nation, 1920–1960*. New York, Hill & Wang, 1965.

Osofsky, Gilbert. *Harlem: The Making of a Ghetto. Negro New York, 1890–1930*. New York, Harper & Row, 1966.

Preston, William, Jr. *Aliens and Dissenters: Federal Suppression of Radicals, 1903–1933*. Cambridge, Mass., Harvard University Press, 1963.

Ruland, Richard. *The Rediscovery of American Literature: Premises of Critical Taste, 1900–1940*. Cambridge, Mass., Harvard University Press, 1967.

Russell, Francis. *The Shadow of Blooming Grove: Warren G. Harding in His Times*. New York, McGraw-Hill, 1968.

Santayana, George. *The Genteel Tradition: Nine Essays by George Santayana*. Edited by Douglas L. Wilson. Cambridge, Mass., Harvard University Press, 1967.

Seldes, Gilbert. *The Seven Lively Arts*. Revised Edition. New York, Sagamore Press, Inc., 1957.

Sinclair, Andrew. *Prohibition: The Era of Excess.* Boston, Little, Brown & Co., 1962.

Sklar, Robert. *F. Scott Fitzgerald: The Last Laocoön.* New York, Oxford University Press, 1967.

Slosson, Preston William. *The Great Crusade and After, 1914–1928.* New York, The Macmillan Company, 1930.

Soule, George. *Prosperity Decade. From War to Depression: 1917–1929.* New York, Holt, Rinehart and Winston, 1947.

Stein, Maurice R. *The Eclipse of Community: An Interpretation of American Studies.* Princeton, N. J., Princeton University Press, 1960.

Susman, Warren I. "A Second Country: The Expatriate Image," *Texas Studies in Literature and Language,* vol. 3, no. 2, Summer, 1961, pp. 171–183.

Ward, John W., "The Meaning of Lindbergh's Flight," in Joseph J. Kwiat and Mary C. Turpie, editors, *Studies in American Culture; Dominant Ideas and Images.* Minneapolis, University of Minnesota Press, 1960.

Ware, Caroline F. *Greenwich Village, 1920–1930: A Comment on American Civilization in the Post-War Years.* Boston, Houghton Mifflin Co., 1935.

Wiebe, Robert H. *The Search for Order, 1877–1920.* New York, Hill & Wang, 1967.

White, William Allen. *A Puritan in Babylon: The Story of Calvin Coolidge.* New York, The Macmillan Company, 1938.

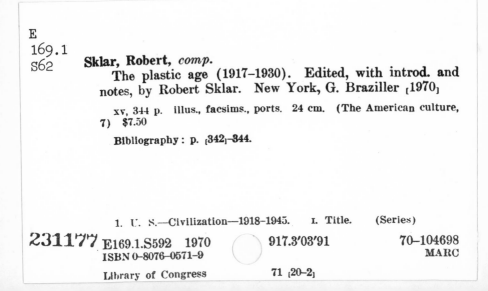

E
169.1
S62

Sklar, Robert, *comp.*
   The plastic age (1917–1930). Edited, with introd. and
notes, by Robert Sklar. New York, G. Braziller (1970)

   xv, 344 p. illus., facsims., ports. 24 cm. (The American culture,
7) $7.50

   Bibliography: p. (342)–344.

1. U. S.—Civilization—1918–1945.   I. Title.   (Series)

231177 E169.1.S592   1970   917.3'03'91   70–104698
       ISBN 0-8076-0571-9   MARC

       Library of Congress   71 (20–2)